Reforming Turkish Energy Markets

Izak Atiyas · Tamer Çetin · Gürcan Gülen

Reforming Turkish Energy Markets

Political Economy, Regulation and Competition in the Search for Energy Policy

Springer

Izak Atiyas
Arts and Social Sciences
Sabanci University
34956 Istanbul
Turkey

Tamer Çetin
Department of Economics
Yildiz Technical University
Yildiz Kampusu
34349 Istanbul
Turkey

Gürcan Gülen
Bureau of Economic Geology
University of Texas at Austin
1801 Allen Parkway
Houston, TX 77019
USA

ISBN 978-1-4614-0289-3 ISBN 978-1-4614-0290-9 (eBook)
DOI 10.1007/978-1-4614-0290-9
Springer New York Heidelberg Dordrecht London

Library of Congress Control Number: 2012934654

Printed on acid-free paper

Springer is part of Springer Science+Business Media (www.springer.com)

Acknowledgement

The authors would like to thank Değer Boden Akalın and her colleagues at Boden Law Office, Tuncay Babalı, Haluk Bilgiç, Ercüment Camadan, Sibel Çetinkaya, Erkan Erdoğdu, Prof. Mustafa Özcan Ültanır and Ceren Uzdil for many helpful conversations, comments and suggestions. We have benefited greatly from their knowledge and advice. Research on energy markets in Turkey owes a lot to the pioneering efforts and contributions of Prof. Dr. Osman Sevaioğlu, which we gratefully acknowledge. Thanks are also due to Deniz Sanin for excellent research assistance. As usual, all remaining errors are the responsibility of the authors.

Contents

Chapter 1
Introduction

The Turkish energy sector reforms should be studied within the context of global restructuring and energy market trends. Energy industry is global with increasing interconnections of electricity and pipeline networks, increased trade of oil, products, and natural gas (both in liquefied form as LNG and via pipelines); climate change is another factor that brings countries together to focus on emissions from the energy industry. Turkey is, in some ways, a leader and, in many other ways, a follower of sector trends. As a country that is heavily dependent on energy imports but one that is also playing an increasingly important role as a conduit between resource-rich regions of the Caspian and Middle East and consumers in Europe and elsewhere, Turkey learned from the experiences of others as the country restructured its energy sectors but also has a lot to offer in lessons learned.

Since the late 1980s, starting with Chile, electricity sector restructuring has been tried in many jurisdictions around the world. Since most countries had an integrated state monopoly, restructuring called for unbundling and privatization, or at least corporatization. The World Bank and other donor agencies as well as the International Monetary Fund (IMF) often required such power sector reforms and privatization of state assets as a precondition of their assistance packages; Turkey was no exception. The main drivers for restructuring was the inability of state monopolies to keep up with investment needs of growing economies and the desire to increase efficiency, especially in wholesale and generation markets. Since each country differed in terms of their geography, availability of domestic resources, energy trade balance, composition of their economy, and sociopolitical conditions, the restructuring approach differed but fundamental principles such as unbundling of generation, transmission and distribution assets; open access to the transmission grid; establishment of an independent regulator; and competition in the wholesale market remained the same.

Today, some of these experiments can be considered successful but others are not. Politics of reforming electricity, which remains a political commodity rather than a market commodity in most jurisdictions; and opposition of incumbent interests have undermined reform efforts. But equally important is the instantaneous

I. Atiyas et al., *Reforming Turkish Energy Markets*,
DOI: 10.1007/978-1-4614-0290-9_1,

nature of electricity markets, which do not always send the price signals necessary for timely investment in generation capacity to balance base, intermediate, and peak load needs, raising resource adequacy concerns. As a result, the 'one-size-fits-all' approach to sector reform has proved misguided and been dropped by the donor community in favor of a more nuanced approach customized according to conditions of each jurisdiction. The desire to introduce renewables and reduce greenhouse gas emissions also impacted these considerations.

In some ways, Turkey initiated electricity sector reform prior to Chile and other early adopters. In the early 1980s, the country attempted to attract private investors, especially for power generation via innovative contract schemes (Chap. 2). Also in the 1980s, Turkey started to import natural gas from Russia via the Western pipeline (Chap. 3). As a country that was, and still is, heavily dependent on imported energy, adding natural gas to the fuel mix from Russia, a non-traditional source of energy at the time, was seen as a strategy of risk diversification to enhance energy security. Natural gas' cleaner burning qualities relative to coal and oil products were also important considerations as air pollution had become a serious health risk in Ankara and İstanbul, especially in winter months.

A state monopoly, BOTAŞ, was responsible for building and operating natural gas pipelines both for imports and domestic transportation and distribution. More importantly, BOTAŞ was responsible for signing long-term import contracts that included take-or-pay clauses backed by Treasury guarantees. Natural gas was the fuel of choice for most of the private generators, who signed power purchase agreements (PPAs) with the state power utility. These PPAs also included take-or-pay clauses backed by Treasury guarantees. This confluence of long-term contracts in both gas and power sectors intricately connected the two sectors and laid the foundation for stranded costs and incumbent interests that would have to be dealt with during the reform process.

1 Energy Sector Restructuring

Throughout the 1980s and 1990s Turkey tried various schemes to engage private sector investments in the electricity industry to meet the energy needs of a rapidly growing economy. These schemes, discussed in Chap. 2, entailed granting Build Operate Transfer (BOT)—Turkey was one of the first countries to do so, Build Operate (BO), and Transfer of Operating Rights (TOR) contracts that included take-or-pay clauses and Treasury guarantees. These schemes faced numerous legal problems: as per decisions of the Constitutional Court, they were designed as concession contracts under Administrative Law. They were therefore subject to judicial review by the Council of State and could not benefit from international arbitration. These factors were seen to discourage international investors. Further, the purchase guarantees meant that plants built under these contracts were protected from competition. These factors had already directed the bureaucracy to search for a more fundamental reform.

1.1 Role of Economic Crises

A number of factors help explain the emergence of the new regulatory regime in the early 2000s.[1] One factor is the presence and influence of international actors such as the IMF and the World Bank supporting the liberalization agenda. After a decade of severe macroeconomic instability Turkey signed a stand-by agreement with the IMF in 1999 as part of an exchange-rate-based macroeconomic stabilization program. In her Letter of Intent, Turkey committed to "legal amendments will be passed by parliament to define energy as a sector subject to the Turkish commercial code."[2] It was hoped that such legal amendment would facilitate privatizations through sale of TOR contracts. The Economic Recovery Loan agreement signed with the World Bank in May 2000 went further; Turkey committed to the enactment of an electricity reform law to establish an independent regulatory agency "with full authority over tariff policy, further liberalize the electricity sector and ensure an adequate competitive environment" and to adopt a plan to establish a regulatory authority and demonopolize the gas sector (World Bank 2000). A similar move toward the independent regulatory agency model was also envisaged for the telecommunications industry. These commitments were reinstated in a new Letter of Intent sent to the IMF in December 2000.[3]

The stabilization program resulted in a severe financial-cum-balance of payments crisis in 2000 and early 2001. A new recovery program was adopted in May 2001, and energy sector reform was a component of this recovery program, along with other structural reforms (International Energy Agency 2001; Airaudo et al. 2004). The reform laws for electricity and gas had already been enacted by that time (February and April 2001, respectively). The international literature on the political economy of economic reform underlines the role of crises in facilitating the enactment of radical economic reforms. The experience of Turkey seems to be consistent with this view.

1.2 Role of European Union

One should also emphasize the role of European Union. Turkey had already enacted a competition law in 1994 (Law No. 4054 on the Protection of Competition) and established a Competition Authority as a precondition of entry into a Customs Union with the EU. EU accession guided regulatory reform in a wide range of

---

[1] See Özel and Atiyas (2011) for a discussion of the factors that guided "regulatory diffusion" for the case of Turkey.

[2] Letter of Intent dated December 9, 1999, http://www.imf.org/external/np/loi/1999/120999.HTM accessed December 16, 2011.

[3] Letter of intent dated December 18, 2000, http://www.imf.org/external/np/loi/2000/tur/03/index.htm accessed December 16, 2011.

policy areas, including network industries such as electricity, gas, and telecommunications. As will be discussed in the following chapters, the legal and regulatory frameworks adopted for electricity and gas in the early 2000s were already consistent with those in the EU.[4]

2 Renewables

Partially driven by energy security concerns and partially to follow EU principles, especially regarding environmental standards, Turkey started promoting renewable energy technologies and energy efficiency, passing the Renewables Law in 2005 and the Energy Efficiency Law in 2007 (Chap. 4). Carbon dioxide emissions per capita are one of the lowest in the OECD. In terms of economic activity, emissions per dollar of GDP at market exchange rates are among the highest in the OECD although at purchasing power parity they are not that high. Regardless, since 1990, Turkey has doubled its CO_2 emissions, among the largest increases observed in OECD (IEA 2009). Moreover, the CO_2 intensity of electricity and heat production in 2007 was among the highest, although it has been declining since 1990. In addition, ambient air pollution due to sulfur dioxide and nitrogen monoxide exceeds national air quality standards.

The country always generated large amounts of electricity from hydro resources (more than 40% of total generation in the 1990s but 25% in 2010), but it also added more than 1,600 MW of wind since the passage of the Renewables Law in 2005. Turkey's goal of 30% renewables by 2023 seems quite achievable. Still, other than hydro, most of which is based on large dams, installed renewables capacity is about 3% of total installed capacity in the country; the share of renewables (other than hydro) in generation is often much less.

Some geothermal and biomass facilities are also under construction but solar continues to struggle as the most expensive technology in the absence of high enough tariff support. The Renewables Law has many of the standard clauses such as requiring energy suppliers to provide a certain percentage of their electricity from renewable resources, providing price support, and ease of access to rights of way for interconnection. However, Turkish feed-in-tariffs (FITs) are much lower than those offered in most EU countries, especially for solar. Turkey started offering bonus payments for local content but it is too early to judge the effectiveness of these payments although they may be challenged by international suppliers at the World Trade Organization. Still, the Turkish strategy can be more sustainable than higher FITs, which were shelved by many EU governments in response to the financial and economic crises that engulfed most EU members.

Small hydro facilities are encouraged by the Renewables Law and implementing regulations but in many locations, host communities object to construction of these facilities out of concern for the local environment and impact of the facility on the

[4] See, for example, the various chapters in Hoekman and Togan (2005).

river flows, local ecosystem, and their livelihoods. Perhaps more relevant for Turkey's hydro ambitions is the history of tensions among Turkey, Syria, and Iraq regarding the sharing of the waters of Fırat (Euphrates) and Dicle (Tigris) rivers that start in Turkey but supply almost all of freshwater needs of Syria and Iraq. With the risk of changing rainfall patterns due to climate change, the water shortages can be more severe in the region, raising tensions further. Sharing of water resources by riparian countries is a serious and growing issue across and growing many parts of the world; there are efforts to develop international standards and agreements, of which Turkey should be aware. These issues are discussed further in Chap. 4.

3 Nuclear

At the same time, Turkey is closer to its first nuclear facility that the country has been pursuing since the 1970s. The official goal is 5% nuclear by 2020. Given that renewables are still costlier than conventional technologies and intermittent, and have low capacity factors, nuclear offers another option for Turkey to diversify its energy portfolio with an emissions-free technology. For a variety of reasons, including public opposition, high capital cost and financing difficulties, and insufficient governance and management capacity on the part of the state agencies, Turkey has not been able to build its first nuclear plant yet. But, now there is an intergovernmental agreement between Russia and Turkey. A state-owned Russian company offered an economically attractive price of 12.5 cents per kWh (in 2019 prices when the plant's first unit is supposed to start operations) to build the facility. However, the Akkuyu site, which was first licensed in the 1970s, is now seen as inappropriate by some experts due to its proximity to an active fault line. Local opposition has been strong for years but gained further strength after the Fukushima accident. Perhaps, the biggest concern is the lack of an independent nuclear regulator and a "safety culture" in state institutions that is commensurate with the risks inherent in nuclear operations. A five-page nuclear law is not sufficient to instill confidence that Turkey is institutionally ready to build and operate a nuclear facility, and manage radioactive waste properly. The Fukushima accident might have been a striking reminder to Turkish officials of the shortcomings of the institutional framework for nuclear in Turkey; new legislation is reportedly under development to address safety and waste management concerns in full coordination with the IAEA. We will discuss these issues in Chap. 4 in more detail.

4 An Accounting of Restructuring Efforts

As with any restructuring experience, there are many unintended consequences, unfulfilled promises and timelines due to numerous implementation challenges ranging from resistance from incumbent interests to politically motivated manipulation of market dynamics and institutions, and from incompetency and inexperience of implementing agencies and the private sector to old school thinking (Chaps. 2, 3).

4.1 Electricity

Electricity restructuring has been driven by a privatization strategy and the revenues that can be generated from privatization rather than a desire to instill healthy competition in the sector. The key strategic role given to privatization in the restructuring process have also led the Turkish authorities to initiate restructuring in the distribution segment, where the possibilities of competition are limited, rather than generation, where the real productivity gains would be expected in the medium term. Overall, 10 years passed since the 2001 restructuring bill but competition is still limited to a relatively small segment of the electricity industry, most generation remain in state hands and distribution privatizations were delayed significantly. The privatization method entailed selling of operating rights to the highest bidder and did not include any competition in terms of service (in contrast to the method adopted for the natural gas distribution companies). Privatization of distribution franchises, finally being implemented, is expected to reduce the system losses and improve reliability. System losses (technical and illegal use) can be quite high in Turkey (14–19% as national average depending on the source of data) and range from 5.6 to 73% across regions, highest in the east and southeast. Technical losses is said to be around 7–8%. But data is not always reliable and consistent across different sources. Power outages are common in Turkey, adversely affecting economic activity. Turkish businessmen report on average four power outages per month, which are particularly severe for the manufacturing sector (World Bank Group 2009). While interruptions seem to be more common in eastern and southeastern Anatolia, in early January 2012 there was a widespread blackout that lasted three hours in major industrial cities of the northwest. There was a similar outage of six hours across 13 cities in 2006 in the western part of Turkey.

The Turkish reform model was largely inspired by the New Electricity Trading Arrangements of the UK, and it was envisaged that most trade would take place through bilateral contracts and real-time equality of supply and demand would be implemented through a balancing market. However, in actuality the balancing market acted as a pool, where most trade took place most of the time and the development of the bilateral contracts market proceeded much more slowly than initially envisaged. Although the restructuring process has recorded some significant achievements, for example, in terms of the establishment of a wholesale market, private investment was late to respond (though eventually private investment did respond) and progress in terms of competition or efficiency and productivity gains is still to be seen. In effect, Turkey represents an interesting case underlining the pros and cons of a restructuring model driven predominantly by privatization. These issues are discussed in Chap. 2.

4.2 Natural Gas

Introducing competition into the gas market has proved to be even more elusive. Turkey already had developed long-term supply contracts via BOTAŞ with several suppliers in the region. As a result, developing competition meant the transfer of portions of these contracts to private entities, which acquired an import license from the regulator. Both the release program and the liberalization of gas imports were severely delayed. At the risk of stating the obvious in hindsight, it was always going to be difficult to convince suppliers such as Gazprom to switch to private importers from BOTAŞ, with which they had long-term contracts that included oil-indexed pricing, take-or-pay clauses, and Treasury guarantees. With the expiration of the first Western pipeline contract in late 2011, there is now an opportunity to reduce the share of BOTAŞ in import volumes. BOTAŞ has not renewed the contract for long term, but had to sign a one-year agreement to ensure supply adequacy in the market because private importers' negotiations with Gazprom have not resulted in any contracts by the end of 2011. The delay in these negotiations raises concerns about the inexperienced private importers' ability to sign fair deals with experienced suppliers such as Gazprom. The Russian side may be expecting a bigger involvement from the Turkish government in selection of the private partners in lieu of guarantees as part of the increased intergovernmental cooperation between Turkey and Russia. Also, BOTAŞ is reportedly selling gas in domestic market at lower prices than its cost to import gas. These subsidies are not only a significant burden on BOTAŞ' finances but also form an obstacle for private firms since they cannot compete in the domestic market as long as subsidies continue even if they are able to get as good a deal from Gazprom as BOTAŞ.

On the other hand, since late 2009, about 25 companies acquired spot LNG import licenses from the Energy Market Regulatory Authority (or EPDK, Enerji Piyasası Düzenleme Kurumu); in 2010, a record amount of spot LNG was imported—8% of total imports. Although the country's first private LNG import terminal, EgeGaz, completed in 2002, was not given an import license until late 2008, competition in wholesale supplies of natural gas seems to have finally started. The success of this trend depends largely on the commitment of government officials to the market opening process as companies negotiate with suppliers who traditionally dealt with BOTAŞ. The 2008 deal of the Ministry of Energy and Natural Resources with Egypt to import gas with BOTAŞ as the agent of the state was a blow to the process although, given recent developments in Egypt and Syria, this deal is not likely to materialize in the near future.

In contrast, the licensing of distribution franchises appears to be quite successful, offering lessons to other jurisdictions around the world that are trying to get distribution networks built by private investment (Chap. 3). The great majority of the cities was connected within several years and is now supplied natural gas. The auction process implemented by EPDK led to "zero" bids for distribution tariffs and even "zero" connection charges in several franchise areas and low tariffs in general. This way, licensed companies built distribution networks

Table 1.1 Share of energy imports in total imports

2002	2003	2004	2005	2006	2007	2008	2009	2010	2011
12%	17%	15%	18%	21%	20%	24%	21%	21%	22%

Source. www.tcmb.gov.tr

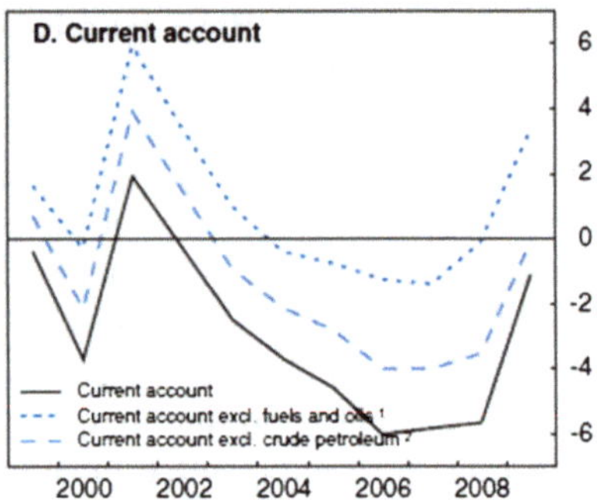

Fig. 1.1 Current account (as percent of GDP). *Source.* OECD (2010), p 36

and connected customers at very low fees, which were fixed for eight years. As some of the first licenses are completing their initial eight-year period, the companies are seeking higher tariffs but these distribution charges represent a small share of the total gas bill for customers and any increase to be approved by the regulator should not have much impact. The success of this approach raises questions about why a similar auction method was not pursued for the privatization of electricity distribution networks.

5 Energy Security

Energy security considerations continue to influence Turkish energy policy, and must have gained renewed importance after the rapid increase in oil prices in the 2000s. Since Turkey imports almost all of its oil and all of its gas at prices indexed to the price of oil, gas prices increased significantly along with the price of oil. The share of energy imports in total imports peaked at 24% in 2008 when the oil and gas prices peaked and remains above 21% as compared to 12% in 2002 (Table 1.1). As in other countries with large oil and gas imports, increasing cost of these fuels negatively impacts trade and current account balances (Fig. 1.1). In 2010, current account deficit increased to 6% of GDP again with the relative recovery of the economy and energy prices as compared to 2009. As of the end of 2011, energy imports were equivalent to about half of the country's trade deficit and two-thirds of current account deficit.

When the contract for the Western pipeline expired in late 2011, Turkey did not renew it via BOTAŞ but some private companies are negotiating with Gazprom for about four billion cubic meters (bcm); another six bcm is also available for private companies. This action does not necessarily help with enhancing energy security because it maintains the share of Russian gas in total gas imports but it has the potential of lowering the cost of gas via competitive importers, especially if gas prices can be set independent of the price of oil. But, private entities have not been able to secure import contracts in place of BOTAŞ at the time of writing.

Increased competition has occurred via spot LNG imports. In 2010, Turkey imported a record amount of spot LNG cargoes—8% of total imports, some of which was imported by private entities (Chap. 3). These spot cargoes were not based on oil-indexed prices and were priced lower. Western Europe is moving away from oil-indexed pricing for gas imports,[5] either via pipeline or as LNG. This transition is at least partially driven by the competitive pressures created in EU countries as gas sector reforms outlined in EU and national regulations are finally taking hold. Increasing LNG imports by many countries as well as imports from North Africa helped to diversify supply sources. The global supply of natural gas and trade of LNG and piped gas have been increasing. The shale gas revolution in the US has been having a deflationary impact on the Atlantic basin trade of LNG, which was already under some pressure due to global economic slowdown since 2008. On the other hand, the oil market remains tight. On the demand side, oil and natural gas stopped being close substitutes since oil use for power generation practically disappeared in most of OECD economies. Under these conditions, leaving the natural gas price tied to the price of oil would unnecessarily inflate it.

Turkey has significantly increased its energy collaboration with Russia, including the intergovernmental agreement on the Akkuyu nuclear facility, renegotiation of gas contracts from the Western pipeline and some take-or-pay obligations of BOTAŞ, and the Turkish support for Russia's South Stream pipeline under the Black Sea all seem to be parts of this collaboration. The South Stream pipeline will not supply gas to Turkey but it might reduce the amount of gas that will be shipped via Turkey, hence reducing transit revenues. In exchange, Turkey seems to be getting an attractive price for the nuclear electricity and a lower gas price for new Western pipeline contracts. A transparent accounting of these deals is necessary to conclude whether Turkey benefits from these arrangements or not. It also remains to be seen whether this bi-national collaboration increases Turkey's dependence on Russia for energy or it helps Turkey in its international dealings to pursue an energy diversification strategy. Both South Stream and Nabucco remain speculative projects at this time given their costs and complexity of supplier deals, and as new projects based on Shah Deniz gas from Azerbaijan seem to be more realistic and advancing fast. The Turkish strategy of "having multiple irons on the fire" may turn out quite astute at the end—see discussion on transit options in the following section.

Another opportunity for Turkey to diversify its natural gas supplies is the potential to increase domestic production. Exploration efforts by TPAO, the national oil company, have intensified in recent years. The offshore Black Sea potential attracted major international companies such as ExxonMobil and

[5] For example, see Stern and Rogers (2011).

Petrobras. Smaller companies have been exploring across the country but especially in the Thrace Basin and offshore Black Sea. There are no major discoveries yet. Turkey has some shale deposits that can be developed once their geologic characteristics are better understood. The higher price environment is conducive to developing unconventional and marginal resources that were previously considered too expensive.

However, the upstream investment frameworks of the country are dated and do not create a consistent environment for exploration and development with an independent upstream regulator and regular bidding rounds for exploration or development blocks. The frameworks do not address peculiarities of unconventional resources. A modern petroleum framework and a more commercially oriented and organized TPAO can lead to increased upstream activity in Turkey. Only with increased exploration efforts, resources can be fully assessed and developed if commercially viable. It is absolutely necessary to develop the proper safety and environmental protection standards and institutional capacity to regulate operators to prevent accidental spills or water pollution, and to properly mitigate damages if accidents occur.

The contribution of modern renewables other than hydro is very small. Despite the support framework created since the passage of the Renewables Law in 2005, only investments in wind (about 1,600 MW of new capacity and 4,600 MW under construction) have been noteworthy. There is no significant solar investment and only about 114 MW of geothermal capacity in operation although another 314 MW is under construction. Given their low capacity factor, wind facilities cannot be expected to supply more than a few percent of total demand in the country for the foreseeable future. Altogether, modern renewables other than hydro will not be able to enhance Turkey's energy security in any significant way for some time to come unless Turkey increases support programs substantially, especially for solar.

6 Turkey as a Transit Country

In addition to its own increasing energy needs, Turkey also acts as a bridge between hydrocarbon resources of the Caspian and Middle East regions and consumers in Europe. Although the country's Ceyhan port on the Mediterranean acts as an outlet for Caspian oil for the world market, increasingly it is natural gas that is of interest. In 2007, Turkey started exporting gas but relatively small volumes (less than one bcm per year). However, there are many major pipeline projects, including Interconnector Turkey–Greece–Italy (ITGI), Trans-Anatolia, Trans-Adriatic Pipeline (TAP), and the largest, Nabucco, which is planned to transport gas from Azerbaijan, Turkmenistan, and Iraq, among others. Although BOTAŞ is a partner of the Nabucco project company, recent developments raised questions about Turkey's commitment to the project. In last days of 2011, Turkey signed on Russia's alternative to Nabucco, the South Stream project, by allowing access to Turkish waters in Black Sea. The South Stream pipeline is designed as a bypass of Ukraine, which had conflicts with Russia in the past regarding gas supplies and prices, and as an alternative to the Nabucco pipeline. These conflicts led to curtailment of gas supplies to Ukraine by Gazprom and Ukraine using gas destined to Europe, including Turkey, and leaving customers in those regions without gas in the middle of winter.

In September 2011, BP, the operator of the Shah Deniz project in Azerbaijan, which was targeted to supply much of the initial gas to the Nabucco pipeline, proposed an alternative in South-East Europe Pipeline (SEEP). The proposal envisions using existing pipeline capacity in Turkey and Europe and building only about 800 miles of new pipeline, or about a third of the total distance between Shah Deniz and customers in Europe. A later agreement between Turkey and Azerbaijan, and the announcement of Trans-Anatolia pipeline project under the leadership of SOCAR, national oil company of Azerbaijan, gave further support to SEEP and undermined Nabucco further.

These projects target the Shah Deniz gas of about 10 bcm per year. As such it is conceivable that a version of Nabucco can still survive if and when Iraqi and Turkmen gas become available for exports to Europe via Turkey since larger pipeline capacities will be needed. Given that Nabucco has the backing of EU and has developed the appropriate legal framework, a "merger" of SEEP, Trans-Anatolia and Nabucco can be possible to expedite the approval process.

However, much more worrying for Nabucco is Turkey's support of the South Stream project because that is the Russian alternative to Nabucco to supply gas from Russia and Caspian/Central Asian resources to Europe. As a subsea pipeline in the hostile environment of Black Sea this project is quite expensive, with estimates ranging from 15 to 25 billion dollars, but the examples of Blue Stream and Nord Stream show that Russia can get these challenging subsea projects built. Nabucco is cheaper at an estimated 10–15 billion dollars but it is in need of supplies from multiple sources including Azerbaijan, Turkmenistan, and Iraq. Recent announcements indicate that gas from Azerbaijan will flow via alternative pipelines; gas from Turkmenistan remains challenging as it would have to be routed either via Iran or via Azerbaijan. Both routes face problems. For example, building necessary infrastructure in Iran by international investors can be subject to sanctions; Iran's own need for gas may create a situation similar to Ukraine interfering with gas flows from Russia. The legal rights of littoral states of the Caspian Sea are not yet resolved; as such, the Trans-Caspian pipeline remains on paper. Hence, gas from Iraq is now a priority. Nabucco shareholders OMV and MOL are developing gas fields in northern Iraq. It is possible that Iraq might have the potential to fill Nabucco alone, in which case, other pipelines may not mean the death of Nabucco project.

It is also possible that Europe will need gas from all of these pipelines as many countries consider shutting down their nuclear plants in reaction to the Fukushima accident and coal plants to reduce greenhouse gas emissions. In any case, Turkey is well placed to take advantage of its strategic location between major gas producers to its east and southeast and the consumers in Europe while, at the same time, meeting its own growing demand from an increasingly diversified group of exporters.

7 Looking Ahead to a Dynamic Energy Scene

The discussion above suggests a multidimensional framework with which to evaluate the Turkish experience with energy sector reform. On the one hand, restructuring of the electricity and gas industries aim at developing competitive industries and reduce the burden of energy on the public budget. Restructuring alone, however, is not likely to address concerns raised in terms of energy security, dependence on imports and the possible adverse effects of these on the current account, and macroeconomic stability. These concerns require a broader energy policy. Components of such a broader policy already exist with regard to, for example, renewables and energy efficiency. Whether these are sufficient is a central question this book will try to address.

With regard to restructuring, although 10 years have passed since the passage of electricity and natural gas restructuring laws in 2001, the implementation of key requirements were delayed significantly but Turkey is finally entering a period when the results of electricity and gas restructuring will start to be seen. Privatization of electricity distribution companies started late but is near completion; the companies will be judged on their performance in reducing system losses per EPDK regulation. Privatization of generation assets still under state ownership, also delayed for years, is scheduled to start in 2012. Regional cross-subsidies (national tariff) are scheduled to expire also in 2012. If these actions can be completed as planned, Turkey should have a more competitive electricity market with more private participants.

But, the state remains as a key player. The country's first nuclear plant may get built based on an intergovernmental agreement between Turkey and Russia. On the gas side, BOTAŞ still holds a great majority of the long-term contracts and the government is signing new deals with suppliers such as Russia and Egypt. Since gas-fired generation is an important part of the generation portfolio in the Turkish electricity market, both in terms of overall generation and also in terms of cycling flexibility to provide peak load service and cycling back-up for renewables, the ability to import reliable and affordable natural gas is crucial for power sector performance and affordable electricity prices as well.

Turkey is importing gas from multiple sources although more than 40% comes from Russia. There are multiple transit pipeline projects to Europe that can increase supplies from Azerbaijan in the short term and, eventually, from Turkmenistan and Iraq not only to Europe but also to Turkey. There are emerging signs of reducing BOTAŞ' share. Private investors are negotiating with Gazprom to replace BOTAŞ as importers from the Western pipeline after the expiration of the 1986 contract. The large number private companies with a spot LNG import license is also encouraging not only in terms of diversifying supply sources and increasing competition but also in terms of lower gas prices since these cargoes do not have to be oil-linked.

In the rest of the book, we will evaluate progress with the restructuring process so far and discuss prospects looking ahead for both electricity and natural gas sectors, which are closely linked. We will also assess most recent developments in the Turkish energy scene, namely the promotion of renewables, energy efficiency, and nuclear energy. These alternatives are not likely to survive in a fully competitive market environment, since they are costlier than market-supported technologies such as gas-fired power plants that private investors would most likely pursue. The marriage of support programs for these alternatives and the efforts to complete restructuring of gas and power sectors create interesting dynamics. Similarly, as an import dependent and transit country, Turkey is trying to balance energy security and regional energy trade relations with gas market restructuring. We will try to balance these complex interactions and dynamics in our policy recommendations chapter at the end of this book.

References

Airaudo, M., Derviş, K., Gros, D., Öztrak, F. Bayar, F. and Y. Işık (2004) "Stabilising Stabilisation" Center for European Studies, EU-Turkey Working Papers No. 7. http://www.ceps.be/ceps/download/1001 accessed December 16, 2011.

Hoekman, Bernard and Subidey Togan (2005) *Turkey: Economic Reform and Accession to the European Union*, Washington DC: Word Bank Publications.

International Energy Agency (2001). Energy Policies of IEA Countries – Turkey 2001 Review, Paris: IEA.

IEA (2009); Energy Policies of OECD Countries: Turkey 2009 Review, IEA/OECD, Paris.

OECD (2010). OECD Economic Surveys, Turkey.

Özel, Işık and İzak Atiyas (2011). "Regulatory Diffusion in Turkey: A Cross-sectoral Assessment" in Tamer Çetin and Fuat Oğuz (eds.) *Political Economy of Regulation in Turkey*, New York: Springer, 51–74.

Stern, Jonathan and Howard Rogers (2011). *The Transition to Hub-Based Gas Pricing in Continental Europe*. NG 49, The Oxford Institute for Energy Studies.

World Bank (2000) Loan Agreement (Economic Reform Loan) between Republic of Turkey and International Bank For Reconstruction and Development, Loan No. 4549 TU. http://www-wds.worldbank.org/external/default/WDSContentServer/WDSP/ECA/2004/12/15/FB1944A5BDD9DEA285256F03001638BC/1_0/Rendered/PDF/FB1944A5BDD9DEA285256F03001638BC.pdf accessed December 22, 2011.

Chapter 2
Regulatory Reform and Competition in the Turkish Electricity Industry

1 The Structure of the Electricity Industry

1.1 Demand, Capacity, and Production

The growth of electricity demand in Turkey has historically been high, growing at an average rate of about 7% per year between 1990 and 2010. As seen in Fig. 2.1, there have been a number of years with exceptionally low growth, namely 1999, the year of a devastating earthquake, and the years 1994, 2001, and 2008–2009, which were years of severe economic crises.

Imports and exports of electricity are negligible. As of the end of 2010, total capacity is about 50 GW. The composition of total capacity according to fuel type is given in Table 2.1. The table shows a steady increase in the share of natural gas from less than 15% in the early 1990s to over 35% by 2010. This expansion occurred at the expense of coal, fuel oil, but especially hydro. Replacing coal and fuel oil with gas helps with reducing emissions but displacing hydro may negate such benefits.

An important part of the increase in gas-fired plants is accounted by new plants built by the private sector. The evolution of generation capacity by legal status is given in Table 2.2. In the Table EÜAŞ is the state owned Electricity Generation Corporation (Elektrik Üretim A.Ş.). The term "concession companies" refers to enterprises that had generation and distribution concessions and were taken over by EÜAŞ in 2003. The table shows that the share of private sector plants, comprising autoproducers, production companies and companies holding transfer of operating rights (TOR) contracts, has increased from about 19% in 2000 to almost 51% in 2010. The item "production companies" includes both independent power producers (IPPs) and companies with build operate transfer (BOT) or build operate (BO) contracts. As discussed below, the competitive implications of these two classes of generators are of course quite different, since BO and BOT contracts entailed take-or-pay clauses shielding these plants from any type of commercial

I. Atiyas et al., *Reforming Turkish Energy Markets*,
DOI: 10.1007/978-1-4614-0290-9_2,

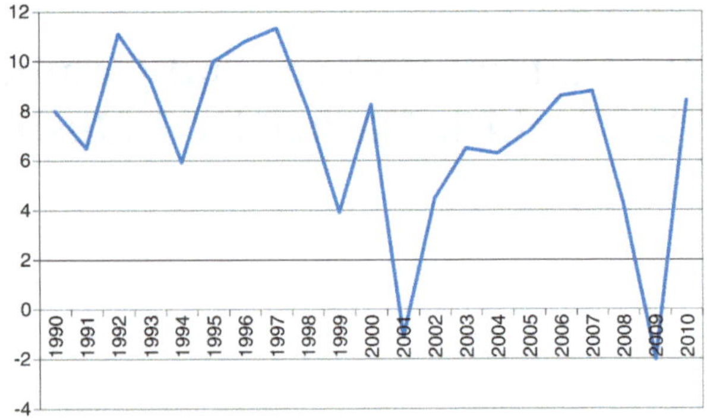

Fig. 2.1 rowth of demand for electricity (%). *Source* TEİAŞ

Table 2.1 Installed capacity by primary energy sources (MW)

	Coal	%	Fuel Oil	%	Natural Gas	%	Other	%	Total Thermal	%	Hydro	%	Wind	%	Total	%
1990	5,206	32	1,202	7	2,210	14	918	6	9,536	58	6,764	41	0	0	16,318	100
1995	6,374	30	1,149	5	2,925	14	626	3	11,074	53	9,863	47	0	0	20,954	100
2000	6,989	26	1,261	5	7,044	26	759	3	16,053	59	11,175	41	19	0	27,264	100
2005	9,117	23	2,253	6	13,774	35	759	2	25,902	67	12,906	33	20	0	38,844	100
2010	11,950	24	1,549	3	18,420	37	358	1	32,279	65	15,831	32	1,320	3	49,524	100

Source TEİAŞ

Table 2.2 Installed capacity by legal status (MW)

	1990	1995	2000	2005	2010
EÜAŞ (1)	14,729	15,574	17,968	20,431	20,368
%	90	88	66	53	41
Affiliated Partnerships of EÜAŞ		3,284	3,284	2,154	3,834
%		19	12	6	8
Concessionary companies	378	716	610		
%	2	4	2		
Autoproducers	1,194	1,345	2,996	4,062	3,143
%	7	8	11	10	6
Transfer of operation rights (TOR)			330	650	650
%			1	2	1
Production companies	16	35	1,985	10,797	21,265
%	0	0	7	28	43
Mobile power plants			91	750	263
%			0	2	1
Turkey	16,318	17,670	27,264	38,844	49,524
%	100	100	100	100	100

Note Production Companies include BO, BOT and IPP plants
Source TEİAŞ
(1) Including generators in the privatization programme

Table 2.3 Generation by legal status 2010

	GWh	%
EÜAŞ	79,258	38
EÜAŞ affiliated partnerships	16,274	8
Production companies	98,904	47
Autoproducers	12,447	6
TOR	4,324	2
Total	211,208	100

Note Production companies include BOT, BO and IPP plants.
Source TEİAŞ

Table 2.4 Generation by primary energy source 2010

	GWh	%
Coal	55,046	26.1
Fuel oil, diesel naphtha	2,180	1.0
Gas	98,144	46.5
Renewables and waste	458	0.2
Total thermal	155,828	73.8
Hydroelectric	51,796	24.5
Geothermal and wind	3,585	1.7
Total	211,208	100.0

Source TEİAŞ

risk including competition. The private competitive segment of the market consists of IPPs, autoproducers, and autoproducer groups.[1] The share of IPPs has also increased over time. In 2005, total capacity of IPPs was about 2.2 GW, less than 6% of total capacity in the industry. By 2010, an additional 10 GW of capacity was added by IPPs, raising their share to about 25% of total capacity.

As of 2010, total electricity production in Turkey reached about 211 thousand GWh (Table 2.3). The share of EÜAŞ and its partnerships[2] in total generation was about 46% and that of the private sector was about 54%. However, the share of independent power producers was 19% and the share of autoproducers was nearly 6% (Camadan 2011). The share of gas-fired plants in total generation is about 47% and that of hydroelectric plants is about 25% (Table 2.4).

[1] Autoproducers are established primarily to consume the electricity they generate by themselves. According to the Energy Market Law, they have the right to sell 20% of the electricity they produce to the market. Under exceptional circumstances the Board of the regulatory authority may increase this ratio. The ratio has been set at 40% by the Board in December 2011. However, any sale in excess of the ratio set by the Board would require a generator's license. An autoproducer group is similar, except that it generates electricity not only for itself but for its affiliates. In what follows the term autoproducer will be used to refer to both autoproducers and autoproducer groups.

[2] EÜAŞ affiliated partnerships are companies where EÜAŞ' ownership share is above 50%.

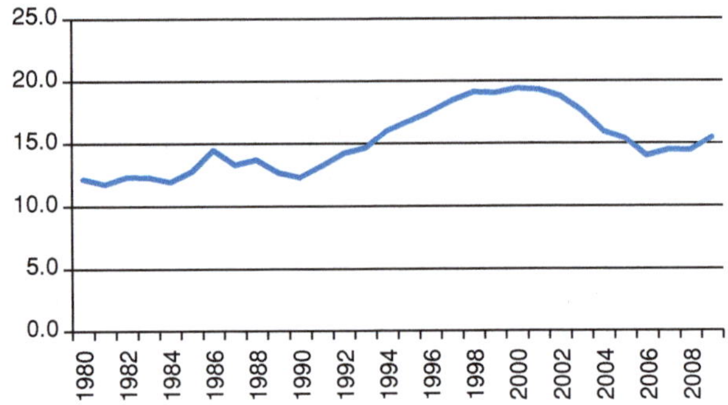

Fig. 2.2 Transmission and distribution losses as a share of total consumption (%). *Source* TEİAŞ

1.2 The Problem of Distribution Losses

An important issue that any reform effort had to face was the problem of losses and theft. There are two sets of data provided on technical and "non-technical losses" in Turkey.[3] Figure 2.2 shows the ratio of total (transmission and distribution) losses as a percentage of total consumption in Turkey, as reported by the Turkish Electricity Transmission Corporation (Türkiye Elektrik İletim A.Ş., TEİAŞ). The loss ratio increased between 12 and 15% in the early 1990s to a high of over 19% by the year 2000. It has since declined to around 15% by 2009.

The second source of data on losses, the Turkish Electricity Distribution Company (Türkiye Elektrik Dağıtım A.Ş., TEDAŞ), reports technical losses and theft as the difference between total energy purchased by TEDAŞ and total energy sold. Figure 2.3 shows distribution of losses as a percentage of total energy purchased according to TEDAŞ data. The ratio has reached a peak at 21.6% in 2000, declined until 2008 to 14.4% but has increased again, reaching 18.6% in 2010. The TEDAŞ data are different from those provided by;TEİAŞ the overall trend seems similar; however, TEDAŞ reports larger increases in 2009.[4]

Compared to international averages these ratios are extremely high. As shown in Fig. 2.4, as of 2008 the average ratio of transmission and distribution losses to total supply was less than 7% among OECD countries and 8.5% in the world. Among OECD countries Turkey has the highest loss ratio after Mexico.

The distribution of losses across regions is highly uneven. In 2009, the ratio of losses to total consumption in two distribution regions of Eastern Anatolia was above 50% (Table 2.5).[5] Istanbul had the second highest level of losses in terms of absolute

[3] The term "non-technical losses" most often refers to theft of electricity. Hence "theft" and "non-technical losses" will be used interchangeably. The term "losses", when used alone, refers to the sum of technical and non-technical losses.

[4] As of December 2011, TEİAŞ loss data for 2010 were not available.

[5] The provincial composition of regional distribution companies is provided in Table 2.7 below.

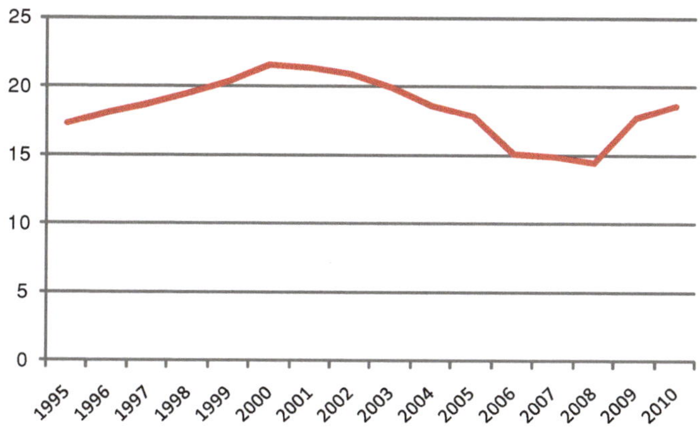

Fig. 2.3 Distribution losses (percentage of energy purchases by TEDAŞ). *Source* TEDAŞ Annual Report 2010

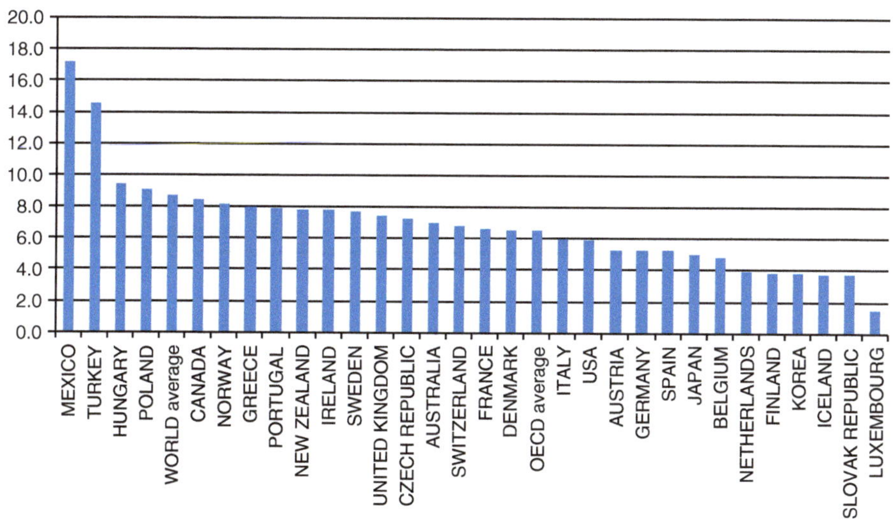

Fig. 2.4 Transmission and distribution losses among OECD countries (2008) *Source* OECD, as reported by TEİAŞ

quantities. The increase in the loss ratio in the 1990s probably reflects both an overall breakdown of governance Turkey experienced during the 1990s as well as insufficient investment. The fact that loss ratios were highest in provinces that have suffered most from violence associated with the Kurdish problem also suggests the presence of deeply rooted social factors. There is anecdotal evidence that theft is also high in shanty towns in some urban centers (most notably in Istanbul) and that in some cases industrialists engage in large amounts of theft in areas where law enforcement is weak.

Table 2.5 Distribution losses across distribution regions (2009)

	Ratio to total purchases (%)		MWh
DİCLE EDAŞ	73.01	DİCLE EDAŞ	11 337 581
VANGÖLÜ EDAŞ	55.57	BOĞAZİÇİ EDAŞ (Istanbul West)	1 975 682
ARAS EDAŞ	27.70	VANGÖLÜ EDAŞ	1 626 976
FIRAT EDAŞ	13.63	TOROSLAR EDAŞ	1 316 381
ÇORUH EDAŞ	11.51	GEDİZ EDAŞ	1 032 424
YEŞİLIRMAK EDAŞ	10.63	AYEDAŞ (Istanbul East)	693 489
BOĞAZİÇİ EDAŞ (Istanbul West)	9.68	ARAS EDAŞ	655 366
AKDENİZ EDAŞ	9.18	ULUDAĞ EDAŞ	654 357
MERAM EDAŞ	8.54	AKDENİZ EDAŞ	599 040
TOROSLAR EDAŞ	8.30	MERAM EDAŞ	520 595
ÇAMLIBEL EDAŞ	7.71	YEŞİLIRMAK EDAŞ	481 844
GEDİZ EDAŞ	7.67	TRAKYA EDAŞ	396 108
AYEDAŞ (Istanbul East)	7.48	FIRAT EDAŞ	320 788
GÖKSU EDAŞ	6.93	OSMANGAZİ EDAŞ	313 725
TRAKYA EDAŞ	6.41	ÇORUH EDAŞ	298 543
OSMANGAZİ EDAŞ	6.08	GÖKSU EDAŞ	266 195
ULUDAĞ EDAŞ	5.59	ÇAMLIBEL EDAŞ	179 407

Source TEDAŞ Statistics 2009

2 Historical Background and the Road to Reform

As in many other countries, the main player in the electricity industry in Turkey was a vertically integrated publicly owned enterprise, the Türkiye Elektrik Kurumu (Turkish Electricity Authority, TEK). TEK was established in 1970 with the purpose of uniting activities related to the supply of electricity under a single integrated publicly owned entity.[6] In 1993, TEK was separated into two corporatized entities, the Turkish Electricity Generation and Transmission Company (TEAŞ) and the Turkish Electricity Distribution Company (TEDAŞ).

In the 1980s and 1990s, there were several attempts to attract private capital to the electricity industry. These efforts can partly be explained by the significant

[6] The only exceptions were municipally-owned transmission and distribution facilities and three regional concession companies. The municipal facilities later came under TEK's control in 1982.

transformation in the overall economic policy regime that took place in the 1980s. In the post World War II era in Turkey was engaged in a policy regime often labeled import substitution industrialization (ISI) in the economic development literature. This policy regime was characterized by heavy involvement of the state in economic activities, in particular widespread government ownership of enterprises in critical industries, such as energy, telecommunications, petrochemicals, iron, and steel. The state also played a critical role in the allocation of financial resources especially through stateowned banks. A major balance of payments crisis in the second half of the 1970s (and a military coup in 1980) marked the end of the ISI regime. The 1980s witnessed massive liberalization of domestic markets, international trade, and finance. In this new market-oriented regime privatization was seen as a means of eliminating what was perceived to be widespread inefficiencies in the public sector. In addition, there was a strong public finance reason for privatization: throughout the 1990s Turkey experienced high public deficits and mounting public debt. Forecasting high growth in electricity demand, and high investment requirements to build the necessary generation capacity, Turkish governments wanted to reduce the burden on the public budget by attracting private investment to the industry.

An important attempt to privatize TEK through sale of ownership rights was undertaken in 1994 through Law 3974. This was struck down by the Constitutional Court. The Court decision was generally perceived to determine the boundaries of privatization policies until an amendment to the Constitution in 1999. The Court was concerned about foreign ownership in a strategic industry and about the fact that the law did not envisage any remedies to prevent monopolization or cartelization. It also objected to the law's attempt to characterize contracts engaging the private sector in the electricity industry as governed by private rather than public law. The Court stated that electricity was a public service and therefore private sector provision was regulated under public law and had to be organized as a concession under the judicial review of the Council of State (Danıştay).[7]

The attitude of the Constitutional Court was widely regarded as barring privatization models that entailed transfer of ownership rights over state-owned electricity assets. In the 1980s and 1990s, attempts to engage the private sector took the form of designing investment schemes such as BOT, BO, and transfer of operating rights (TOR) contracts. The first law that established a legal framework for private sector participation in the electricity industry was enacted in 1984 (Law No. 3096). This law introduced two types of contracts: BOT contracts for new generation facilities and TOR for existing generation and distribution facilities. A BOT was a concession through which a company would build and operate a generation plant for 99 years (later reduced to 49 years) and then transfer the plant to the state at no cost. A TOR was a lease-like arrangement under which the private company would operate and,

---

[7] For the various constitutional and legal problems with private participation in the electricity industry in Turkey see Gülen (1998); Bilgiç et al. (1999); Çetin and Oğuz (2007); Ulusoy and Oğuz (2007) and Atiyas and Oder (2007).

where necessary, rehabilitate a government-owned facility for a specified period of time. The attractiveness of the BOT projects was enhanced in 1994 through Law No. 3996, which provided tax exemptions and authorized the treasury to grant guarantees. In 1997, the BO model was introduced through Law No. 4283. Investments under the BO model were also eligible for treasury guarantees.

An important feature of these generation contracts was purchase agreements between the private company and TEAŞ or TEDAŞ that included take-or-pay clauses that committed the buyer to purchase a specified amount of electricity at prespecified prices or price formulas over duration of 15–30 years. In the end, the amount of generation capacity built under these contracts has been limited (about 4,000 MW started operating between 1997 and 2004, see Atiyas 2006, p. 75). However, these contracts have been quite controversial, for several reasons: first, some contracts (especially some BOT contracts awarded under law 3996) were awarded without a competitive procedure. Rather, contracts were awarded on the basis of bids collected from preselected companies (Çakarel and House 2005, p 7). Second, tariffs under the contracts were heavily front loaded to allow for early recovery of costs. Hence, especially during the early years of the contracts, electricity purchased by the state was expensive. Third, there have been allegations in reports prepared by the Turkish High Court of Accounts, as well as other official audit bodies that there have been irregularities in the design and implementation of these contracts (Atiyas 2006). At the least, it is believed that the state did not negotiate these contracts sufficiently rigorously, and obtained poor bargains: the government has retained most of the commercial risks, while providing the private sector with substantial rewards, especially in the form of treasury provided guarantees to cover critical commercial take-or-pay payment obligations, such as minimum electricity generation levels and minimum quantities of gas in power station gas purchase contracts, at associated predetermined prices in US dollars over the life of the contracts. On the other hand, project owners contend that the high initial prices were a reflection of Turkey's high international risk rating which translated into a high cost of capital for these debt financed energy generation projects.

There were other problems as well. Attempts by successive governments to treat these contracts as governed by private law were turned down, as abovementioned, by the interpretation of the Constitutional Court which meant that private sector provision had to be organized as a concession. This, in turn meant that contracts were to be reviewed by the Council of State (Danıştay) which could be a lengthy process. Also, concessions did not have recourse to international arbitration. These issues were finally resolved through a constitutional amendment in 1999 which stated that public services can be provided by private investors under private law contracts as long this is specified in law (Atiyas and Oder 2007; Ulusoy and Oğuz 2007).

Finally, fiscal implications of the contracts eventually raised serious concerns. The contingent liabilities created by the treasury guarantees provided to the contracts added further strain to the rapidly deteriorating public finances of the 1990s. As part of a general stabilization program that was put together with the support of the IMF, by the early 2000s Turkey had pledged to end treasury guarantees in future contracts.

In hindsight, a more structural problem with the BOT and BO contracts was that they did not contribute to the development of competitive electricity markets in Turkey, and indeed, neither were they intended to. The take-or-pay clauses meant that generators did not need to compete *in* the market and all commercial risk was transferred to the state. To the extent, that contracts were awarded through a tender procedure (and in some cases they were not) private investors competed *for* the market, and the fixed price nature of the contracts implied that generators did have incentives to minimize costs. However, there were no mechanisms that would ensure that any cost savings would eventually be passed on to consumers. In any case, when a more competitive model was adopted for the electricity industry in the 2000s, the BOT and BO contracts became stranded costs.

The controversy around these contracts created another important implication for the future: the energy bureaucracy became extremely averse to concluding contracts with the private sector, and as discussed below, this aversion did influence the evolution of the competitive model that was launched in the 2000s. Further, the fiscal problems of the 1990s and the role of electricity contracts in it made the fiscal gatekeepers of the state, namely the Ministry of Finance and the Treasury, extremely cautious about the fiscal implications of any state involvement in the participation of the private sector in the electricity industry.

Dissatisfaction with the BOT–BO model of private participation in electricity had already led the bureaucracy to search for more competitive models of electricity supply. A stabilization program supported by the IMF and the World Bank became instrumental in pursuing a more fundamental restructuring of the electricity industry through the adoption of the electricity market law (EML, Law No. 4628) in 2001. EML envisaged a competitive market, liberalization of both supply and demand and the creation of an independent regulatory authority.

3 Market Structure and Regulation Under the EML

The EML provided a fairly broad and detailed framework for the organization of markets and activities in the electricity industry.[8] First, it established a new regulatory authority, the Electricity Market Regulatory Authority (Elektrik Piyasası Düzenleme Kurumu, EPDK) as the regulator of electricity markets with wide powers to issue secondary legislation. After the enactment of Gas Market Law in 2001 and Petroleum Market Law in 2003, the EPDK was also given authority over the natural gas and oil industries. Its name was also changed to Energy Market Regulatory Authority (Enerji Piyasası Düzenleme Kurumu, EPDK).

The EML describes the EPDK as an "independent, administratively, and financially autonomous public institution". It is governed by its own board which

[8] For reviews of the regulatory environment in electricity see Atiyas and Dutz (2005); Güney (2006); Atiyas (2006); Hepbaşlı (2005); Erdoğdu (2007); Ulusoy and Oğuz (2007).

consists of nine members and a president, appointed for 6 years by the Council of Ministers. The Board members cannot hold jobs in the industry for 2 years after their term in office is completed. The decisions of the Board of the EPDK can be appealed at the Council of State, or Danıştay.

The main functions of the ETKB with respect to the electricity industry include implementing the licensing regime, preparing and implementing secondary legislation for the electricity and gas (and later oil) markets, regulating distribution and transmission activities and the provision of retail services to noneligible consumers, monitoring compliance and imposing penalties and fines in cases of noncompliance.

Under the new regime, public assets were legally unbundled into separate public companies: TEAŞ was separated into EÜAŞ, the Electricity Generation Corporation, TEİAŞ, the Turkish Electricity Transmission Corporation, and TETAŞ, Turkish Electricity Trading and Contracting Corporation, a wholesale trading company. It was envisaged that assets owned by EÜAŞ and TEDAŞ would be privatized. Transmission activities, on the other hand, would remain under public ownership. The primary task of TETAŞ was to take over all energy sale and purchase agreement of TEDAŞ and TEAŞ, including energy purchase and sales agreements entered into under BOT, BO, and TOR contracts and also export and import contracts. Also, initially EÜAŞ would sell all the electricity it has generated to TETAŞ. The idea was that the relatively expensive electricity purchased through BOT, BO, and TOR contacts would be balanced by what was perceived to be relatively cheap electricity purchased from EÜAŞ and the electricity would be sold under a uniform price to TEDAŞ. Hence essentially, TETAŞ would work under an average cost pricing scheme.

The market model envisaged by the EML consisted of two fundamental components: a market for bilateral contracts and a balancing mechanism to ensure real-time equality between supply and demand. The balancing market would be run by the National Load Dispatch Center (Milli Yük Tevzi Merkezi, MYTM) established in TEİAŞ and accounts among participants would be settled by the Market Financial Reconciliation Center (Piyasa Mali Uzlaştırma Merkezi, PMUM). The EML did not mention a spot market and the balancing mechanism became truly operational only in 2006. This delay in the establishment of the balancing market had important implications for private investment, an issue discussed further below.

The market model adopted in the EML seems to have been inspired by the New Electricity Trading Arrangement (NETA) of England and Wales which was also launched in 2001. NETA was preceded by the Pool, which was a centralized and mandatory market for wholesale trade in electricity. The NETA relied on bilateral contracts and a balancing mechanism to equate demand with supply in realtime. The Pool was faulted for a number of problems, including giving rise to excessive market power by the participating generators.[9] The Turkish policy

[9] It seems the California crisis played a role in this choice as well. The California model also had an exchange similar to the Pool, and there were strong indications that exercise of market power played a significant role in the development of the crisis.

makers seem to have been impressed by these criticisms and opted for a more decentralized arrangement.[10]

The EML provided for a wide variety of activities, including generation, wholesale trade, transmission, distribution, and retail supply. Entry into any of these activities required obtaining a license, which would be granted by EPDK presumably to any investor that met the conditions in the law. Hence the supply side was liberalized through a licensing regime.

Generation would be carried out by EÜAŞ, private generators who have obtained a generation license, autoproducers and autoproducer groups who generate electricity for their own use, but can sell surplus electricity in the market. Distribution companies would be able to engage in retail supply as well, provided they obtained a retail license.

The demand side was liberalized as well: every year EPDK would determine a threshold level of consumption, such that consumers with annual consumption exceeding that level would be designated as "eligible consumers" and would have the freedom to choose their own suppliers. A question that arises in this context, and one with important implications for the development of bilateral contracts, is whether eligible consumers would be able to purchase electricity from the retail arms of distribution companies. The EML stated that "In cases where there are consumers unable to purchase electricity and/or capacity from another supplier in the region served by any distribution company, then such distribution company is obliged to obtain a retail sale license, and engage in electricity sales to such consumers on a retail basis and/or provided retail sale services." In practice, eligible consumers have been able to choose distribution companies as their suppliers.

The EML has a number of provisions designed to facilitate the development of competition:

- The EML required that the holder of a distribution or transmission license to provide nondiscriminatory system access and use of system rights to all real persons and legal entities. Further, the terms of such access were to be regulated by EPDK.
- The EML introduced accounting separation, that is, operators which have more than one license or more than one plant had to keep different accounts for the different activities or plants. This remedy would facilitate the determination of regulated tariffs.
- Generation companies could enter into affiliate relationships with distribution companies without having controlling power over them.
- The EML stated that total market share of generation facilities operated by a particular private sector generation company and its affiliates could not exceed 20% of total installed capacity in Turkey in the preceding year.
- In the original version of the EML, distribution companies were allowed to operate generation facilities but the amount of the annual electricity generated by

[10] There were academics and experts in the UK who were not uncritical of the transition from Pool to NETA. See for example, Helm (2003) and Newbery (2005).

Table 2.6 Regulated tariffs

Activity	Regulated Price/Charge	Method
Transmission	Connection Charge	Project based
	System operation price	Revenue cap
	System use price	Revenue Cap
	Market Management Price	Revenue Cap
Distribution	Connection Charge	Project based and Standard Connection Charge
	Use of System Price	Revenue cap
Retail	Retail Sale Service Price	Revenue Cap
	Retail Sale Price	Price Cap
	Average Loss and Theft Price Cap	Price Cap
Wholesale (TETAS)	Average Wholesale Price	Cost based

Source EPDK; The Electricity Market Tariff Regulation and associated communiqués

them could not exceed 20% of the total electricity consumption in the region. Later this upper limit was removed through an amendment to the EML, apparently to increase the attractiveness of the distribution assets for privatization.

In addition, the EML also stated that in the context of privatization activities, foreign real persons and legal entities engaged in the market activities cannot have a market share that will enable them with a control power in the electricity generation, transmission, and distribution sectors. Presumably, this was intended to address the concerns of the Constitutional Court regarding foreign ownership.

The EML identified tariffs that would be regulated by EPDK. These were stated as: transmission tariffs, distribution tariffs, connection and use of system tariffs, retail tariffs for noneligible consumers, and the tariffs of TETAŞ. Eligible consumers would also be subjected to regulated tariffs until such consumers would choose their own suppliers through bilateral agreements. Tariffs for bilateral agreements, including those of eligible consumers at the retail level would be freely determined. The details of tariff regulations have evolved somewhat overtime. Table 2.6 provides a summary of the regulated tariffs and the methodologies used in regulation as of December 2011.

Distribution and transmission connection charges are intended to cover the costs (connection assets and costs incurred in their construction) incurred when users connect to the grid. Users of the distribution system are also subjected to a standard connection charge that depends on connection capacity and distance. Tariffs for transmission services entail three additional components, all regulated through revenue caps: use of transmission system tariffs, transmission system operation tariffs, and market management tariffs. Use of transmission system tariffs are designed to cover the investment, operation, and maintenance costs of the network. These are calculated on a regional basis and separately for consumers and producers.[11] The system transmission operation tariff captures the costs of services provided by the National Load Dispatch Center and fixed costs associated with ancillary services. These prices are uniform across all regions. The Market Management Tariff reflects the costs of operating the Market Financial Settlement Center. All of these components are regulated through revenue caps. The retail sale price applied to noneligible consumers reflects the average cost of energy purchased by retail companies plus a gross profit margin cap. The retail service sale price is intended to cover costs associated with provision of retail services and is also regulated through a revenue cap. Retail prices for eligible consumers are not regulated. Finally, the TETAŞ wholesale price is intended to cover average costs of wholesale electricity procured by TETAŞ and to ensure TETAŞ financial viability.

In general, regulated tariffs are proposed by the respective institutions and approved by EPDK. Proposals for the subsequent year have to be presented before the end of October in the current year and EPDK is expected to approve them by December 31 of the current year. EPDK may choose not to approve the tariffs and request revisions.

The presence of technical losses and theft, especially in the distribution system, represented a complicating factor faced by the new model. As described above, the ratio of losses varied highly across regions. With liberalization, it was expected that prices would closely reflect costs, and this would have meant large variations in electricity prices across regions. The law also attempted to provide instruments that would potentially be used to protect consumers from the asymmetries that could be generated by these high and variable distribution losses. It stated that "in cases where consumers in certain regions and/or in line with certain objectives need to be supported, such subsidy shall be provided in the form direct cash refunds to consumers without affecting the prices". The authority to design such subsidies was given to the Council of Ministers.

In hindsight, it can be said that the EML had a number of behavioral and structural measures in anticipation of significant competition problems similar to those that emerged, for example, in the European Union (EU). The structural measures included elements of vertical as well as horizontal separation, whereas the most important behavioral remedy was the provision for regulated third party

---

[11] As of December 2011, 14 regions have been defined for the purposes of transmission system use prices.

access. It may be useful to compare these provisions with those that existed in the European Union (EU). In 2001, electricity markets in the EU were still under the regime of the so-called 1st liberalization package, the main component of which was the electricity directive (Directive concerning common rules for the internal market in electricity, 96/92/EC). This directive liberalized electricity generation, but allowed member states to choose between an authorization procedure, similar to the option chosen in Turkey and a tendering procedure, whereby it would be up to the state to decide where and when a generation plant should be installed. Hence, Turkey had chosen a more market oriented and decentralized liberalization path. Regarding access, the directive allowed for both regulated *and* negotiated third party access, the latter undoubtedly a less competitive option given the high bargaining power of vertically integrated incumbent operators. Hence, regarding access Turkey had chosen an option that protected entrants relative to incumbents. Significantly, while the EU directive did require accounting separation, it did not contain any structural measures for further vertical unbundling of transmission assets. Again, the EML was more procompetitive that the European directive at the time. It was not until the adoption of the 2nd liberalization package in 2003 that the EU took significant steps regarding both access and unbundling.

It would also be useful to compare the Turkish model against a benchmark distilled through the worldwide restructuring experience over the last three decades. The key components of such a benchmark "textbook" model is provided by Joskow (2008) as follows: (1) privatization to increase incentives, prevent politization and end soft budget constraints, (2) vertical separation of competitive segments from naturally monopolistic segments, (3) horizontal restructuring to establish a minimum number of players to ensure a minimum degree of competition, (4) creation of voluntary wholesale public spot energy and operating reserve markets, (5) establish rules to ensure efficient access to the transmission network, (6) unbundling of retail tariffs, (7) in cases where competition in retail markets are seen unlikely to develop, ensure that distribution companies are suppliers of last resort, (8) creation of independent regulatory agencies, and (9) design and implementation of a transition mechanism. The Turkish model as reflected in the EML seems to cover most of these components except for two items: the first is the voluntary wholesale spot energy market and the second is the transition mechanism. The implications of the absence of a wholesale market will be discussed below. Regarding the transition mechanism, while the general characteristics of the target market model seems to have been clear, the strategy to get there would only be clarified after the passage of three more years, by the publication of a strategy document (SD) in 2004.

4 Implementation Strategy

The most important step in the restructuring of the industry was the privatization of generation and distribution assets. As indicated above, transmission assets would remain under public ownership. The EML mentioned privatization but did not provide a time table. A time table for the next steps of the implementation of the EML, as well as an outline of the general strategy, was introduced through a "Strategy Document" (SD)[12] issued in March 2004.

The SD reiterated the central role of privatization in the restructuring of the electricity industry. Moreover, the SD stated that privatization would start with distribution assets and then proceed to generation assets. The stated reason for this sequencing was the hope that successful privatization of distribution companies would create credible contractual counterparts for existing and new entrant generation and wholesale companies.[13] It is generally believed that if distribution companies remained under state ownership, they would continue to be badly managed. Moreover, civil servants acting managers would be unwilling to sign contracts with the private sector, especially given the public suspicion about the BOT, BO, and TOR contracts signed under the previous regime. In addition, it seems policy makers thought it would be difficult for public sector managers to resolve the loss theft problem in the distribution segment and that the private sector would have had an easier time.

In the mean time generation assets would be grouped into portfolio generation companies (excluding some hydro generation assets, which would continue to sell their output to TETAŞ). The basic principles to be followed in the creation of portfolio companies were attaining financial feasibility and preventing market power. The privatization of generation plants would start after significant progress in the privatization of distribution companies.

These priorities reflected in the SD deserve a few comments: first, the central role given to privatization process in the restructuring strategy in practice meant that competition obtained a secondary role. After all, it is generally believed that ultimately it is competition that is expected to generate efficiency gains and higher consumer welfare over the long run, not a transfer of ownership. While privatization may encourage efficiency gains by making profit maximization the primary objective of enterprises, without competition such efficiency gains do not translate into higher consumer welfare. Clearly, the possibility of injecting and increasing competition is much higher in generation, nil in distribution and limited in retail supply. Given these considerations, many alternative strategies could have been designed. For example, one alternative strategy that emphasized competition could have started with the creation of portfolio companies, appointment of professional managers with the mandate to run their companies as independent profit maximizers, soon to be followed by their privatization. In the meantime, new competent management could have been appointed to distribution companies and eventually they could be privatized as well. The fact that the Turkish strategy did not follow this route is possibly explained by several factors. There was a general pessimism

---

[12] Decision No. 2004/3 of the High Planning Council, Official Gazette 17.3.2004.

[13] According to Price Waterhouse Coopers (2008) "Metering and billing problems coupled with loss & theft ratios much higher than the OECD median constituted the main imperatives behind the policy decision to grant a priority to the distribution segment" (p 17).

about the degree to which state-owned companies could be reformed and their efficiencies increased. Second, the government had its eye on potentially high revenues that could be raised through the sale of monopoly rights. As discussed further below, it seems generation of revenues for the public coffer has been an overriding objective of the restructuring process in the electricity industry.

As part of the transition period, the SD stipulated that several types of transitional or vesting contracts will be implemented. These included:

- Transitional contracts between TETAŞ and EÜAŞ hydroelectric plants. Some hydro plants will not be included in the generation portfolio companies and they will continue to sell their output to TETAŞ as long as it is deemed necessary to achieve an average TETAŞ sales price that reflects the expected market price. The idea was to use hydro plants to lower market prices in cases where they were deemed too high.
- Transitional contracts between TETAŞ and the distribution companies. Electricity purchased by TETAŞ from EÜAŞ and existing contracts will be distributed among distribution companies.
- Transitional purchase and sale contracts between distribution companies and generation groups. It was envisaged that these contracts would last at most 5 years, to be replaced by market based contracts. In effect they have been renewed at the end of the 5 years.
- Distribution companies would make agreements with suppliers for an amount covering at least 85% of estimated consumption of noneligible consumers.

Regarding distribution, Turkey was divided into 21 distribution regions, and a regional distribution company was created for each region (Table 2.7). Licenses for distribution activities would be at most for 49 years. Since the restructuring strategy depended crucially on the privatization of distribution assets, the SD included steps that were perceived to reduce uncertainties and increase the attractiveness of these assets to potential investors. Tariffs would be specified on a multiannual basis and the first tariff application period would be 5 years.

The SD also introduced a significant departure from the EML in the handling of interregional differences in distribution costs. Instead of direct subsidies to consumers, the SD stipulated that a "price-equalization scheme" would be introduced for a transitional period that ends in 2010. This meant that cross subsidies from low-loss regions would be used to finance losses in high-loss regions. As this required new legislation, Law No. 5496 introduced an amendment to EML and gave the EPDK the authority to design the equalization scheme. It is generally believed that the main reason for this change is the unwillingness of the Ministry of Finance and the Treasury to create any additional burdens to the budget. Relying on cross subsidies instead precludes direct support from the public budget.

Additional measures were intended, apparently with the objective of making distribution assets more attractive to potential buyers. Originally the SD stated that the threshold for eligible consumers would be set at 7.8 GWh until 2009, in effect limiting the extent of retail competition. However, this was not adhered to and the threshold for eligible consumers has been reduced along a faster schedule down to

Table 2.7 Distribution regions

Region No.	Distribution Companies	Provinces
1	Dicle Elektrik Dağıtım A.Ş.	Diyarbakır, Şanlıurfa, Mardin, Batman, Siirt Şırnak
2	Vangölü Elektrik Dağıtım A.Ş	Bitlis, Hakkari, Muş, Van
3	Aras Elektrik A.Ş.	Erzurum, Ağrı, Ardahan, Bayburt, Erzincan, Iğdır,Kars
4	Çoruh Elektrik Dağıtım A.Ş.	Trabzon, Artvin, Giresun, Gümüşhane, Rize
5	Fırat Elektrik Dağıtım A.Ş.	Elazığ, Bingöl, Malatya, Tunceli
6	Çamlıbel Elektrik Dağıtım A.Ş.	Sivas, Tokat, Yozgat
7	Toroslar Elektrik Dağıtım A.Ş.	Adana, Gaziantep, Hatay, Mersin, Osmaniye, Kilis
8	Meram Elektrik Dağıtım A.Ş.	Kırşehir, Nevşehir, Niğde, Aksaray, Konya,Karaman.
9	Başkent Elekrik A.Ş.	Ankara, Kırıkkale, Zonguldak, Bartın, Karabük, Çankırı, Kastamonu
10	Akdeniz Elektrik A.Ş.	Antalya, Burdur, Isparta
11	Gediz Elektrik Dağıtım A.Ş.	İzmir, Manisa
12	Uludağ Elektrik Dağıtım A.Ş.	Balıkesir, Bursa, Çanakkale, Yalova
13	Trakya Elektrik Dağıtım A.Ş.	Edirne, Kırklareli, Tekirdağ.
14	İstanbul Anadolu Yakası Elektrik Dağıtım A.Ş. (AYEDAŞ)	İstanbul Anatolian Side
15	Sakarya Elektrik Dağıtım A.Ş.	Sakarya, Bolu, Düzce, Kocaeli
16	Osmangazi Elektrik Dağıtım A.Ş.	Eskişehir, Afyon, Bilecik, Kütahya, Uşak
17	Boğaziçi Elektrik Dağıtım A.Ş (BEDAŞ)	İstanbul European Side
18	Kayseri Elektrik Dağıtım A.Ş.	Kayseri
19	Menderes Elektrik DağıtımA.Ş.	Aydın, Denizli, Muğla
20	Göksu Elektrik Dağıtım A.Ş.	Adıyaman,Kahramanmaraş
21	Yeşilırmak Elektrik Dağıtım A.Ş.	Samsun, Amasya, Çorum, Ordu, Sinop

Source Privatization Authority

30 MWh by end of 2011. Finally, as discussed before, restrictions on the extent to which distribution companies can integrate backwards into generation were lifted through Law No. 5398.

The SD provided clear deadlines for the different components of the strategy. Privatization of all distribution companies was to be completed by 2006; as of December 2011 they have still not been completed. The privatization of generation portfolio companies was to have started by July 2006 and as of December 2011 there have been no significant privatizations of generation assets.

5 Developments and Issues Under the New Regime

5.1 Progress with Privatization

5.1.1 The Privatization Model for Electricity Distribution

While privatization was to play a crucial role in the strategy for restructuring the electricity industry, implementation has been significantly delayed. The SD had stated that "the main target will be to privatize all distribution companies/regions until 31 December 2006." The privatization of only three regions (Başkent, Sakarya and Ayedaş) was launched in 2006 with the intention of completing them by March 2007. However, these tenders were cancelled just before the tender date.

Among the official reasons put forward by the authorities was the completion of the infrastructure works to take above ground middle voltage (MV) lines to underground (Price Waterhouse Coopers 2008).

One important reason for the delay was the search for the appropriate legal form of ownership of the distribution assets. While some authorities preferred a model that transferred the ownership of the assets to private parties, others preferred a model whereby ownership would be retained by the state and private parties would be granted rights to operate the assets. In the end, with the nudge of a recommendation delivered by the Council of State, it was decided that privatization would not entail the transfer of ownership rights, and instead the TOR backed share sale model ("TSS model") was adopted.

The model was as follows: first, the Privatization Authority (PA, Özelleştirme İdaresi Başkanlığı) established a distribution company in each of the distribution regions established in the SD. In the Kayseri region (region no. 18), the distribution company was already partially private and had obtained operating rights in 1990. That company had its contract renewed and granted a license in 2009. Two additional companies, Menderes and Göksu were granted operating rights in the context of Law No. 3096 and were handed over to private companies outside the privatization program. Hence out of the 21 regional companies there were 18 left to be privatized.

Each of these distribution companies signed a TOR agreement with TEDAŞ and each obtained a distribution license and a retail sales license, as well as vesting contracts with EÜAŞ and TETAŞ.[14] The TOR was such that all of the existing assets as well as new assets to be created after the privatization would remain under the ownership of TEDAŞ. The investor would purchase the shares of the company that would own the rights to operate all distribution and related assets (such as buildings, vehicles, and machine parks) as well electricity distribution and retail licenses in the region. While there would be other companies in the region with retail licenses, the distribution company would be the only operator that holds a distribution license. The privatization would transfer 100% of the share of the company to the purchasing investor.

5.1.2 Tariffs Structures for Distribution and Retail Companies

The tariff structures under which the distribution companies would operate were determined as follows: the period 2006–2010 was identified as the "transition period"[15] at the end of which tariffs would become fully cost based. Because of delays in privatization, the transition period was later extended until the end of 2012.[16] During the transition period tariffs would entail various types of

---

[14] The following is drawn from Privatization Authority (2009).

[15] Through Law No. 5496, Article 6.

[16] As per Law No. 5784 enacted in 2008.

crosssubsidies across regions as well as consumer groups, through the application of a price equalization scheme. As a result, there was a single national tariff structure uniform across regions but differentiated according to consumer groups. The price equalization scheme was adopted to prevent large variations in technical losses and theft across regions (see Table 2.5) from resulting in large variations in end-user tariffs. As mentioned above, the EML had envisaged the use of direct income transfers to consumers to compensate for regional disparities in costs associated with losses and thefts, but the SD (and later Law No. 5496 adopted in 2006) introduced instead a price equalization scheme that entailed a cross subsidy mechanism. Accordingly, the application of a national tariff would generate surpluses and deficits for each distribution company, depending on their specific costs, especially theft, and losses. These surpluses and deficits would be cleared through financial transfers across regions. The cross subsidies and the price equalization scheme are supposed to be terminated by the end of the transition period.

The end-user tariffs and revenue requirements of the distribution companies for the duration of the transition period were already determined prior to privatization. Interestingly, while EML gave EPDK the exclusive authority to regulate tariffs, through an amendment to the Law introduced in 2006 EPDK was required to approve, without changes, tariff offers made by TEDAŞ for the "first implementation period" (i.e., 2006–2010).[17] Hence, effectively EPDK did not have the opportunity to scrutinize the tariff offers presented by TEDAŞ.

Revenue requirements cover projected expenses for distribution and retail services and provide an allowance for target level technical and "non-technical losses" (i.e., theft). As per the EML and the Electricity Market Tariff Regulation the end-user tariff is unbundled into four components: retail sales, retail services, distribution, and transmission. Since 2011, a component capturing the cost of technical and nontechnical losses has been unbundled as well. The retail sales tariff contained a price cap reflecting the cost of energy purchased by the distribution company. Retail services and distribution components have "revenue caps" that cover operating expenses and investment requirements related to distribution and retail services. Transmission tariffs are determined on a cost-plus basis.

The national tariffs approved for the first implementation period are given in Table 2.8. The following revisions could be made to these tariffs: (1) the revenue caps for 2006–2010 were to be adjusted for inflation through the Electricity Market Index announced by EPDK (or through the Consumer Price Index until the Electricity Market Index was available). Further, revenue caps are guaranteed irrespective of consumption levels; and (2) a pass-through mechanism was instituted according to which distribution company could reflect changes in its energy costs to the retail price cap. In fact in July 2008, the High Planning Council, adopted a "Cost-Based Pricing Mechanism" to be instituted by state-owned enterprises in the energy sector. According to this mechanism retail electricity tariffs set for the transition

[17] Article 6 of Law No. 5496 enacted in 2006, adding provisional article 9 to the EML.

Table 2.8 Transition period national tariffs (Turkish Kuruş)

	2006	2007	2008	2009	2010
Industrial MV	11.63	11.52	11.40	11.30	11.19
Industrial LV	11.63	11.63	11.63	11.63	11.63
Commercial	14.75	14.50	14.15	13.87	13.62
Residential	12.40	12.40	12.64	12.89	13.14
Agricultural irrigation	11.19	11.19	11.19	11.19	11.19
Lighting	11.97	12.00	12.04	12.07	12.10

Source Privatization Authority (2009)

period are to be adjusted every 3 months. Hence, actual tariffs have been higher than those depicted in Table 2.8 because of, for example, increases in gas prices.

The tariff structure was based on the logic of incentive regulation. Tariffs were based on specific theft and loss targets for each distribution company. Any improvements beyond target loss ratios could be appropriated by the company, hence the tariff structure entailed strong incentives to cut losses and thefts. There were additional sources of savings. In the construction of the regulated retail tariff, part of the energy purchases by the distribution company were priced through various reference prices. Hence, "The investor is allowed to retain the savings achieved through procuring energy at a lower cost than the regulated reference price." (Privatization Authority 2009, p 10). Further, "the investor is allowed to retain excess value derived from outperforming the predetermined operational improvement targets approved by the Regulator" (ibid.)[18]

The extension of the transition period until the end of 2012 meant that the price equalization scheme and the energy sales agreements (see Sect. 5.1.4) were extended until the end of 2012 as well. In March 2010, the EPDK announced that for the purposes of regulation of tariffs, the "second implementation period" is determined as the period between January 1, 2011 and December 31, 2015. This time the procedure leading to the determination of tariffs for the second implementation period was managed by the EPDK. The second implementation period includes some aggressive targets. One of the important targets is to reduce national theft and losses to 10.3%. As shown in Table 2.9, for some distribution regions this means very substantial reductions in theft and losses (for example, from 46–22% for Vangölü and 60–30% for Dicle). Since regulated tariffs are determined on the basis of these targets, failure to reach the targets will mean financial losses.

An important issue that arises in this regard is the future of cross subsidies. For the time being, the termination of the transition period at the end of 2012 means that cross subsidies will be terminated and cross reflective tariffs will be implemented. However, variations in costs due to differences in loss ratios are still

[18] The teaser for the privatization prepared by the Privatization Authority (2009) argued that "at each distribution company, substantial operational efficiency improvement is achievable through optimizing core business processes, such as billing and collections, arranging and redesigning work flows, enabling effective coordination between divisions, improving information systems, and infrastructure and optimizing personnel productivity."

Table 2.9 Loss targets for distribution companies for the second implementation period

	2011	2012	2013	2014	2015
Akdeniz	8.86	8.45	8.05	8.02	8.02
Aras	22.92	19.04	17.62	16.30	15.08
AYDEM	9.80	9.34	8.90	8.49	8.09
AYEDAŞ	7.12	6.79	6.61	6.61	6.61
Başkent	8.46	8.07	7.88	7.88	7.88
Boğaziçi	9.12	8.69	8.28	7.90	7.57
Çamlıbel	7.72	7.36	7.02	6.92	6.92
Çoruh	10.90	10.39	10.15	10.15	10.15
Dicle	60.96	50.63	42.06	34.93	29.01
Fırat	12.59	11.65	11.11	10.59	10.09
Gediz	8.48	8.08	7.70	7.34	7.00
Göksu	10.03	10.03	10.03	10.03	10.03
Kayseri	10.01	10.01	10.01	10.01	10.01
Meram	8.59	8.28	8.28	8.28	8.28
Osmangazi	7.21	7.21	7.21	7.21	7.21
Sakarya	7.66	7.31	6.96	6.64	6.33
Toroslar	9.38	8.94	8.52	8.12	7.74
Trakya	7.70	7.70	7.70	7.70	7.70
Uludağ	6.96	6.90	6.90	6.90	6.90
Vangölü	46.15	38.33	31.84	26.45	21.97
Yeşilırmak	10.35	9.87	9.41	8.97	8.78

Source EPDK (2010)

substantial. Since it is unlikely that these differences in costs will be borne by consumers, it is expected that either some sort of support for consumers in high cost regions will be developed or the application of national tariff will be extended.

5.1.3 Investment Requirements

The investor that purchases the distribution company would also bear responsibility to undertake necessary investments. In fact, having private investors finance the required distribution system and network improvements and expansions and thereby remove the burden of such investments away from the state budget was identified as a key objective of privatization (Privatization Authority 2009, p 6). The costs of these investments are to be recovered through tariffs. Any portion of investments that is not recovered through tariffs will be paid by TEDAŞ to the

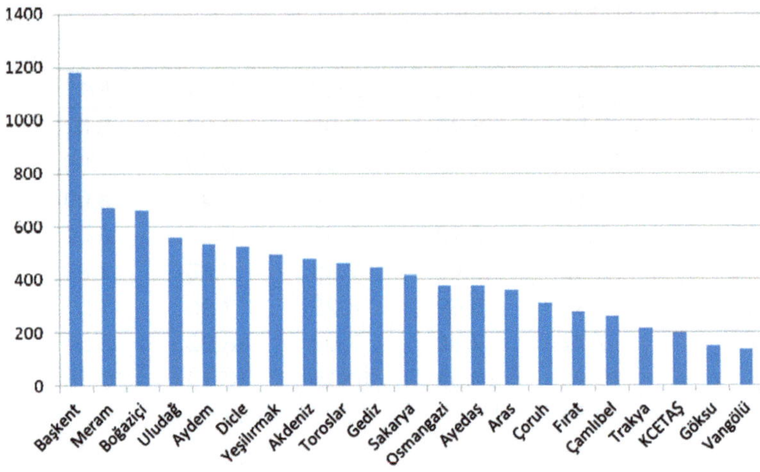

Fig. 2.5 Distribution investments for 2011–2015 (million TL). *Source* EPDK (2010)

investor on the expiration or termination of the contract. The investment program and expenditures of the distribution companies are to be monitored by EPDK.

One indicator for the need for investments in the distribution system is the extent of outages experienced by businesses. According to the results of surveys carried by the World Bank, Turkish firms experience on average 4.1 power outages per month (World Bank Group 2009). This is more than twice the number of outages experienced in the EU-10 countries.

Investment requirements for the first implementation period (2006–2010) were already determined and their costs included in the end-user tariffs. In effect, for the period 2006–2009 actual investments in the distribution system (3.5 billion TL) was higher than originally committed (2.5 billion TL). For the second implementation period, a total of about 9 billion TL of investments have been approved by the EPDK. Figure 2.5 shows the distribution of investment plans across regions.

After the transition period, distribution companies will prepare annual investment plans and present them to EPDK for approval. EPDK is also authorized to monitor the implementation of investment plans.

5.1.4 Vested Contracts for Distribution Companies

According to the SD, during the transition period distribution companies are to procure 85% of their estimated regional demand for electricity by noneligible consumers from TETAŞ and portfolio generation companies created out of EÜAŞ assets. Each distribution company has therefore been given Energy Sales Agreements (ESA) with TETAŞ and portfolio companies, which will remain valid until the end of 2012, the extended deadline for the transition period.

Table 2.10 Privatization of distribution companies—status as of December 2011

Company	Date of Tender	Privatization High Council Decision	Date of Transfer of Operating Rights	Data date	Consumption (billed, MWh))	No. Subscribers	Purchase price (USD)
Başkent	01.07.2008	19.09.2008-57	28.01.2009	2008	11,161,478	3,078,870	1,225,000,000
Sakarya	01.07.2008	19.09.2008/58	11.02.2009	2008	8,760,455	1,307,982	600,000,000
Meram	25.09.2008	30.04.2009/16	30.10.2009	2008	5,858,905	1,530,509	440,000,000
Aras*	25.09.2008	-	-	2008	1,655,806	725,151	128,500,000
Osmangazi	06.11.2009	22.04.2010/16	31.05.2010	2009	4,846,186	1,311,267	485,000,000
Yeşilırmak	06.11.2009	07.06.2010/35	29.12.2010	2009	4,049,650	1,521,182	441,500,000
Çoruh	06.11.2009	07.06.2010/36	30.09.2010	2009	2,295,105	1,017,555	227,000,000
Çamlıbel	18.02.2010	26.07.2010/57	31.08.2010	2009	2,146,351	746,002	258,500,000
Vangölü	18.02.2010	01.11.2010/93	-	2009	1,300,787	408,620	100,100,000
Fırat	18.02.2010	01.10.2010/86	31.12.2010	2009	2,032,633	680,237	230,250,000
Uludağ	18.02.2010	24.06.2010/42	31.08.2010	2009	11,049,990	2,388,421	940,000,000
Boğaziçi	09.08.2010	11.04.2011/26	-	2009	18,434,621	3,954,871	2,990,000,000
Gediz **	09.08.2010	11.04.2011/28	-	2009	12,436,056	2,389,838	1,920,000,000
Trakya	09.08.2010	11.04.2011/29	-	2009	5,780,809	792,766	622,000,000
Dicle	09.08.2010	11.04.2011/27	-	2009	4,190,977	1,100,754	228,000,000
Ayedaş	07.12.2010	11.04.2011/31	-	2009	8,582,325	2,242,140	1,813,000,000
Toroslar	07.12.2010	11.04.2011/32	-	2009	14,538,958	2,742,119	2,075,000,000
Akdeniz	07.12.2010	11.04.2011/30	-	2009	5,927,658	1,550,026	1,165,000,000

* Tender cancelled by the Council of State
**Purchaser failed to carry out commitments
Source Kurna (2011) and authors' compilation

5.1.5 Outcomes of Privatization of Electricity Distribution

The privatization of distribution companies finally started to take place in 2008. The current situation is summarized in Table 2.10. The privatizations whose tenders took place in 2008 and 2009 were completed with the exception of Aras, whose tender was cancelled by the Council of State. The operating rights of these companies were transferred in the year following the tenders. However, Privatizations of 2010 were problematic. In many cases the parties who won the tender failed to put together the necessary financing or called off the purchase altogether. In such cases the Privatization Authority negotiates with the second or third highest bidders. As of December 2011, this process was still going on. The purchase prices depicted in Table 2.10 refer to prices offered by the highest bidder; actual prices that are realized as highest bidders are eliminated will likely be lower.[19] In the case of Gediz, there were only two bidders to start with. When they abdicated, the tender had to be cancelled.

Figure 2.6 provides some crude measures on the dispersion of prices offered during the tenders. Top offers are scaled by number of subscribers and annual

[19] It turns out the bids of the top three bidders are not that far apart, except for Bedaş, where the two top bids (1.813 and 1.812 billion USD, respectively) were substantially higher than the third and fourth highest bids (1.459 and 1.321 billion USD, respectively).

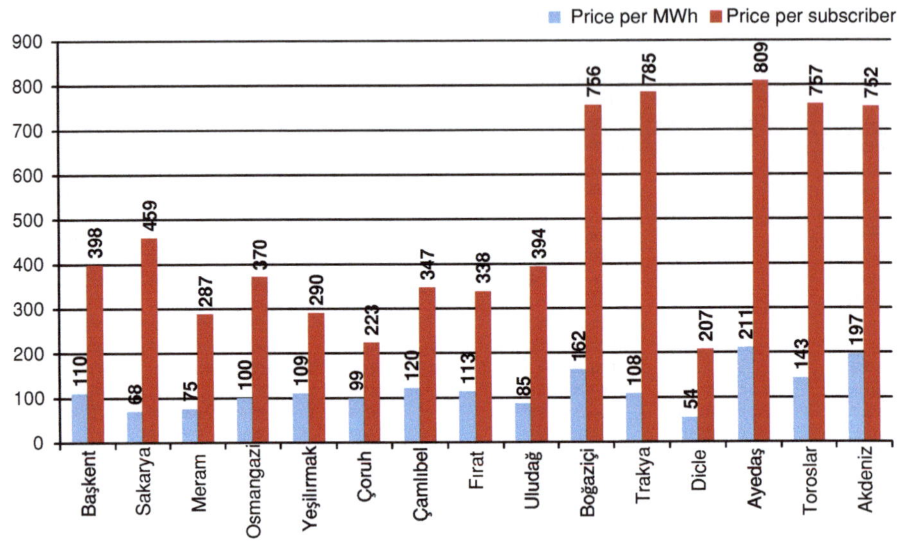

Fig. 2.6 Highest bids per subscriber and MWh (USD). *Source* Table 2.11

consumption levels. Average bids per subscriber are especially high in Boğaziçi, Ayedaş, Toroslar, Trakya, and Akdeniz. This reflects the fact that consumptions per subscriber is high in these regions. Still, there are quite high variations in price per MWh, ranging from a low of $50–70 in Dicle and Sakarya to $211 in Ayedaş. There have been worries that in some cases the heat of competition has led investors to offer excessively high prices during privatization tenders, raising concerns about the financial viability of the companies.[20]

5.1.6 Privatization of Generation Companies

Preparations for the privatization of generation companies are under way. As of December 2011, a number of generation plants have already been privatized. ADÜAŞ (141 MW) was privatized in 2008. In 2009 tender process for 52 run-of-river hydroelectric plants have been started; these have been completed by 2011. The prices realized in these tenders have been quite high, creating worries about financial problems in the future (Deloitte 2010).

It has been decided that four plants will be privatized individually. In addition, 9 portfolio companies will be created. The capacities of the companies to be

[20] In reference to data presented in Fig. 2.7, note, again, that the privatization process for Boğaziçi, Trakya, Dicle, Ayedaş, Toroslar, Akdeniz, Vangölü have not been completed and the data may change.

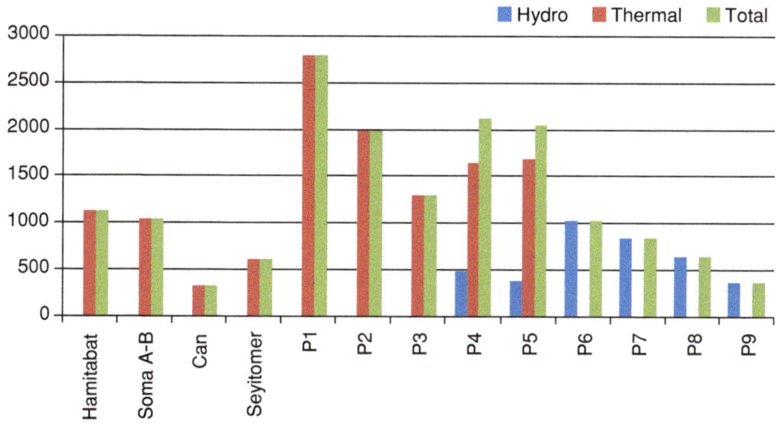

Fig. 2.7 Installed capacities of generation portfolios scheduled for privatization. *Source* Deloitte (2010)

privatized range between 320 MW and 2,795 MW. The companies to be privatized are listed in Fig. 2.7.

5.1.7 Privatization: An Assessment

To summarize, then, 10 years after the adoption of the EML and 7 years after the publication of the SD, the privatization of distribution companies, which was the crucial step in the restructuring strategy, has still not been completed. Since, most potential efficiency gains from restructuring were contingent on progress with privatization, harvesting such efficiency gains has also been postponed. Delays in privatization have meant that so far progress with the development of competition has been limited.

Another important characteristic of the privatization process in electricity is that it has been revenue driven. The whole strategy of privatization has been to sell the assets to whoever is willing to pay the highest price. In the case of distribution assets, the price investors are willing to pay depend very closely on their expectations about the path of future regulated prices, which are not completely exogenous. One problem that may arise when auctions are designed in this way is that they may attract not necessarily the most efficient investor but rather investors who are more confident that they may influence the regulatory process. Another concern is that, irrespective of the particular characteristics of the investors, high prices paid for obtaining the assets may translate into higher tariffs for consumers ex-post despite declarations by the regulatory authority to the contrary. Hence higher prices may represent simply a form of taxation. In this regard, as discussed in detail in Chapter 3 the authorities have been more innovative in the privatization of gas distribution companies where they

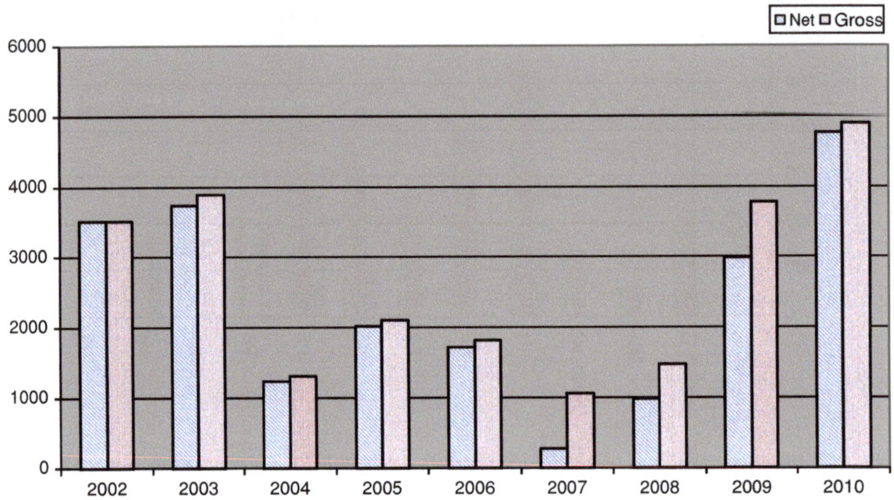

Fig. 2.8 New additions to capacity (MW). *Source* TEİAŞ

have attempted to select not investors willing to pay the highest price, but investors who were willing to provide services and undertake investments at lowest cost.

So far, the main benefit of the privatization process has been fiscal in nature. Given the nature of tariff regulation, one should expect significant improvements in losses and theft in the future. It remains to be seen the extent to which efficiency gains resulting from reductions in losses and theft are going to be translated into higher consumer welfare.

5.2 Private Investment Response

During the early years of the new regime the investment response of the private sector was extremely weak. Figure 2.8 shows a measure of investments, namely new additions to capacity. "Net" additions are calculated by subtracting from gross additions retirements of existing capacity or revisions to declared capacity. The EML was adopted in 2001, the new capacity that appears in 2002 and 2003 was mostly natural gas plants that were started to be built before the adoption of the law.[21] The figure shows that additions to capacity were very low until 2009, even though there was general expectation of rapid growth in demand. In fact, it is generally accepted that were it not for the crisis of 2008–2009, which reduced the growth of demand for electricity significantly during those years (see Fig. 2.1),

[21] Many of these plants are small auto-producers; there were some IPP and BO plants as well. Plants that were of more significant size were gas-fired and there was one plant based on imported coal.

Turkey was going to face significant capacity shortages and possibly blackouts by 2009 (Atiyas and Ferer 2007). This lack of investment response led the authorities to take additional precautions for resource adequacy (see Sect. 5.7). A closer look into the dynamics behind the lack of investment response is worthwhile.

There were several reasons for the poor investment response. A significant delay in the privatization of distribution companies was one important reason. As mentioned above, the whole point of the specific sequencing adopted by the restructuring strategy (privatize distribution first and generation later) was to ensure that generators would face credible buyers. It was hoped that once under private management distribution companies would be willing to develop bilateral contracts with generators, and thereby encourage new entry. It was also hoped that such bilateral contracts would help new entrants in obtaining external finance. Public managers were not willing to develop contracts with private generators. The bad publicity of previous experience with BOT and BO contracts possibly had a hindering effect.

However, a more important problem had to do with distortions in or indeed absence of price signals that would provide incentives for new investments. Until the balancing market was launched in 2006, all the prices in the system were administratively determined. TETAŞ purchased power from EÜAŞ and from plants under existing BO and BOT contracts and determined a wholesale price on the basis of average costs. TEDAŞ bought electricity on the basis of that price and sold electricity basically at a price that presumably covered costs including losses.

In a market system, the price of electricity would be determined by the marginal cost of the marginal plant. In an environment of impending scarcity, one would expect that some (especially peak) prices would start to rise, providing signals for additional investment. In the Turkish case, these signals were absent until 2006.

Lack of prices that reflect the scarcity value of power even in the short run has created problems for existing private generators as well. Private generators in the market (autoproducers, autoproducer groups, and independent power producers) were competing with TEDAŞ for the patronage of eligible consumers and selling at a discount of 10–15%. Most private producers ran gas-fired plants. Starting in mid-2004 prices of natural gas supplied by BOTAŞ started to increase. At the same time, the government was unwilling to increase TEDAŞ retail prices. In fact, between June 2004 and August 2006 BOTAŞ gas prices increased by almost 60% while TEDAŞ retail prices remained constant. The consequence was that autoproducers and independent power plants were faced with a severe margin squeeze. This is captured in Fig. 2.9 which plots the ratio of retail TEDAŞ prices (tariffs for industrial consumers) to BOTAŞ gas prices for eligible consumers. The figure shows that while in 2002–2004 the TEDAŞ retail price was about 4–5 times the BOTAŞ gas price, toward the end of 2006 it was less than three times higher. Everything else constant, this implies a significant drop in the margins of private producers. Private producers complained that some prices determined by government agencies (such as those of power produced by EÜAŞ hydro-plants) were superficially low, reflecting a desire by the government to prevent increases in regulated retail prices. In 2006, the margin squeeze led some producers to

Fig. 2.9 Ratio of TEDAŞ retail prices to gas cost. *Source* BOTAŞ, TEDAŞ

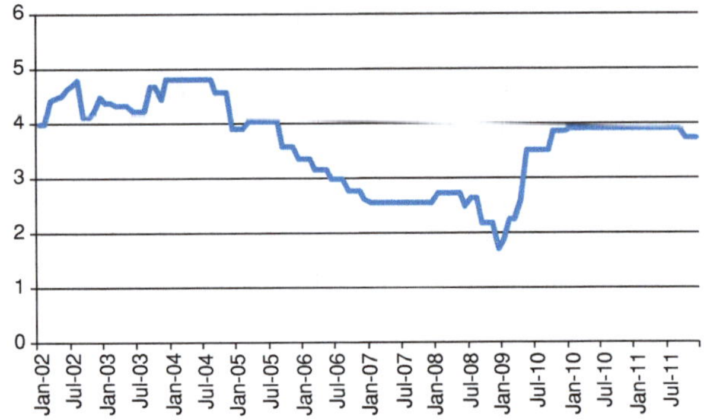

announce that they may start closing loss-making plants down. In the summer of 2006 there was a blackout that affected 13 provinces in Western Anatolia and the Aegean Coast. Finally, the balancing market was launched in August 2006. The balancing market produced prices that better reflected the scarcity prices of marginal generation capacity. As a result, most generators cancelled their bilateral contracts and started to sell to the balancing market. Note that as shown in Fig. 2.9 that ratio of regulated retail prices to gas prices continued to decline well into 2009, but this further decline became irrelevant for private electricity producers thanks to the availability of the balancing market.

Besides adverse movements in prices, however, the lack of investment response by the private sector reflected a lack of regulatory credibility as well. Given especially the seeming unwillingness of the government to adjust retail prices in response to what the private sector saw as rising costs, potential investors were not sure that fair or cost-reflective prices would be available in the future once new plants came on line.

Several explanations have been advanced for the government's unwillingness to raise prices. One explanation is that the government was worried that any increase in energy prices could have hurt the disinflation program that had successfully reduced inflation from over 50% in the early 2000s to 10–12% by 2006. Another hypothesis was that the government was not willing to raise prices before the elections of 2007 for fear that it could generate a loss of votes (Sevaioğlu 2007). Needless to say, failure to adjust prices to reflect costs created financial losses and led to accumulated debt and arrears among different state-owned energy enterprises. It has been reported that by the end of 2006 total debt of state-owned energy companies to BOTAŞ, including interest, was about 10.6 billion TL (about 6 billion Euros), of which about 8.7 (5 billion Euros) was by EÜAŞ.[22] EÜAŞ, in turn, had accumulated claims on TEDAŞ, etc. It was customary to issue special laws to clean those arrears.

[22] The daily Referans, 21.9.2007.

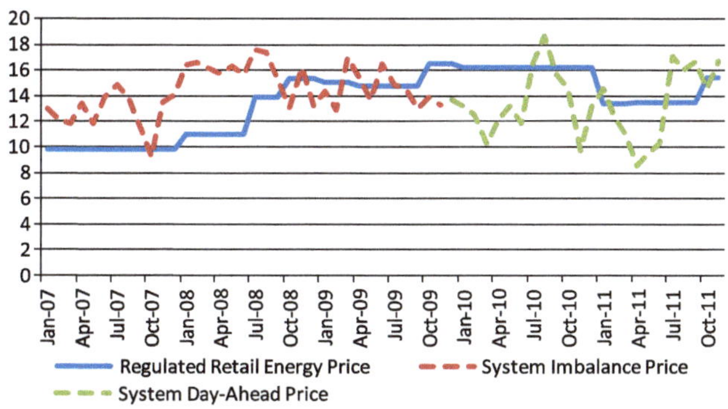

Fig. 2.10 Regulated retail prices versus prices in the balancing market. *Source* TEİAŞ and TEDAŞ

However, the dynamics behind the lack of investment response points out to factors that go deeper than manipulation of the retail prices. Especially, during periods of relatively tight capacity (which was the case in 2005–2006) cost reflective regulated retail prices can often be lower than the marginal cost of marginal capacity. This is because regulated prices often reflect average costs of electricity purchased over plants with varying degrees of variable costs. By contrast, during periods of tight capacity, and under some sort of merit order, the marginal cost of marginal capacity would almost by definition reflect costs of more expensive plants. Hence in principle market design should be able to accommodate such situations. In other words, when there is unsatisfied demand and available capacity that can be used to meet that demand, market design should be able to ensure that such capacity is kept within the system even when it is more expensive than the average cost of inframarginal units. This is almost the definition of short-term supply security. If the expensive units could not sell to eligible consumers, then, as long as there is unsatisfied demand, they could have sold electricity to distribution companies. However, as described above, distribution companies were not willing to buy directly from private generators. If there had been a spot market, IPPs could sell to the wholesale market and distribution companies could have purchased anonymous electricity from the spot market. In the Turkish case there was no spot market either. The lesson seems to be that the institutional features of the market design at the time was so rigid that it did not allow any of these solutions. In effect when the balancing market was launched, it acted as a spot market.

In any case, Fig. 2.9 also shows that investment response has recovered after the launch of the balancing mechanism. Significant new capacity has been added in 2009 and 2010. The construction of at least some of these plants probably started after the launch of the balancing mechanism and appearance of prices significantly higher than TEDAŞ retail prices.

Figure 2.10 provides some idea about prices in the balancing markets and regulated retail prices. The "system imbalance price" and the "system day-ahead

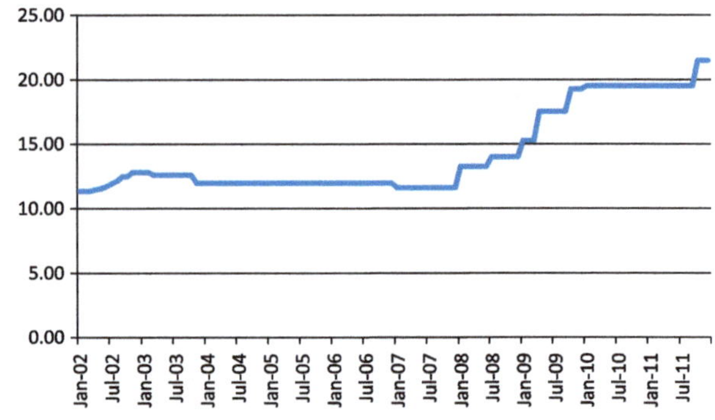

Fig. 2.11 TEDAŞ Industry tariffs (Kr/kWh)

price" are prices established in the balancing market (the different names reflect the different periods in the evolution of the balancing market, see the discussion below). The regulated retail price refers to the retail price of energy provided by distribution companies before the addition of unbundled retail sale service, distribution, and transmission components. Hence this is a rough measure of the regulated price against which private generators compete. The figures show that especially in 2007 and 2008 the imbalance market has generated prices higher than regulated prices. This seems to have changed in 2010 and 2011, reflecting both the adjustments made to regulated retail prices and possibly the effect of additional capacity.

5.3 *Tariffs*

Figure 2.11 plots the national retail tariffs of distribution companies for industrial users. It shows how prices have been kept constant between 2003 and 2008 despite increases in gas costs. Electricity prices were raised by EPDK in January 2008 for the first time after almost 5 years. Prices almost doubled between 2008 and 2010.

The increase in prices after 2008 probably reflects a change in political attitude towards electricity prices, whereby political authorities must have finally realized the damage caused by keeping prices excessively low. Another important policy innovation undertaken in 2008 also reflects this change in attitude. To ensure that changes in fuel costs are reflected in tariffs, the High Planning Council accepted a cost-based pricing mechanism (CBPM) effective since July 2008.[23] The CBPM covers four main state economic enterprises in the energy industry (Turkish Coal Enterprises, BOTAŞ, EÜAŞ and TETAŞ) and 20 regional distribution companies. The mechanism requires BOTAŞ to adjust its tariffs on a monthly basis, whereas other companies are required to adjust their tariffs in January 1, April 1, July 1, and October 1. Accordingly, retail tariffs are also adjusted on a quarterly basis. It was hoped that such an automatic adjustment mechanism would eliminate politically induced manipulation of energy prices and add regulatory credibility to the privatization process.

[23] High Planning Council Decision No. 2008/T-5 dated 14.2.2008.

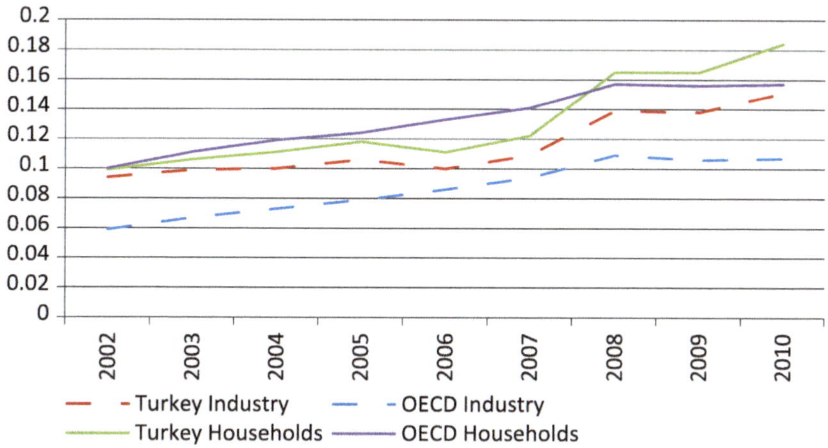

Fig. 2.12 Industry and household electricity tariffs: Turkey versus OECD (USD/kWh). *Source* IEA (2011)

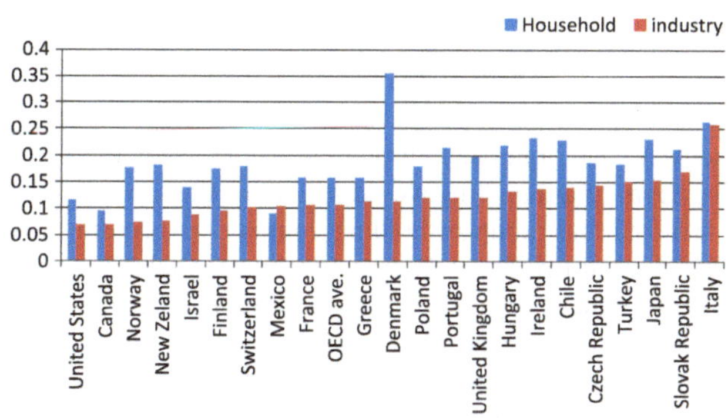

Fig. 2.13 Household and Industry Electricity Prices in OECD countries (USD/kWh, 2010). *Source* IEA (2011)

Figure 2.12 provides data on the path of industry and household retail prices. Household prices in Turkey are close to (and recently a bit higher than) OECD averages whereas prices for industry are substantially higher.

Figure 2.13 shows household and industry electricity prices among members of the OECD, ranked according to industry prices. Again, Turkey has the 4th highest electricity price for industry, whereas household prices, while higher than the OECD average, is lower than a large number of countries. One should note that this situation may partly be reflecting taxes. According to the IEA (2011, p 47) tariff data are inclusive of nonrefundable taxes. In Turkey, taxes on electricity for industry are especially high (18.5%) relative to many OECD countries (only two countries have higher taxes, Norway and Italy, and the OECD average is about 9%), whereas taxes on electricity for households (21.5% in Turkey) are close to OECD average (19.7%).[24]

5.4 Vertical Unbundling

Unbundling of transmission and distribution networks, the natural monopoly components of the electricity industry, from the potentially competitive segments of generation and retail supply is a significant component of any restructuring effort that has as its objective the creation of a competitive market. The main purpose of vertical unbundling is to prevent market foreclosure. The concern is that those who control naturally monopolistic network elements in the industry may prevent competitors in potentially competitive segments (generation and retail supply) from having nondiscriminatory access to the network. Even in cases where access tariffs are regulated, incumbent operators that control the transmission or distribution network may discriminate against competitors through non-price means. A recent sector inquiry undertaken by the European Commission has uncovered various forms of nonprice discrimination that incumbents utilize to foreclose markets to new competitors (European Commission 2007).

There are various forms of vertical unbundling. Accounting separation would require the vertically integrated entity to hold different accounts for its activities in the different segments of the industry. Legal unbundling would require activities in the different segments to be organized through separate legal entities (e.g., separate companies). This form of unbundling would still allow the separate legal entities to be owned by the same capital group or holding company. Accordingly, ownership unbundling is the strongest form of separation, whereby a capital group active in a network segment cannot have control over an entity in a different segment of the industry.

The 2009 Electricity directive of the EU[25] provides for different unbundling regimes for transmission and distribution networks. Regarding transmission, the original intention of the Commission was to achieve ownership unbundling both with respect to generation and retail supply. In the event, the directive ended up stipulating three different forms of unbundling, ownership unbundling being one of them.[26] The interesting question is whether in its current form TEİAŞ obeys the EU rules on unbundling given that both TEİAŞ and EUAŞ are state owned. European Commission's explanatory note on unbundling (2010) states that the rules on unbundling apply equally to private and public entities. It also states that two separate public bodies "should therefore be seen as two distinct persons and should be able to control generation and supply activities on the one hand and transmission activities on the other provided they are not under the common influence of another

[24] IEA (2011), pp 335 and 336.

[25] Directive 2009/72/EC 13 July 2009 concerning common rules for the internal market in electricity and repealing Directive 2003/54/EC.

[26] See European Commission (2010) for an extensive discussion and clarification.

public entity in violation of the rules on ownership unbundling". In other words, "the public bodies concerned must be truly separate". It seems therefore that TEİAŞ can be considered to comply with ownership unbundling.

In the case of the distribution network, the EU electricity directive requires that in cases where the distribution company is part of a vertically integrated undertaking, it should be legally unbundled from other activities of the vertically integrated undertaking not related to distribution; in addition it should be "functionally unbundled" in order to ensure its independence from other activities of the vertically integrated undertaking. Functional unbundling requires "management separation", that is, that persons responsible for the management of the distribution company do not participate in the day-day operation of other activities in the integrated structure, and that the distribution company has "effective decision rights", for example, over the assets used in its operations. Furthermore, the distribution company is required to establish a compliance program, "which sets out measures taken to ensure that discriminatory conduct is excluded and to ensure that observance of this prohibition is adequately monitored" (European Commission 2010, p 26). The main purpose of a compliance program is to provide a formal framework for ensuring that the distribution company complies with the principle of nondiscrimination.

As already mentioned, the EML required accounting unbundling of all activities. In addition, the original version restricted distribution companies' procurement of energy from affiliated generators to 20% of total consumption in the relevant distribution region. This restriction was removed in 2005 in an amendment to the EML.[27] This was largely seen as a step to increase the attractiveness of distribution companies to be privatized (Sevaioğlu 2005).

As a result of this amendment distribution companies could fully integrate into generation and retail supply, creating a seriously precarious situation with respect to competition. What changed the situation was an intervention by the Competition Authority during the privatization process. In Turkey, the privatization is regarded as a takeover and the Competition Board can intervene in the privatization process in two instances: first, under specific circumstances (such as if the entity to be privatized has market share above 20%) then an advance notification needs to be provided to the Competition Board before the tender is announced to the public, so that the Board can provide its views on the proper method of structuring the sale of the privatization assets. Second, to become legally effective, the privatization transaction requires a Board approval, in particular if an advance notification was necessary.[28] In its opinion regarding the privatization of distribution companies the Competition Board stated that the preferred option for ensuring competition was ownership separation between

[27] Law No. 5398, July 2005. An important restriction imposed on the distribution company was that the price of the electricity purchased from its subsidiary or affiliated companies could not be higher than the country average wholesale electricity price. This price is determined by EPDK and has been set equal to the average price established in the day-ahead market.

[28] See Atiyas (2009) for a discussion.

distribution and retail supply. Short of that, at a minimum the tender documents should state that distribution activities will be required to be legally separated from retail supply by the end of the transition period. The Board also stated that the strategy for distribution privatization has predominantly taken into consideration issues of security of supply and encouragement of foreign investments, but has insufficiently considered the institution of competition and protection of consumers. The Competition Authority did not specify any conditions regarding unbundling between distribution and generation, presumably because vertical integration was specifically allowed by the 2005 amendment to the EML.[29] This intervention by the Competition Authority proved effective and presently, as per an amendment to EML introduced in 2008, distribution companies are required to move any generation and retail supply activities into separate legal entities by January 1, 2013.[30]

While the 2008 amendment is a significant improvement, it is not clear that legal unbundling is sufficient to ensure nondiscriminatory access to the distribution network. The remedy falls short of the EU approach since it does not specify conditions for functional separation and any form of a compliance program.

5.5 Development of the Wholesale Market

5.5.1 Evolution of the Balancing Market

The first version of the balancing and settlement regulation (BSR) was actually first adopted in November 2004. This was seen as a step towards a more complete wholesale market and was called "Temporary" (T-BSR). Under the T-BSR, the financial settlement of transactions implemented to maintain the physical balance of the system was carried out through bid and offer prices proposed by TETAŞ and approved by EPDK.

The balancing market started operations in August 2006, as an emergency response to a blackout that covered western Turkey. The basic principle behind the mechanism was that the results of the balancing mechanism were to be settled together with the quantities of bilateral contracts. The system worked as follows (EPDK 2010): participants prepared their daily production programs. They submitted offers for producing above ("up-regulation") and below ("down-regulation") their production programs. The offers were accepted by the National Load Dispatch Center (MYTM) with a view to keep the system in balance. Payments related to accepted offers and imbalances between accepted offers and actual values of energy injection and withdrawal were settled by the Market Financial Settlement Center

[29] Competition Authority (2005). Competition Authority (n.d.) provides the internal report that provided the basis for the Board Decision.

[30] Law No. 5784 of July 2008.

(MFSC) at the end of each month. The accepted offers produced hourly system marginal prices (SMP). The system imbalance prices (SIP) were calculated as averages of the SMP for three periods: night, day, and peak. Financial settlements were carried out using the SIPs.

The workings of the balancing market were changed through the adoption of the so-called "final" Balancing and Settlement Regulation (F-BSR) in April 2009, effective since December 2009. Through this regulation, day-ahead balancing was separated from real-time balancing. Day-ahead balancing would take place in the Day-Ahead Market and real-time balancing would take place in the Balancing Power Market. The Day-Ahead Market was to be preceded by a preparatory period called Day-Ahead Planning. The Day-Ahead Market was to be launched in May 2011 and it has started operations after some delay in December 2011.

It is envisaged that most of the balancing activities are undertaken in the Day-Ahead Market and that imbalances arising in real time are dealt with in the Balancing Power Market. The planning market works as follows: the system operator presents system constraints and demand forecasts. Each market participant presents demand forecast, the daily production program, bilateral contracts, upregulation and downregulation price offers. The system operator determines System Day-Ahead Prices (SDAP), and delivers to the participants instructions to produce above or below program. Settlement for transactions in the Day-Ahead Market is done through the SDAP on an hourly basis (whereas under the F-BSR there were only three time periods).

The purpose of the Balancing Power Market is to eliminate in real time imbalances time that may arise, for example, because of unexpected changes in consumption or unexpected plant failures. Real-time balancing are activities performed by the MYTM. These activities include increase of the productions of the balancing units through acceptance of the upregulation offers; reduction of the productions of the balancing units through acceptance of the downregulation offers and thereby procurement of the tertiary reserve necessary for frequency control. In the real-time balancing markets each participant delivers a production program and price offers to produce above or below program. The SMP is determined as the highest accepted upregulation or lowest accepted downregulation bid. SMP is used for settlement of transactions in the Balancing Power Market.

An important innovation introduced with the Day-Ahead Market is more active participation by the demand side. In the Day-Ahead-Planning system, consumers had to declare consumption levels irrespective of prices. Under the Day-Ahead Market, consumers may bid schedules that are sensitive to prices; hence, the Day-Ahead Market will involve more active participation of the demand side (Deloitte 2009; Ongün 2011). Another important change introduced through the Day-Ahead Market is the possibility of market splitting and zonal pricing.[31] The F-BSR authorizes the system operator to undertake necessary studies to determine long term, large scale and enduring possible congestions in the transmission system,

---

[31] See Kölmek (2011) for a discussion.

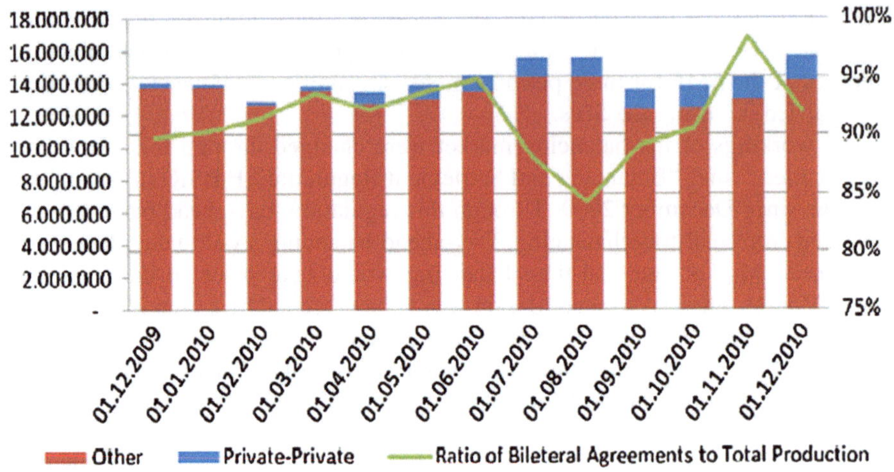

Fig. 2.14 Volume of bilateral contracts (MWh). *Source* EPDK (2010)

and to divide the national electricity system into trade zones. It is hoped that market splitting and zonal pricing will provide better signals for the location of generation plants and transmission investments. The regulation that will govern the implementation of zonal pricing has not been issued as of December 2011.

5.5.2 Evolution of the Bilateral Contracts Market

The evolution of the balancing market and improvements that have been achieved over time is a significant accomplishment of the restructuring process. It has played a crucial role in generating price signals that more closely reflect the scarcity value of electricity and in attracting private investment into the industry. At the same time, however, the balancing market started to operate as a wholesale market rather than a balancing market per-se. In response to the opening of the balancing market in August 2006, most independent power producers have terminated their bilateral contracts and have sold their electricity to the balancing market instead. Hence, while in a bilateral markets model it is expected that a small portion (say 10–15%) of electricity would be traded for balancing purposes, the balancing market in Turkey has attracted almost all electricity supplied by private competitive generators. In effect, the balancing market has been operating more like a spot market for electricity.

As a result the market for *private* bilateral contracts, say between eligible consumers and independent generators, has remained underdeveloped. Figure 2.14 shows the evolution of the bilateral contracts market in 2010. The total volume of bilateral contracts is about 14 TWh. However, only about 10% of this entails

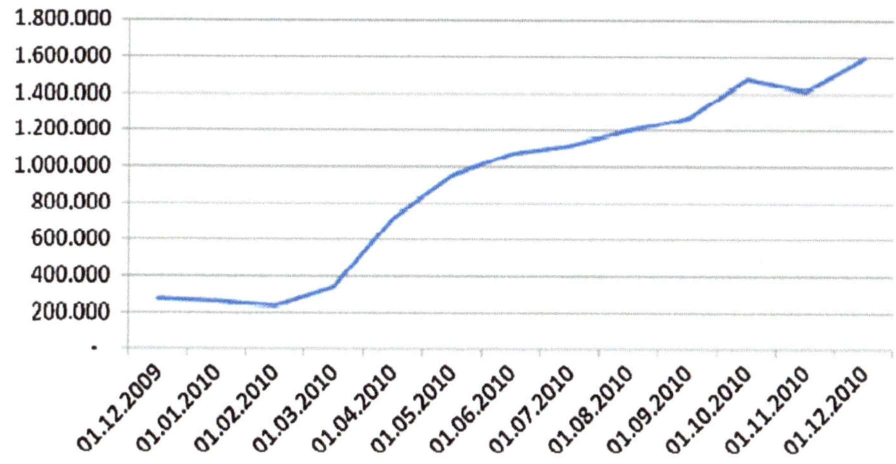

Fig. 2.15 Volume of private-to-private bilateral contracts (MWh)

contracts where both parties are private persons (see also Fig. 2.15), though this ratio is increasing. One advantage of bilateral contracts is that it provides a hedge against volatility of spot prices. One would expect that as players in the market learn about this property of bilateral contracts and as trust builds over time, the attractiveness of such contracts for independent generators and eligible consumers should increase.

5.6 Competition Issues

It is well know that wholesale electricity markets are especially susceptible to problems of unilateral exercise of market power, much more so than markets for other goods and services.[32] In most markets problems of unilateral market power are closely related to the degree of concentration. In electricity markets, the possibility of capacity constraints creates conditions, whereby a generator may be able to raise prices by reducing output or withdrawing capacity even when its market share is not high by traditional standards. Incidents where exercise of such market power has contributed to increase in prices during periods of high demand have been extensively reported in the literature. Given that the price elasticity of electricity demand is often low, higher prices often do not translate to high deadweight losses. However, price spikes do generate large redistributions of wealth among the players in electricity markets, including possibly from consumers to producers or traders. In many jurisdictions ex-post application of

[32] See, for example, Borenstein and Bushnell (2000); OECD (2003); Garcia and Reitzes (2007) and Wolak (2005).

competition law is not seen as a sufficient weapon against unilateral exercise of market power, if anything because investigations under competition law often take a long time. Additional remedies, often of ex-ante nature, are implemented. Such remedies range from restraints on generation behavior regarding bids or capacity actions, to transparency rules. At the very least, special effort is devoted to monitor market developments and take precautions if there are developments in the market that may facilitate unilateral exercise of market power (Garcia and Reitzes 2007).

The problem of unilateral exercise of market power has not become an issue in the Turkish context yet. However, the privatization of generation companies is going to make a significant change in the market environment. EÜAŞ has not been behaving as a profit maximizing generator. If anything, EÜAŞ assets have been used to keep electricity prices low, or to moderate their increases. With privatization, these assets are going to be managed by profit maximizing entities, with every incentive to use market power if possible. So far there have been no preparations to deal with market power issues that may arise. At the very least, either the Ministry, or EPDK or TEİAŞ should undertake periodical studies about whether transmission constraints are likely to arise in the next few years. If that is the case, then the nature of proper remedies may be discussed.

5.7 Resource Adequacy

The lack of investment response by the private sector and the blackout of 2006 has raised resource adequacy as a major concern. Law No. 5784 introduced a number of amendments to the EML to address the resource adequacy problem. The changes require the Ministry to prepare a report on electricity supply security every year. They authorize TEİAŞ to open bids to have energy plants established or to rent capacity from existing generation plants under the auxiliary service agreements to meet regional system needs. Distribution companies and suppliers which meet the demands of eligible consumers are required to inform EPDK about supply resources they are going to use to meet demand (in the case of distribution companies the reports have to cover the next 5 years). In addition, the law provided a tender mechanism to address resource adequacy issues: the council of ministers may announce a tender if energy investments are not sufficient to meet demand. If the Ministry determines that the tender process is not adequate to meet energy demand, the council of ministers may authorize EUAŞ to build electricity generation plants.

The amendment also mentions the establishment of capacity mechanisms. In fact it required the Ministry to prepare a regulation regarding procedures to be followed for the establishments of capacity mechanisms within 6 months of the publication of the law (i.e., by January 2009) but this has not been done. It seems the authorities' perceptions about the urgency of capacity mechanisms have been diminished because of the increase in private sector investments and the recession that Turkey went through in 2008–2009. Even though there were some studies undertaken for the authorities, they have not been made public.

5.8 Prospects for Retail Supply

By the end of 2012, distribution companies holding retail licenses will have to organize retail activities under separate legal entities. The purpose of this legal separation is to help develop competition in the retail supply market. Accordingly, the threshold for eligible consumers has been reduced continuously over time down to 30 MWh in 2011. That means that consumers representing about 75% of total consumption are eligible to choose their suppliers (Camadan 2011). The actual level of consumption of eligible consumers who have used their rights to switch suppliers to total consumption is lower, representing about 18% of total consumption in 2010 (EPDK 2010a, p 74). The degree of statutory market opening is planned to reach 100% in 2015 (Camadan 2011).

The degree to which competition in the retail supply market can develop is an issue where there is less agreement relative to other dimensions of electricity restructuring.

Table 2.11 reports one the most widely used statistics to measure the degree of effective competition in the retail supply market, namely the ratio of customers that switch from the incumbent to new suppliers. The numbers are discouraging, even for large industrial consumers. In Great Britain, the frontrunner in market opening, the switching ratio among small business and households is less than 20%.

International experience seems to suggest that retail supply may generate higher efficiency gains when real-time pricing is possible at the retail level. This would require a more advanced technological infrastructure, including the installation of smart meters. Smart metering would make it possible for consumers to respond to fluctuations in wholesale prices. This, in turn, would create margins for new products and services that can be provided by competitive retail suppliers (Joskow 2000). In principle, retailers may provide a variety of contracts that can be selected by consumers with different degrees of potential for risk taking, ability to switch consumption over hours of the day, etc. But the challenge for retail competition remains to be the lack of interest on the part of small consumers (households and small commercial) in managing their daily use of electricity. Smart in-home devices, programmable thermostats, online management of home appliances, smart phone applications are technologies that can help, especially with younger generations. Better yet is the remote control of key appliances such as refrigerators and air conditioners by system operators but this raises privacy issues. Overall, the evidence for retail competition based on real-time pricing is weak for small consumers.

An important issue to consider in this regard is whether any regulation of retail prices should continue after full market opening. The problem is that regulated prices are often seen as an impediment to the development of competition in the retail markets.[33] When regulated tariffs are too low relative to spot prices, eligible

---

[33] The Sector Inquiry of the European Commission (2007) states: "Regulated retail tariffs can have highly distortive effects and in certain cases pre-empt the creation of liberalised markets" (p 14).

Table 2.11 Customer switching rates in the European Union (%, 2009)

	All Retail Market	Large Industry	Medium Industry	Ssmall industry and household
Austria	1.3	8.3	7.9	1.3
Belgium	6.9	NA	NA	NA
Bulgaria	0.004	37	0.008	0
Cyprus	0	0	0	0
Czech	1.5	73	22	1.5
Denmark	6.2	NA	16.5	6.1
Estonia	NA	NA	NA	0
Finland	8.1	NA	NA	NA
France	3.4	NA	NA	3.6
Germany	4.8	15.6	5.9	4.7
Great Britain	NA	NA	NA	18.4
Greece	0.03	0	5.15	0.03
Hungary	NA	NA	NA	NA
Ireland	20.5	16.8	38.53	20.39
Italy	4.5	25.7	37.3	12.2
Latvia	0.01	0	0.5	0
Lithuania	0	0	0	0
Luxembourg	0.2	3.3	0.46	0.17
Malta	0	0	0	0
Northern Ireland	0.75	3	14	10
Norway	8.1	NAP	7.9	8.1
Poland	NA	NA	NA	NA
Portugal	2.3	32.7	24.6	2.2
Romania	0.013	13.32	4.17	0.004
Slovak	0.9	NA	NA	0.88
Slovenia	1.4	0	5.7	1.4
Spain	NA	NA	NA	NA
Sweden	11.2	10	10	11.4
The Netherlands	11	NA	NA	11

Source European Commission (2010b)

consumers may prefer to remain with (the retail arms of) incumbent distribution companies which may in turn make competitive entry into the retail supply industry difficult. In fact, as reported by Camadan (2011) in the Turkish case whether such a "supplier of last resort" will remain after market opening is not clear. Given bleak prospects for the development of retail supply for many residential consumers, the authorities will likely choose to retain a supplier of last resort for some time, and this will likely be the incumbent distribution company or its retail arm.

The position of the European Regulator's Group for Electricity and Gas is that regulation of end-user prices should be terminated and that protection of vulnerable consumers does not require the regulation of end-user prices (ERGEG 2007). This is possibly correct, but if the prospect of retail competition is high. Hence, it seems the question of whether or how long retail price regulation should continue also is closely connected to measures that would help develop competition in the retail markets. Again, looking ahead, installation of smart meters is one potential measure that needs to be seriously considered. In addition to that, measures and services to increase consumer information and awareness are also likely to be very important.

5.9 Distributional Concerns

The development of competition, elimination of cross subsidies, reductions in illegal use and establishment of cost-reflective tariffs are all likely to have significant distributive consequences. Realignment of prices may have strongest effects on households with low incomes. Based on the 2003 Household Expenditure Survey of Turkey, Bağdadioğlu et al. (2007) show that households in the decile with the lowest income spend an average of nearly 50% of their income on electricity. For the highest income group, this ratio is about 4%. The authors recognize that the very high ratio for the lowest income group "may arise because low income households generate a significant part of their income in kind rather than money, so that any money expenditure appears as a very high proportion of (money) income." Still, it is clear that changes in prices are likely to have a much greater impact on low income than on high-income households.

It is also likely that illegal use is more widespread among poorer households. Bağdadioğlu et al. (2007) show that a larger share of households reporting no expenditures live in provinces with high network losses, and also that amongst the lowest decile of households 50% of households reported no expenditure on electricity, while the corresponding proportion for the richest decile is only 17%. Hence, reductions in illegal use would impact disproportionately low-income households.

Another dimension of the problem has to do with rebalancing of tariffs among different consumer groups, especially among industry and households. Data from IEA (2011) reveals that the ratio of electricity tariffs for households to tariffs for industry are much lower in Turkey relative to OECD averages. At the start of the restructuring process in 2002, this ratio was 1.0 for Turkey whereas it was 2.0 on average for European OECD members and 1.7 for all OECD. By 2010 the ratio improved for Turkey somewhat, reaching a ratio of 1.2. However, it is still one of the lowest among OECD countries and significantly lower than OECD averages (1.5 for all OECD countries). Hence one should expect further increases in tariffs paid by households relative to those paid by industry. In fact, Bağdadioğlu et al. (2007) conduct an experiment to evaluate the consequences of increasing the ratio of industry to household prices to OECD average and find that while the impact of such a change on electricity expenditures increases with income, the impact as a proportion of disposable income decreases with household income, from about 5.5% for the lowest income household to less than 1% for the richest decile. The introduction of a fixed fee, representing fixed cost of retail services, is also likely to have regressive effects.

Distributional effects of electricity restructuring often also entails considerations of access. This is less of a problem in Turkey as an overwhelming majority of households are already connected to the network. Hence, the main channel through which distributional effects are likely to register is through changes in tariffs.

All of this suggests that the restructuring process needs to be supplemented by a policy to address issues of affordability and distributional consequences. This is also important to maintain the political viability of the restructuring program, and to reduce political incentives to manipulate prices, as TEDAŞ prices were before they were adjusted after 2008. The EML was cognizant of the possible need to address these concerns, as it envisaged that in cases where support for consumers were needed, this should be carried out through direct income transfers. However, no additional work has been undertaken in this area. Affordability of energy among low-income households and likely adverse distributional consequences of restructuring represent priority areas that need to be addressed.

5.10 Institutional Issues

The performance of a regulatory regime is generally believed to depend both on the general design of the restructuring program, the quality of regulations and their implementation, and on the institutional characteristics of the way the process is governed. The history of economic governance in Turkey has not been exemplary in that regard. Even the enactment of the EML has often been criticized by various stakeholders, including the bureaucracy, for not having been prepared in a participatory manner and for having been adopted without adequate public consultation. Throughout the 1990s privatization efforts have been conducted in a manner that attempted to bypass the legislature and centralize discretionary authority in the executive in a nontransparent way and many such initiatives were cancelled by the constitutional court (Atiyas 2009). Initially, BOT projects were granted without any transparent and competitive tender mechanisms, raising concerns about favoritism. There have been improvements in the 2000s, but there are a number of issues that still need to be highlighted.

Turkey would benefit from a clearly articulated and cohesive long-term energy strategy that is the product of a participatory process that includes various shareholders such as universities, consumer groups, professional associations, and the private sector. Governmental agencies including the ETKB and EPDK have various strategic documents but, although useful, these are bureaucratic documents that have not resulted from a stakeholder process, have not benefited from public consultation and more importantly do not present and discuss alternative options and tradeoffs. Similarly, much more effort needs to be spent on the evaluation of the impact of policies and regulations adopted. The Electricity Market Report of EPDK (2010) is an important step forward in this regard. Impact evaluations should go beyond descriptive analysis of the evolution of regulations and markets and evaluate the effect of developments on targeted outcomes. To give an example, the authorities have so far not undertaken a critical analysis of why bilateral markets have not developed as expected and why the balancing market is acting like a pool.

An important shortcoming has to do with the fact that EPDK regulations and decisions are published without justifications. Requiring regulatory authorities to provide justifications for their decisions is an important tool that improves transparency and accountability and provides a source of discipline that increases the quality of regulations. A good example in this regard is the Competition Authority: the law that founded the Competition Authority required that the decisions of its Board be published both with a justification and with a summary of the internal report that provides the analytical background to the decisions. Recently, the Information Technologies and Communication Authority, the regulatory agency overseeing electronic communications markets, has also been required to provide justifications for the decisions of its governing board.

Similarly, the exact methodologies used for the more technical aspects of the regulations are not made public. For example, the EPDK has not disclosed what sort of an approach it used to calculate the target loss ratios for the 2011–2015 period to the public. The calculations behind the determination of other key parameters in tariff regulations are also not public. Making these methodologies open to public scrutiny would represent an immense step towards transparency and accountability.

By contrast, the public consultation process especially as regards to EPDK regulations and some of the decisions of its Board seems to be working: draft regulations or decisions are published to solicit comments. However, comments provided by different parties are not disclosed. Making these comments publicly available would also enhance transparency.

Another important issue has to do with appointments to the Board of the EPDK. Regulatory credibility requires that Board members are not under political influence when they perform their duties. There is no universally agreed on methodology for appointments that would ensure such political independence. In the case of the EPDK, Board members are appointed by the Council of Ministers. Political independence of the Board may be enhanced if appointments are made in a more transparent and accountable way. For example, there may be hearings in the parliament that would give members of parliament a chance to question the candidates. The ultimate authority to appoint would still remain by the Council of Ministers, but such hearings may provide incentives to the government to make their appointments more merit based.

The government recently passed a new "decree with the force of law"[34] which gives ministries the authority to "inspect" the activities of regulatory authorities associated with them. While the clause does not give ministries authority to change or overturn the decisions of the regulatory authorities, or intervene in their management, it does give ministries the ability to harass agencies by subjecting them to inspections. As of December 2011, there have been no examples of exercise of such inspection authority, but the move by the government has been interpreted by the press as a step towards reducing the independence of the regulatory authorities.

6 Electricity Restructuring: An Assessment

The results of the Turkish experience with restructuring in the electricity industry are mixed. On the one hand, the legal environment and the organization of the industry have changed in fundamental ways. Significant progress has been achieved in establishing a balancing market that can provide much more correct signals about the scarcity price of electricity. The establishment of the balancing market was also instrumental in attracting new private investment into the industry. In that sense, to the extent that the purpose of restructuring was to relieve the state budget of the burden of electricity investments, one should admit a degree of success. In effect, compared to the 1990s, the new model has been successful in attracting private investment for distribution privatization under competitive conditions, without granting any concessions, subsidies, or government guarantees.

However, the main purpose of restructuring ought to be efficiency gains and increases in consumer welfare. The fundamental means of achieving these objectives are through the development of competition in generation. In that regard, after 11 years of the enactment of the EML and after 7 years of adoption of the SD, one has to admit that so far little has been achieved. True, in the special case of Turkey high losses and theft in the distribution system provided another important source of efficiency gains and the targets set by the EPDK for the 2011–2015 period seem quite aggressive. But that does not change the fact that these efficiency gains are significantly delayed. More importantly, the degree of competition in generation is still very modest and restricted to about a quarter of generation.

The primary reason for this delay is rooted in the fact that the driver of the restructuring process has been privatization, not competition. In addition, privatization itself was driven by the quest of maximizing privatization revenues. An alternative strategy could have been to identify competition as the main driver of the restructuring process. That would have required horizontal breakup and corporatization of generation assets, mandating them with competitive behavior and their privatization if necessary. Competition has less to do with efficiency gains in

[34] A Decree with the Force of Law is basically a law that is enacted by the Council of Ministers rather than the Parliament. Such decrees are based on "authorizing laws" which have been enacted by the Parliament.

the distribution system and these could in principle be achieved under state ownership, through improvement in their management, and corporatization. The Turkish authorities must have thought that reform of public management was more difficult than privatization, but in hindsight, given the difficulties faced in and slow progress of privatization, it is not clear that this was indeed the case. The alternative strategy could have been inspired by Scandinavian countries, especially Norway and Sweden, where state ownership has been extensive but nevertheless substantial success has been achieved in developing competition.[35]

Looking ahead, the degree of reduction in the losses of the distribution system will provide the first true test of the Turkish model. In the meantime, competition in generation can be achieved in a faster manner if the portfolio companies currently being established are quickly corporatized, put under competent management are given a mandate to behave in an independent and competitive manner in the market. Listing these corporations in the stock exchange would result in a major improvement in transparency.

While there has been significant progress in terms of market design, there are some remaining issues that need to be addressed. Regarding resource adequacy, the authorities should undertake a study to see whether the current measures are sufficient or whether instead of burdening EÜAŞ with the task of closing the gap of reserve capacity, a capacity mechanism should be instituted instead. Even though exercise of market power has not yet posed a major problem in the restructuring process, this may potentially become an issue especially once generation assets are privatized. It would be better to examine ahead of time whether in generation and transmission conditions are likely to generate such competition problems, and take remedial action if necessary, rather than wait and act after the occurrence of incidents of exercise of market power.

Turkey is a country where distribution of income is highly unequal. Moreover, inequality of income distribution has significant regional dimensions. Hence there are large number of households who experience problems of affordability and energy poverty. This is likely to present political incentives to manipulate and distort energy prices. The current implementation of national tariffs and the regional cross subsidies it entails are good examples of inefficient outcomes that such incentives may produce. A better approach is to develop a policy that targets energy poverty and affordability issues directly.

References

Amundsen, Eirik S. and Lars Bergman (2006). "Why Has the Nordic Electricity Market Worked So Well?" *Utilities Policy*, 14 (3), 148–157.

Atiyas, Izak (2009) "Recent Privatization Experience of Turkey – A Reappraisal", in Ziya Öniş and Fikret Şenses (Eds.) *Turkey and the Global Economy: Neo-Liberal Restructuring and Integration in the Post-Crisis Era,* New York: Routledge, 101–122.

[35] See, for example, Amundsen and Bergman (2006).

Atiyas, Izak. (2006). Elektrik Sektöründe Serbestleşme ve Düzenleyici Reform, Istanbul: Tesev Publication, http://www.tesev.org.tr/UD_OBJS/PDF/IYIYNTSM/elektrik%20Sektorunde%20Serbestlesme%20ve%20Duzenleyici%20Reform.pdf accessed December 16, 2011.

Atiyas, Izak and Mark Dutz (2005). "Competition and Regulatory Reform in Turkey's Electricity Industry", B. Hoekman ve S. Togan *Turkey: Economic Reform and Accession to the European Union*, The World Bank and CEPR.

Atiyas, Izak and Jorge N. Ferer (2007). "Electricity" in S. Ülgen (ed.) Second Generation Structural Reforms: De-Regulation and Competition in Infrastructure Industries - The Evolution of the Turkish Telecommunications, Energy and Transport Sectors in Light of EU Harmonisation, CEPS Special Reports, http://www.ceps.be/ceps/download/1416 accessed December 16, 2011.

Atiyas, İzak and Burak Oder (2007). *Özelleştirmenin Hukuk ve Ekonomisi*, Ankara:TEPAV, http://www.tepav.org.tr/upload/files/1271234172r8289.Turkiye___de_Ozellestirmenin_Hukuk_ve_Ekonomisi.pdf accessed December 16, 2011.

Bagdadioğlu, N., Başaran A. and C. W. Price (2007) "Potential Impact of Electricity Reforms on Turkish Households" ESRC Centre for Competition Policy and Norwich Business School, University of East Anglia CCP Working Paper 07-8.

Borenstein, Severin ve James Bushnell (2000) "Electricity Restructuring: Deregulation or Re-regulation?", *Regulation*, 23(2), 2000, 46–53.

Camadan, E. (2011). "Why 2012 Will Be So Important for the Restructured Turkish Electricity Market" *The Electricity Journal*, 24 (10) 70–78.

Çetin, Tamer and Fuat Oğuz (2007), "The Politics of Regulation in the Turkish Electricity Market" *Energy Policy* 35, 1761–1770.

Çakarel, E. and J. C. House (2005) "IPP Investment in Turkey's Electric Power Industry" Prepared specifically for distribution at a PESD Seminar: "The Experience of Independent Power Producers in Developing Countries" Stanford University, June 2-3, 2005, http://iis-db.stanford.edu/docs/59/Turkey.pdf, accessed December 16, 2011.

Competition Authority (nd) Türkiye Elektrik Dağitim A.Ş.'nin Özelleştirilmesi Hakkında 1998/4 Sayılı Rekabet Kurulu Tebliği Çerçevesinde Hazırlanan Rekabet Kurumu 1. Daire Görüşü, Ankara. http://www.rekabet.gov.tr/word/gorus/tedasson.doc accessed December 16, 2011.

Competition Authority (2005). "Türkiye Elektrik Dağitim A.Ş.'nin Özelleştirilmesine İlişkin Rekabet Kurulu Görüşü", Ankara. http://www.rekabet.gov.tr/word/gorus/tedasgorus.doc accessed December 10, 2011.

Deloitte (2010). Turkish Electricity Market – Developments and Expectations 2010-2011, Istanbul. http://www.deloitte.com/assets/Dcom-Turkey/Local%20Assets/Documents/turkey-en_er_ElektrikEPiyasasi2010_221010.pdf accessed December 20, 2011.

Deloitte (2009) "Dengeleme ve Uzlaştırma Yönetmeliği Nihai Dönem Düzenlemeleri" presentation, mimeo.

ERGEG (2007) "End-user energy price regulation: An ERGEG Position Paper" Ref: E07-CPR-10-03, http://www.energy-regulators.eu/portal/page/portal/EER_HOME/EER_PUBLICATIONS/CEER_PAPERS/Customers/2007/E07-CPR-10-03_E-UPriceReg_0.pdf accessed December 20, 2011.

EPDK (2010). Electricity Market Report, Ankara. http://www.emra.gov.tr/documents/10615/b8ff3b3a-8853-45ad-8bdd-00428c1857a8 accessed December 20, 2011.

EPDK (2010a). 2010 Yılı Faaliyet Raporu, Ankara. http://www.epdk.gov.tr/documents/10157/34e34f7c-9a18-43ae-a322-c85547239d35 accessed December 20, 2011.

Erdoğdu, Erkan (2007) "Regulatory reform in Turkish energy industry: An analysis" *Energy Policy* 35 984–993.

European Commission (2010). Interpretative Note on Directive 2009/72/EC Concerning Common Rules For The Internal Market In Electricity And Directive 2009/73/EC Concerning Common Rules For The Internal Market In Natural Gas - The Unbundling Regime, Commission Staff Working Paper, Brussels 22 January 2010.

European Commission (2010b). 2009-2010 Report on Progress in Creating the Internal Gas and Electricity Market, Technical Annex. Commission Staff Working Paper. Brussels, 9 June 2010.

European Commission (2007) Communication from the Commission, "Inquiry pursuant to Article 17 of Regulation (EC) No 1/2003 into the European gas and electricity sectors (Final Report)", COM/2006/0851 final, Brussels, 10 January 2007.

Garcia, Jose A. and James D. Reitzes (2007). "International Perspectives on Electricity Market Monitoring and Market Power Mitigation" *Review of Network Economics,* 6 (3) 397-424.

Gülen, S. Gürcan (1998). "Electricity in Turkey; A Legal Battleground in an Ongoing Privatization War." *Power Economics* (December 31, 1998).

Bilgiç, Haluk, Derman, Özgür and Gürcan Gülen (1999) "Review of Legal Battleground in Turkey's Power Privatization War." *Utilities Law Review.*

Güney, Serhat (2006) "Restructuring, Competition and Regulation in the Turkish Electricity Industry", TEPAV 2006 http://www.tepav.org.tr/tur/admin/dosyabul/upload/Restructuring.pdf.

Helm, Dieter (2003). *Energy, the State and the Market: British Energy Policy since 1979.* Oxford: Oxford University Press.

Hepbaşlı, Arif (2005) "Development and Restructuring of Turkey's Electricity Sector: A Review" *Renewable and Sustainable Energy Reviews*, 9, 311–343.

International Energy Agency (2011) Energy Prices and Taxes, Third Quarter 2011.

International Energy Agency (2001). Energy Policies of IEA Countries – Turkey 2001 Review, Paris: IEA.

Joskow, Paul (2000). "Why Do We Need Electricity Retailers? Or Can You Get It Cheaper Wholesale?" http://econ-www.mit.edu/files/1127 accessed December 15, 2011.

Joskow, Paul L. (2008). "Lessons Learned From Electricity Market Liberalization" *The Energy Journal*, Special Issue on the Future of Electricity, pp. 9–42, 2008.

Kayabaş, Çetin and Ercüment Camadan (2011)."2011-2015 Dönemi Elektrik Dağıtım Tarifeleri", *Enerji Piyasası Bülteni,* No. 16, 4-10.

Kölmek, Fatih (2011). "Gün Öncesi Piyasası ve Bölgesel Fiyatlandırma"*Enerji Piyasası Bülteni,* No. 16, 34-38.

Kurna, İbrahim (2011). "Türkiye'de Enerji Sektöründe Özelleştirme" presentation at the ICCI 2011 Conference, http://www.icci.com.tr/dosya/2011sunumlar/O14_Ibrahim_Kurna.pdf.

Littlechild, Stephen (2010) "Why we need electricity retailers: A reply to Joskow on wholesale spot price pass-through" http://www.econ.cam.ac.uk/dae/repec/cam/pdf/WP0008.PDF accessed December 16, 2001.

Newbery, David M. (2005) "Electricity liberalization in Britain: The quest for a satisfactory wholesale market design" *The Energy Journal,* 26, Special Issue, 43-70.

OECD (2003). "Competition Issues in the Electricity Sector", DAFFE/COMP(2003)14, Paris: OECD.

Ongün, A. (2011) "Gün Öncesi Piyasası", presentation. http://enerjienstitusu.com/arsivler/Kasim 2011_Gun%20Oncesi%20Piyasasi%20-%20Abdulkadir%20Ongun.pdf accessed December 16, 2011.

Özel, Işık and İzak Atiyas (2011). "Regulatory Diffusion in Turkey: A Cross-sectoral Assessment" in Tamer Çetin and Fuat Oğuz (eds.) *Political Economy of Regulation in Turkey*, New York: Springer, 51–74.

Price Waterhouse Coopers (2008) "Privatization of the Turkish Electricity Distribution Companies" http://www.pwc.com/tr_TR/tr/assets/ins-sol/publ/privitization.pdf accessed December 16, 2011.

Privatization Authority (2009). "Teaser - Privatization of Turkey's Electricity Distribution Industry", http://www.oib.gov.tr/2009/dosyalar/TEDAS%20Teaser%20Ingilizce%20v05-comments%20removed.pdf accessed December 16, 2011.

Sevaioğlu, Osman (2007). "Subsidizing Electricity Price; How far?" mimeo; on file with the authors.

Sevaioğlu, Osman (2005) "4628 ve Çam Fıstıklı İrmik Helvası", *Global Enerji* July 2005.

Ugaz, Cecilia and Catherine Waddams Price (2003) *Utility Privatization and Regulation: A Fair Deal for Consumers?*, Cheltenham, UK: Edward Elgar.

Ulusoy, Ali and Fuat Oğuz (2007) "The privatization of electricity distribution in Turkey: A legal and economic analysis" *Energy Policy* 35, 5021–5034.

Wolak, Frank (2005a) "Managing Unilateral Market Power in Electricity" World Bank Policy Research Working Paper 3691, Washington DC: The World bank.

World Bank Group (2009) Running a Business in Turkey, Enterprise Surveys Country Note Series, Turkey Country note no. 1 rev. 7/2011, http://www.enterprisesurveys.org/~/media/FPDKM/EnterpriseSurveys/Documents/Country%20Notes/Turkey-09.pdf accessed December 15, 2011.

Chapter 3
The Reform of Natural Gas Market in Turkey

1 Introduction

The use of natural gas in Turkey has increased by 96% during the 2000s. In 2010, total natural gas consumption was around 38.2 bcm per annum but production was only 690 mcm. Accordingly, 98% of gas was imported from Russia, Iran, Azerbaijan, Algeria, and Nigeria via pipelines and LNG. Turkey's natural gas demand is heavily dependent on imports and especially the Russian gas that meets around 45% of consumption in Turkey. Moreover, the dependency of electricity generation on natural gas in Turkey is about 47% and 51% of natural gas is used for electricity production. The natural gas market continues to face crucial issues in terms of evolving energy policies and regulations in Turkey. This Chapter scrutinizes the regulatory reforms, policy issues, and the evolution of market structure in the Turkish natural gas market, and the geopolitical role of Turkey between the gas-rich regions and Europe.

Turkey restructured the natural gas market by the Natural Gas Market Law (NGML) enacted in May 2001. The priority of NGML is to establish a competitive natural gas market. For that reason, it removed BOTAŞ's de jure monopoly rights on imports, storage, distribution, sales, and pricing of natural gas by vertically unbundling the company. EPDK, established as an independent regulatory board by the Electricity Market Law in 2001, is responsible for regulation of the natural gas market activities; third-party access to the transmission and distribution networks, prices and tariffs are regulated by EPDK under non-discriminatory conditions. The law of 2001 requires obtaining a separate license for all market activities to improve competition through participation of different actors in various market activities.

According to the NGML, BOTAŞ was supposed to reduce its market share on imports to 20% by 2009. However, BOTAŞ met 84.1% of Turkey's natural gas imports in 2010, or 32 bcm out of 38 bcm of total imports.

I. Atiyas et al., *Reforming Turkish Energy Markets*,
DOI: 10.1007/978-1-4614-0290-9_3,

An important feature of the reform process is privatization of the public-owned distribution facilities and development of distribution networks in additional cities. EPDK is responsible for organization of the tender processes to select operators of distribution franchises. EPDK considers the financial strength and experience of the potential licensees. Tenders are carried out through competitive bidding and licenses are granted for a minimum of 10 and a maximum of 30 years. As of September 2011, EPDK has conducted 57 tenders and 67 cities have been connected to distribution network, only six cities were connected to the network before 2001. However, the biggest gas distribution company of Turkey, İGDAŞ has not yet been privatized. İGDAŞ is a municipality-owned company and delivers natural gas to 45.8% of the total users in Turkey.

Turkey aims to become an energy corridor for transportation of natural gas from Middle East, Caspian, and Mediterranean areas to Europe. Many projects are underway. The South European Gas Ring or the Interconnector Turkey–Greece–Italy (ITGI) has been in operation since November 2007. The project started as the Turkey-Greece pipeline project and a feasibility study for extending the Interconnector to Italy via a pipeline crossing Adriatic Sea was completed by the end of 2004 by respective companies of Greece, Turkey, and Italy. The offshore pipeline is planned to become operational by 2015.

The Nabucco project aims to transport natural gas from the Caspian, Central Asian, South Mediterranean, and Middle East regions to Europe via Turkey, Bulgaria, Romania, Hungary, and Austria. Terminating in Baumgarten-Austria, the pipeline has a capacity of 31 bcm per annum. The main aim of the Nabucco project is to bypass Russia and to reduce the market power of Russia on the supply of natural gas to Europe. The six-partnered project has been fully supported by an intergovernmental agreement signed between the partners in July 2009 but its start date has been delayed repeatedly.

On December 2011, Turkey and Azerbaijan signed an intergovernmental agreement for the Trans-Anatolia Gas Pipeline (TAGP). This project will transport via Turkey natural gas produced in Shah Sea 2 field of Azerbaijan. The construction of the pipeline will be completed by the end of 2017 by the consortium of SOCAR, BOTAŞ, and TPAO. The pipeline will transport 16 bcm natural gas per annum for the first phase and this volume will reach 24 bcm in the future. While six of 16 bcm will be delivered to Turkey, 10 bcm will be transported to Europe. The TAGP somewhat conflicts with a current project to provide gas to the Nabucco pipeline, the South Caucasus or Shah Sea Project, which includes the Baku–Tbilisi–Erzurum pipeline. Both projects are designed to deliver natural gas from the Shah Sea field in Azerbaijan to the Turkish distribution network and eventually to Europe. It is also expected that natural gas will be transported from Kazakhstan to Europe via these pipelines in the future. Finally, Turkey aims to transport Egyptian, Iranian, and Iraqi natural gas to Europe via some planned projects.

2 Historical Background of Natural Gas Market: The Road to the Reform

In order to understand well the current effects of the reform in the Turkish natural gas market, it is necessary to understand the pre-reform market structure and the road to the reform. Before 2001, a vertically integrated state monopoly, BOTAŞ dominated the market (Fig. 3.1). Ten years after the reform bill, BOTAŞ continues to play a major role in the market as a monopoly in transmission of gas and with significant market share in imports, wholesale market and storage. The company was founded for transportation of Iraq's crude oil to Ceyhan in 1974. BOTAŞ's other functions were to construct natural gas pipelines, to acquire or lease existing pipelines, to transport natural gas via the pipelines, to buy and sell natural gas transported in the pipelines. In 1995, its activities related to natural gas, which started with the import of gas from Russia via the Western route in the mid-1980s, and oil were expanded to include all kinds of petroleum-related activities such as exploration, drilling, production, storage, and refining for the purpose of providing crude oil and natural gas sources abroad (BOTAŞ 2009)[1].

BOTAŞ built natural gas pipelines and related facilities, signed long-term natural gas sale and purchase contracts, and additionally purchased natural gas on the spot markets. However, it could not sufficiently expand natural gas facilities to households and establish a stable market structure. Naturally, BOTAŞ's monopolistic structure in the market obstructed introduction of competition to the market and encouraged the need for a competitive market reform. Source diversity in the form of increased number of suppliers is a crucial part of competition in the natural gas market (Gallick 1993). Competition in natural gas requires downstream customers to have legal rights and ability to choose their supplier of gas, without any regional restrictions (Doane and Spulber 1994).

Private- and public-owned distribution companies could distribute gas to cities, but could not import it from another supplier bypassing BOTAŞ. The introduction of wholesale competition was one of the main drivers of reform.

Another driver was seasonal variation between supply and demand and dependency on imports in natural gas consumption. Natural gas began to be imported to Turkey in 1987 and its consumption increased rapidly. Air pollution in the capital, Ankara, as well as İstanbul was an important reason for importing natural gas.

Turkey's indigenous natural gas production is insufficient to meet demand. Turkey did not and still does not have a world class proven resource base. The legal framework and fiscal regime have been much more demanding than can be justified by the prospective resources; hence, international companies have been reluctant to invest in exploration activities in Turkey. Natural gas exploration is even more challenging than oil because local market has to be ready to absorb the gas; the local

[1] Currently, exploration, drilling, production, and well completion activities in the oil and gas industry of Turkey are carried out by The Turkish Petroleum Corporation (TPAO).

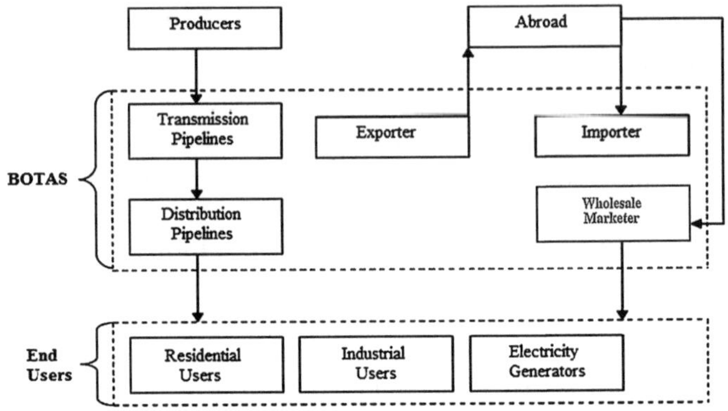

Fig. 3.1 The vertically integrated industry structure before the New Law, 2001. *Source* Çetin and Oğuz 2007a

market capacity was even a bigger constraint in the 1980s when international trade of natural gas was much more limited than today. TPAO, state-owned company responsible for oil and gas exploration in the country, has been either cash-constrained or too politicized to pursue large-scale exploration and production (E&P) projects.

In order to meet growing demand, BOTAŞ signed long-term purchase contracts with Russia, Iran, Turkmenistan, Azerbaijan, Nigeria, and Algeria. But, as a state monopoly, BOTAŞ has not been able to meet demand in an efficient manner with sufficient source diversity.

Under such high import dependency, meeting seasonally volatile gas demand became a concern, especially in the absence of sufficient underground storage capacity. Supplier or transit countries could curtail volumes for economic or political reasons. For example, Ukraine and Iran cut gas exports to Turkey in 2006. In January 2007 and in January 2008, Iran reduced the supply of natural gas two more times. Iran always defended the cuts in supply on the basis of technical problems and a heavy winter. Nonetheless, political reasons also had some role in Iran's behavior although the contract signed with Iran does not require a steady flow of gas throughout the year (Çetin 2010). Ukraine's political troubles with Russia intensified the gas shortage in 2006. During the crisis with Russia, Ukraine consumed domestically some of the gas meant for Turkey. This unexpected supply shortage gave signals about the vulnerability of the market structure and raised questions about the sustainability of the current system.

Such risks of supply interruption can be mitigated via constructing storage facilities and diversifying sources. Storage would be a good tool for smoothing out variations in price. Under the monopolistic structure of BOTAŞ, storage capacity was slow to develop.

Another issue is the interdependence of natural gas and electricity markets. About 62% of gas was sold to power generators in the early 2000s. This amount is still 51%. Such a dependency brings about risk of power shortages in case of gas supply disruptions. In order to overcome this issue, generators in Turkey needed to have multiple and secure sources of gas. In that sense, the introduction of IPPs since the 1980s and the electricity reform in 2001 necessitated a reform in the natural gas market.

Turkey is in a strategically advantageous position in terms of its natural gas market. Being in the middle of Europe and energy-rich countries of Central Asia and the Middle East, it can be an energy corridor between these two regions (Çetin and Oğuz 2007a). The Nabucco and the South Caucasus projects are such projects. It can import gas from a number of countries and diversify its sources; because of its long coastline, it can also import LNG from multiple sources—a strategy many countries in Europe (Spain, France, Italy, and UK) are also pursuing. For that reason, Turkey strives to be the Eurasian Energy Corridor between eastern supply and western demand. A competitive gas market in Turkey could help with the realization of some of these projects, especially if a natural gas hub can be formed. Turkey is expected to attract foreign investments in natural gas in the coming decades (Kılıç 2006; Tunç 2006). It is a natural connection point because of its strategic position between European markets and Central Asian and Middle Eastern producing countries.

Lastly, Turkey is a candidate country for full membership in the European Union (EU). Turkey's regulatory institutional structure has to comply with the EU requirements for accession. Accordingly, the regulatory environment of Turkey's natural gas market needs to comply with directive 2003/55/EC of the European Parliament and of the Council of June 2003. This directive aims to establish common rules for the internal market in natural gas and to increase competition for the member and the probable-member (candidate like Turkey) countries. Compliance with EU Gas Directives was another reason for Turkey to reform its natural gas market. However, similar to the situation in Turkey, many EU countries are not implementing the requirements of EU Gas Directive as quickly as required. Especially countries with dominant state companies such as Gaz de France are slower than others.

3 The Role of Natural Gas in Turkey

Turkey's population has grown rapidly over the last two decades. It has reached 73 million in 2010. It is estimated that the population will reach nearly 90 million by 2020. The Turkish economy has been growing rapidly as well, particularly since the beginning of the 2000s. As shown in the Fig. 3.2, total primary energy supply has also been growing rapidly, with growing economy and population. Growth in total primary energy reached 27% during this decade, with an increase from 76.4 million tons of oil equivalent (mtoe) in 2000 to 97.66 mtoe in 2009 (IEA 2011a).

Especially, the shares of gas and coal are predicted to grow rapidly. The share of natural gas in this energy mix has increased from 5% in 1990 to more than 30% in 2010, as seen in Fig. 3.2. It is estimated that the share of natural gas in the total

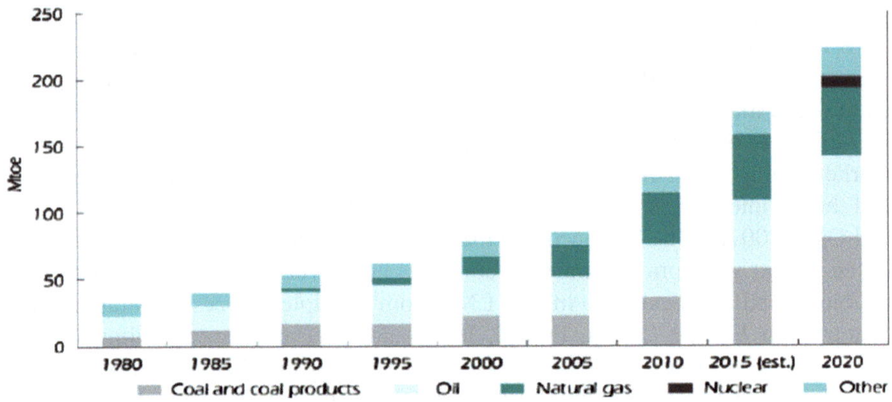

Fig. 3.2 Total primary energy supply and fuel shares. *Source* IEA 2011a

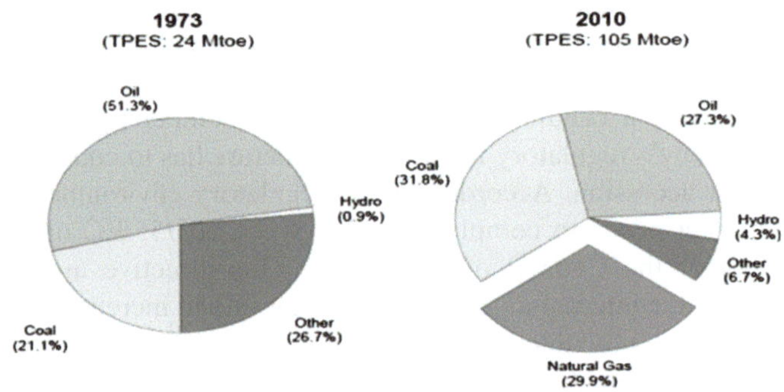

Fig. 3.3 The share of energy sources in Turkey. *Source* IEA 2011b

primary energy will increase more. The use of natural gas in Turkey started at 0.5 bcm in 1987 and reached 3.5 bcm in 1990 and 31.2 bcm in 2006. As of 2011, Turkey is consuming 38.2 bcm of natural gas. In Turkey, as depicted in Fig. 3.3, while there was no natural gas use in 1973, it has the second biggest share of total primary energy consumption with 29.9% of the total after coal with a 31.8% share in 2010 (IEA 2011b).

However, Turkey's natural gas consumption depends heavily on imports. In 2010, Turkey imported 29.9 bcm of natural gas from Russia, Iran, and Azerbaijan by pipeline and 8.2 bcm from Algeria and Nigeria via LNG shipment (IEA 2011b). A comparison of natural gas imports of Turkey and some countries in Europe is provided in Table 3.1. As of the first quarter of 2011, Turkey's total natural gas import is 12.3 bcm. Turkey is among the leading natural gas and LNG importers in the OECD Europe.

Natural gas is especially important in electricity generation; 51% of natural gas was used for electricity generation in 2010 (Fig. 3.4); 32% of natural gas was consumed by household users, and the remaining amount was used by industry users.

Table 3.1 Natural gas imports of some selected countries in the OECD Europe (mcm)

	2008	2009	2010	2011[a]
Germany	92,765	94,572	99,637	30,883
Italy	76,866	69,246	75,348	21,643
France	45,014	45,847	46,199	14,265
Turkey	37,155	35,776	38,037	12,343
Spain	40,760	36,570	36,716	9,779
Netherlands	24,688	24,604	25,775	4,973
Greece	4,210	3,556	3,815	1,295

Source IEA 2011c
[a] First quarter

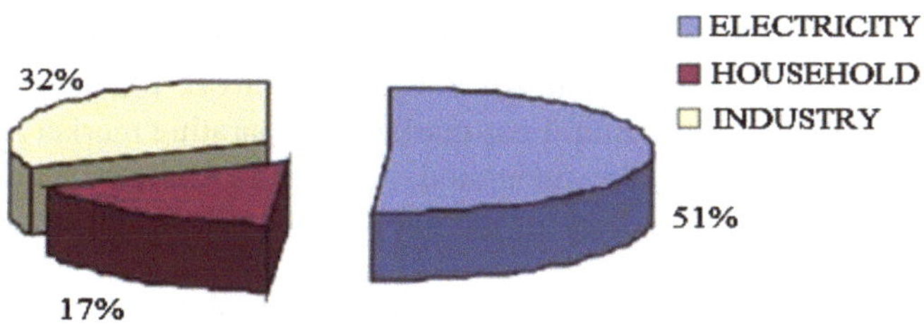

Fig. 3.4 Consumption of natural gas by sectors (2010). *Source* EPDK (2010)

4 Natural Gas Market Law[2]

BOTAŞ's dominant role in the market, the lack of competition, issues of balancing supply and demand in a timely and efficient manner, dependency of electricity generation on natural gas and of natural gas on imports, the absence of storage facilities within the country, Turkey's inability to benefit from its advantageous location in the energy-rich region, and compliance necessity of the internal market to the EU's energy *acquis* brought about the restructuring of the market in 2001.

The regulatory reform aimed:

- To introduce and to institutionalize competition in the market,
- To expand gas transmission pipelines within the country,
- To construct new gas distribution networks for all the cities in the country,
- To increase the use of natural gas,
- To diversify the natural gas sources for security of supply reasons, and
- To develop transit infrastructure between the suppliers in the Caspian Sea and the Middle East and the consumers in Europe.

[2] This section is largely based on Çetin (2010).

With the Natural Gas Market Law[3] (NGML) enacted in May 2001, the objective of harmonizing the Turkish natural gas regulatory environment with the Directive 2003/55/EC has almost been de jure fully achieved. The main components of the Directive are complied within the new Natural Gas Market Law, including the assignment of market oversight to an independent regulatory body, BOTAŞ's unbundling, third party access to pipeline networks, market opening, privatization, and wholesale and limited retail competition (Akçollu 2006). However, the market remains dominated by BOTAŞ after 10 years since the passage of the law.

4.1 The Regulatory Features of the 2001 Law

The NGML is the main regulatory statute of the natural gas market. The main purpose of the new law is to establish a legal framework for developing a fair, transparent, and competitive natural gas market by separating market activities and unbundling BOTAŞ's vertically integrated structure, to reduce state role in the market, and to prepare the ground for the integration to the EU natural gas market by harmonizing regulations.

The NGML designates EPDK as the only regulatory authority and describes the legal environment for regulations in the market. Accordingly, all legal entities are required to obtain licenses from EPDK for transmission, export, import, wholesale, distribution, and storage activities. Licenses are granted for a minimum of 10 and a maximum of 30 years.

EPDK applies an incentive-based rate of return[4] formulation in licenses and sets prices for storage, transmission, distribution, wholesale, and retail facilities. These licenses also include inflation adjustments for prices. EPDK evaluates tariffs, efficiency, and safety of facilities regularly. Thus, the NGML provides the legal ground for supply security and 'fair' rates of return for companies.

The NGML unbundles the market and sets up the legal ground for privatization. Privatization began with city distribution in Adapazarı, Bursa, and Eskişehir regions. Others were privatized in the following years, with the exception of İGDAŞ. The law requires the vertical disintegration of the natural gas activities of BOTAŞ after 2009 by separating it into three state enterprises responsible for trading, storage, and transmission, respectively.

---

[3] Law no.4646, dated 02.05.2001.

[4] Incentive-based rate of return differs from the traditional rate of return model. The rate of return model guarantees some level of return on investment. Firms do not have incentives to reduce costs in this model. Incentive-based rate of return model encourages the firm to reduce its costs. Firms keep any reductions in costs for the contract duration. The Electricity Market Law gives authority to EPDK on cost-price relationships (Çetin and Oğuz 2007b). Fair rate of return refers to an 'acceptable' return over investment. Incentive-based rate of return regulation encourage firms to reconsider their cost during the contract period (Intven and Tetrault 2000).

The law limits the amount an importer company can buy from abroad to 20% of national consumption during any one year. According to the NGML, each year, BOTAŞ needed to sell 10% of its share of gas import contracts to private companies to introduce competition. The sale was aimed to be carried out with a series of annual competitive tenders to sell at least 10% of existing import contracts to new importers so that by 2009, the share of BOTAŞ in total import volumes would be less than 20%. Similarly, potential importers, wholesalers, and distributors cannot have market shares more than 20% to ensure that competition is institutionalized. Distribution companies cannot buy more than half of their gas from a single wholesaler or importer. The law gives discretion to EPDK to change these ratios (Çetin and Oğuz 2007a).

Importers and wholesalers need to inform EPDK about the source and security of their gas imports. Importer entities must contribute to the development and security of the transmission system, possibly via building new lines, upgrading aging infrastructure, adding new technology and similar actions. In addition, the NGML necessitates that importers store 10% of their annual import volumes within five years. Transmission and storage companies and operators of LNG terminals must offer services to their customers under nondiscriminatory conditions, given the availability of capacity and absence of financial risks related to contracts. The NGML gives the right to build storage facilities to any entity that can obtain a license from EPDK for storage activities.

Furthermore, by NGML, licensed companies can construct new pipelines; eligible consumers, which will be determined by EPDK, would choose their own suppliers under the free market conditions; distribution franchises could be built by companies that win a license under a tender; EPDK will determine five different categories for gas prices including connection, transmission, storage, wholesale sales, and retail sales (Mazzanti and Biancardi 2005).

4.2 The Regulatory Authorities of EPDK in the Natural Gas Market

EPDK was initially established as an independent, administratively and financially autonomous electricity regulatory authority, so-called the Electricity Market Regulatory Authority, in 2001 in accordance with Electricity Market Legislation, No.4628, on 03.03.2001. Name of this regulatory board was changed as the Energy Market Regulatory Authority with NGML. The regulatory responsibilities of EPDK were expanded to include the Petroleum Law, No. 5015, enacted in 2003.

Nowadays, the main aim of EPDK is to ensure a financially viable, stable, accountable, and transparent regulatory process on energy markets and to take necessary measures to provide sufficient electricity, natural gas, petroleum, and LPG services of good quality to consumers. The main responsibility of EPDK concerning the Turkish natural gas market is to set up and implement regulations

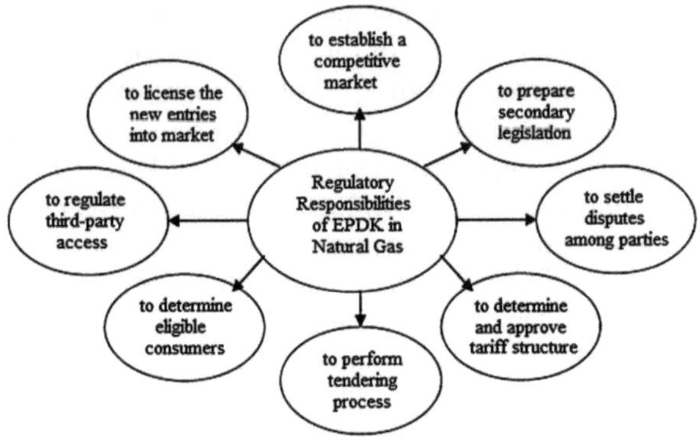

Fig. 3.5 Regulatory responsibilities of EPDK in the natural gas market

to ensure the establishment of a competitive natural gas market, where all market segments will be open to new entrants. BOTAŞ's activities are also regulated by EPDK until BOTAŞ's market share in imports is decreased to 20%.

Although EPDK is administratively independent and financially autonomous, it is administratively related to MENR. It is independent in its authority over the market.[5] Its budget is outside the consolidated state budget and not under the supervision of the Higher Court of Accounts, Sayıştay. The major source of its income is the fees it collects from the industry. When EPDK's income exceeds its expenditures, the remaining part is transferred to the consolidated state budget.

As shown in Fig. 3.5, the regulatory responsibilities of EPDK related to natural gas market are:

- To approve all regulations related to natural gas market activities, on which the Authority has been authorized as per the provisions of the Natural Gas Market Law, and to ensure the execution thereof,
- To ensure the performance of the duties of the Authority for execution of the rights and obligations arising from the international agreements regarding the natural gas market activities,
- To determine and publish secondary legislation and the opinion and suggestions of the Authority with regard to the plans, policies, and applications regarding natural gas market activities,
- To decide on filing applications with any legal or administrative authority for purposes including litigation and enforcement of any penalty or sanction as part of the Board's authority to supervise, carry out preliminary investigations and inquiries concerning the natural gas market operations,
- To enforce regulated third party access, to determine eligible customers over time,

[5] However, a recent decree in August 2011 seems to be limiting the independence of all the regulatory agencies in Turkey. See for more detailed information Decree No. KHK/649 http://mevzuat.dpt.gov.tr/khk/649.pdf.

- To take, implement, and oversee all kinds of decisions regarding issuance of licenses and certificates as provided in the Natural Gas Market Law as well as the compliance with and termination of such licenses and certificates,
- To settle the disputes among legal entities or between legal entities and consumers arising from the implementation of Natural Gas Market Law,
- To organize tendering processes for natural gas distribution licenses of the cities,
- To approve the tariffs regarding the activities indicated in the Natural Gas Market Law or to decide on tariff revisions,
- To regulate procedures and principles regarding the formation of tariff and price structures in transmission and distribution facilities, where competition is nonexistent or insufficient (EPDK 2004; Atiyas and Dutz 2005).

In essence, EPDK regulates and approves transmission, storage, and wholesale tariffs, and all retail tariffs, until competition is well established. The secondary legislation has been issued including regulations for licenses, tariffs, internal installations, market certificates, transmission network operation, distribution, and consumer services and facilities. EPDK is responsible for organizing tenders for natural gas distribution licenses in the cities.

EPDK is responsible for solving disputes of access to the transmission and distribution systems and approve investment plans by transmission and distribution companies. While 64 complaints were received regarding the natural gas market in 2004, the number of applications and complaints in 2010 were 158,571 (EPDK 2004, 2010). It also has responsibility for certain[6] safety regulations, including construction and services of gas facilities. EPDK is also responsible to monitor prices that reflect costs of investment. Companies calculate rates based on future cost projections.

5 Gas Release Program: Contracts and Stranded Costs

In order to encourage competition by abolishing BOTAŞ's dominant role on import and wholesale of natural gas and to diversify natural gas suppliers, the law of 2001 required BOTAŞ to release at least 10% of its import contracts each year. The aim was to reduce BOTAŞ's market share below 20% by 2009. However, although the law prohibited BOTAŞ to sign new contracts, this ban was removed for LNG contracts in 2008. In the scope of the Turkish gas release program, the 2001 law introduced BOTAŞ two ways for reducing its market share on imports to the 20% level: contract release and volume release to private companies. In the contract release, BOTAŞ will transfer all of its rights and obligations stemming

[6] Other government bodies, including the Ministry of Industry and Commerce, have also some regulatory power of social regulations in the industry.

Table 3.2 Contract release amounts

Company	Amount (mcm/year)	Operation Date
Shell Gas	250	December 2007
Bosphorus Gas	750	January 2009
Enerco Energy	2500	April 2009
Avrasya Gas	500	April 2009

Source EPDK 2010

from the contracts to the private companies while, in the volume release, BOTAŞ has to sell the gas to the wholesalers at the Turkish border, still undertaking the contractual obligations. In the case of volume transfer, the price applied by the importer which needs to undertake all cross-border obligations of BOTAŞ cannot be lower than the price in the current contracts. However, primary way was contract transfer by the law.

BOTAŞ failed to fulfill its obligations since no contract or volume release could be achieved up to 2006. In March 2004, EPDK threatened BOTAŞ with fines over the company's failure to meet the target of reducing its market share by 10% per year.

By the end of 2004, a Gas Release Program was initiated which would allow BOTAŞ to partially transfer 6 out of 8 existing contracts to new entrants, specifically contracts with Russia, Algeria, Nigeria, and Iran. Azerbaijan and Turkmenistan contracts were excluded from the program. The amount of gas to be divested each year (16 bcm) corresponded to 60% of the demand in 2005; it is planned that half of the gas imported from Russia should be supplied by companies other than BOTAŞ (Akcollu 2006). BOTAŞ began the first tender process for contract transfer in 2005. In 2006, four companies had the right to transfer a total of 4 bcm per year from the contract signed between BOTAŞ and Gazprom Export in 1998 for 15 years, or 12% of total imports volume (Table 3.2). EPDK granted these companies import licenses; Enerco Energy 2.5 bcm, Bosporus Gas 0.75 bcm, Avrasya Gas 0.5 bcm, and Shell Energy 0.25 bcm. Currently, while Shell and Bosporus Gas have imported 0.25 bcm since 2007 and 0.75 bcm since January 2009, respectively, the other two companies have imported three bcm gas since April 2009. As a result, because the contract release program was postponed several times by 2006, the implementation of contract transfer has been slow and only four bcm of the contract signed between BOTAŞ and Russia (through Bulgaria) was released to private companies by contract transfer in 2005 (BOTAŞ 2009; IEA 2009b).

There are several reasons that lead to entry barriers to the market by deterring potential competitors from the bidding processes. First, import contracts include confidential clauses that cannot be examined by the companies before the tender. Second, there is the requirement for suppliers' consent prior to the tender. Because the contracts, which were signed between BOTAŞ and suppliers, were backed by the Turkish Treasury, suppliers have not been willing to renegotiate contracts with the new companies and they did not give consent to most of the bids. Third, the existence of BOTAŞ's captive customers constitutes a crucial entry barrier in the market for the potential competitors. BOTAŞ still holds contracts with its customers for the delivery of around 27 bcm each year. This situation leads to ambiguity as to how BOTAŞ would release its contracted customers. Fourth, according to the new law, mandatory storage of 10% of the annual import volume means potential extra costs for the new entrants. However, 40 companies bidded in the tender process, but only the bids of the aforementioned four companies were valid. Additionally, even if Enerco Energy, Bosporus Gas, Avrasya Gas, and Shell Energy secure their shares in the contract release process, they have to renegotiate the contract terms with Gazprom as the seller party of contract, to obtain permission to operate from Turkey's competition authority, and to secure import contracts licenses from EPDK (Akçollu 2006; Erdoğdu 2011). The first Western pipeline contract expired in late 2011. BOTAŞ has not signed a new long-term contract. This is an opportunity for private importers to sign deals, but delays in this process raises concerns about these inexperienced players' ability to finalize such deals in a commercially sustainable manner.

6 Unbundling

BOTAŞ's monopoly rights on distribution, storage, the sale of natural gas, and imports were annulled by the 2001 law, as the new industry structure depicted in Fig. 3.6 indicates.

However, the figure also reflects differences between de facto and de jure situations in the market and hence the institutional problems of the industry. Although the 2001 law legally reshapes the industry structure, the transition to this designed market structure will be possible after BOTAŞ's market share falls under 20%. BOTAŞ still has to transfer the discretions on the import facilities and contracts to private sector participants. The nature of BOTAŞ as an incumbent state company with large market power makes transition harder. BOTAŞ has no incentive to follow the legal procedures and continues to be part of the political game (Çetin and Oğuz 2007a).

6.1 Production and Supply

Although the NGML unbundles market activities, the production of natural gas in Turkey is governed under the Petroleum Law, No. 6326 of 1954, according to which, the General Directorate of Petroleum Affairs must grant exploration and development licenses. Although Petroleum Law leaves exploration and production outside the jurisdiction of EPDK, according to the NGML, producers can sell produced gas to wholesalers, distributors, or free consumers only by getting a wholesaler license from EPDK. Producers can sell 20% of their annual production

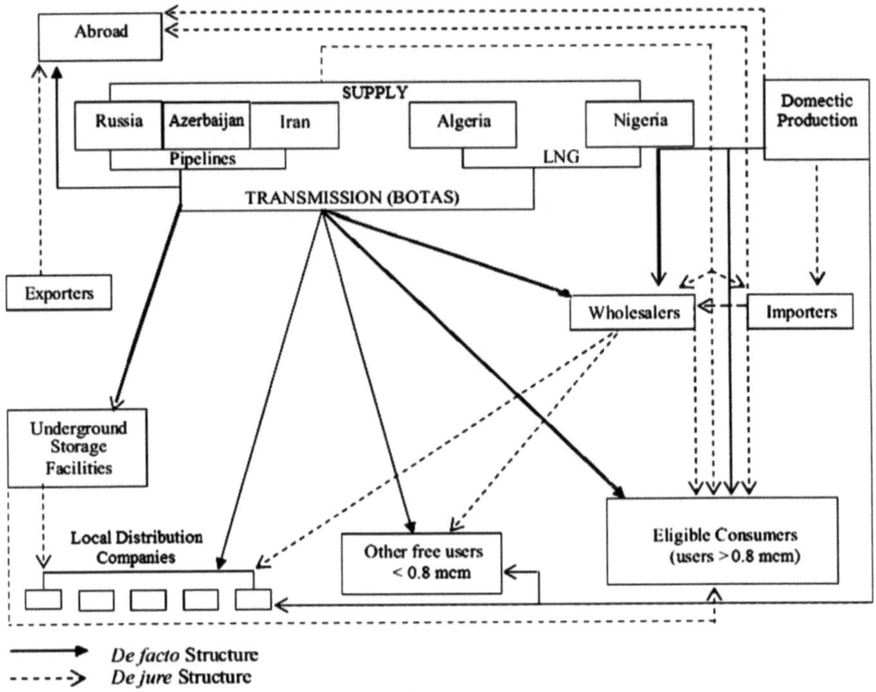

Fig. 3.6 The new structure of the natural gas industry. *Source* according to the current market structure, Çetin and Oğuz 2007a

to free consumers directly. They have to sell the rest through distributors or wholesalers. They can also export the gas by obtaining an exporter license from EPDK.

The Turkish Petroleum Corporation (TPAO), local and foreign private companies participate in natural gas exploration and production in Turkey. Currently, seven companies (TPAO, Amity Oil International Pty. Ltd., Thrace Basin Natural Gas Corporation, Foinavon Energy Inc, Tiway Turkey Limited, Petrol Ofisi, and Transatlantic Exploration Mediterranean Int. Pty Ltd.) that obtained a wholesale license supplies natural gas produced in Northeastern Anatolia, Marmara, and Western Black Sea regions to eligible (free) users, distribution companies, and wholesalers in their own regions. The natural gas production by these companies in recent years is reported in Table 3.3. They produced close to 0.7 bcm in 2010.

The main producer is TPAO, with a 37% share (Fig. 3.7). In 2010, TPAO's natural gas production was 260.7 mcm. Of the total natural gas production 94% was from the Thrace Region, 5% was from the Batman Region, and 1% was from the Adıyaman Region. TPAO owned 16 of the 22 operational fields in Turkey. Most of them are onshore. The North Marmara field in the Marmara Sea that first produced natural gas in 1997 was Turkey's first off shore field. TPAO also conducts gas exploration and production in Kazakhstan, Azerbaijan, Iraq, and Libya.

Table 3.3 Indigenous production of Turkey by company (mcm)

Companies	2008	2009	2010
Amity Oil. Int. Pty. Ltd.	66.67	66.95	67.85
TPAO	488.23	275	260.7
Thrace Basin	338.74	274.2	246.50
Foinavon Energy Inc.	20.56	17.18	15.69
Tiway Turkey Ltd.	61.22	41.51	13.91
Petrol Ofisi	–	9.78	36.38
Transatlantic Exp. Int.	–	–	45.95
Total production	976.44	684.62	687.28

Source The figures are retrieved from EPDK 2010 and www.tpao.gov.tr

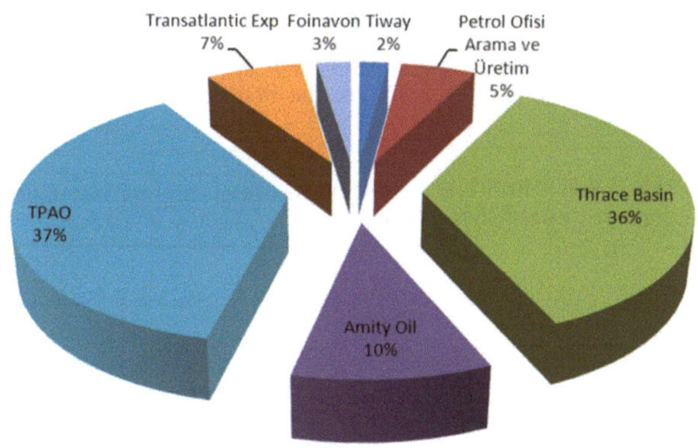

Fig. 3.7 The Production shares of companies that obtained a wholesale license (2010). *Source* EPDK 2010, p 23

TPAO obtained a license for gas exploration in the Mediterranean Sea from North Cyprus Turkish Republic in August 2011.

Turkey's natural gas production has been rather low because of the low level of exploration for gas. Turkey did not and still does not have a significant proven resource base. The legal framework and fiscal regime have been much more demanding than can be justified by the prospective resources; hence, international companies have been reluctant to invest in exploration activities in Turkey. Natural gas exploration is even more challenging than oil because local market has to be ready to absorb the gas; this was even more so in the 1980s when international trade of natural gas was much more limited than it is today. Finally, TPAO, state-owned company responsible for oil and gas exploration in the country has been either cash-constrained or too politicized to pursue large-scale E&P projects (Fig. 3.8). At the end of 2010, while the total natural gas consumption of Turkey was 38,119 mcm, the producer companies in Turkey met less than 2% of this amount, with a production of 690 mcm. Although natural gas production started to increase after 2002, it peaked in 2008, at 976 mcm and started to decline.

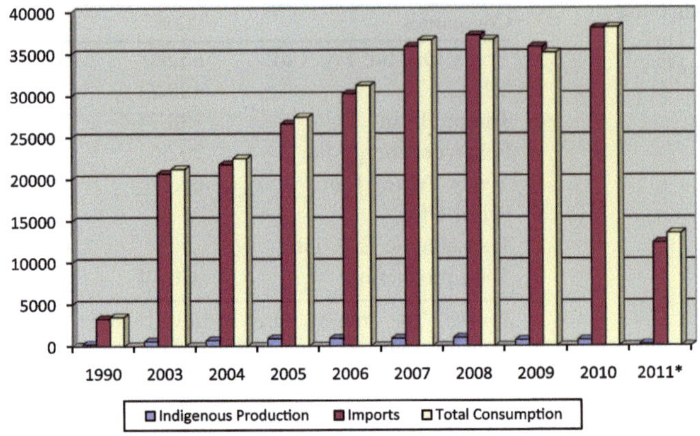

Fig. 3.8 Production and consumption of natural gas in Turkey (mcm). *Source* BOTAŞ 2009; IEA 2007b, 2009a, 2011c. * For the first quarter of 2011

Table 3.4 Distribution companies established before the 2001 law

Distribution region	Company	Date of operation	Ownership
Ankara	EGO	1988	Private
Bursa	BURSAGAZ	1992	Private
İstanbul	İGDAŞ	1992	Municipality
Eskişehir	ESGAZ	1996	Private
İzmit	IZGAZ	1996	Private
Adapazarı	AGDAŞ	2002	Private
İstanbul (Bahçeşehir region)	BAGDAŞ	2003	Private

Source BOTAŞ and EPDK

6.2 Distribution: Privatization and Tenders

In the pre-reform market structure of the Turkish natural gas industry, there were only six major distribution companies owned by municipalities in six big cities along with AGDAŞ established in 2002 (Table 3.4). Due to BOTAŞ's monopoly status on wholesale and imports these municipal utilities had no other choice but purchase natural gas from BOTAŞ (Çetin and Oğuz 2007a).

In order to restructure the distribution segment of the natural gas market, EPDK pursued privatization of the regional distribution facilities owned by municipalities and BOTAŞ, and tenders for private companies to develop new distribution regions established (EPDK 2010). The older grids in Turkey's big cities that were owned and controlled by the municipalities are well developed. The NGML decreed that the state-owned distribution regions have to be privatized within three years after the enactment of the law or within three years following the clearance of the external debt backed by the Treasury (IEA 2007a, p 225). For this purpose,

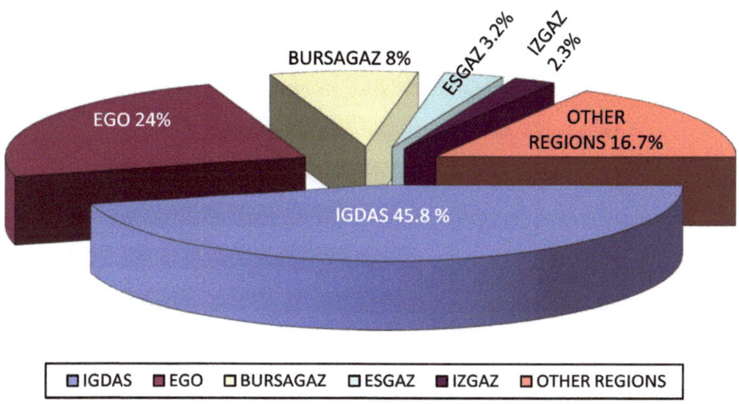

Fig. 3.9 The market shares of distribution regions (2011). *Source* Erdoğdu 2011

the government initiated a privatization process for the grids in the big cities. AGDAŞ, BURSAGAZ, ESGAZ, IZGAZ, EGO (formerly BAŞKENTGAZ), and BAGDAŞ were privatized. İGDAŞ which is under ownership of the İstanbul metropolitan municipality has not yet been privatized. This market structure means that 45.8% of the natural gas consumers in Turkey still depend on the gas supplied by the only state-owned company in the Turkish natural gas distribution market, as depicted in Fig. 3.9.

EPDK conducts the tender processes for new entrants into distribution segment. Tenders for distribution of natural gas to cities are carried out through competitive bidding for a 30-year franchise right via Dutch auctions. The companies have to qualify in terms of financial viability—equity, balance sheets and income statements and documents and letters of intent showing how the investment shall be financed; and experience of the bidder or the firms which will provide design, construction, and operation services to the bidder, in the natural gas and other sectors.

The bids are evaluated over "a unit service and depreciation charge (USDC)" for supply of a cubic meter of natural gas. The companies with lowest three bids participate in a second round of competitive bidding. If there is a tie with a bid of 0 cent/m^3 for USDC, then the Dutch auction continues over "a connection fee" that the firms will charge natural gas users for next five years. The upper limit of this fee is determined in the terms and conditions of the contract by EPDK. This time, the firm offering the lowest connection fee wins the tender. The winning USDC is fixed for eight years. This price determines the firm's profit and how well the firm recovers its investment costs during the first eight years of the project. After the first period, EPDK determines and puts in force a new USDC based on a price cap and a tariff structure offered by the firm.

This fairly unique tender process have proved successful in awarding licenses for a majority of distribution regions (Fig. 3.11), but there are some considerations. First, while the share of USDC in the price regulated by EPDK changes between

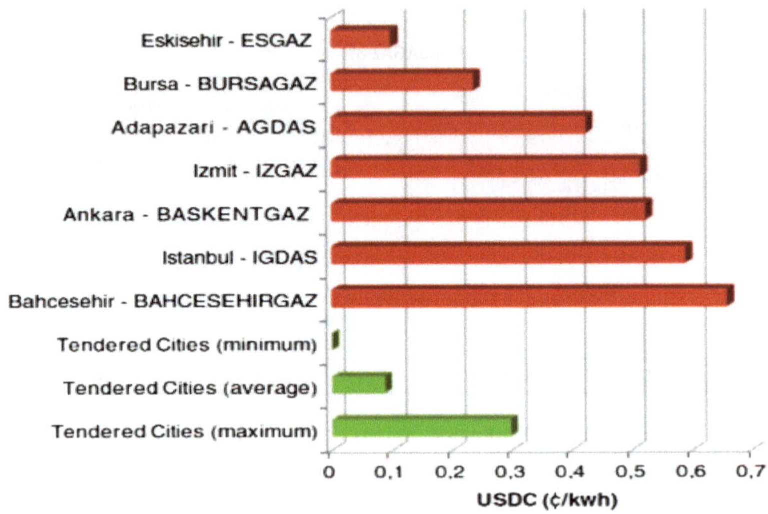

Fig. 3.10 USDC shares in tendered and non-tendered regions. *Source* Erdoğdu 2011

14.1 and 2.4% in privatized and state-owned distribution regions, this share is only between 7 and 0% in the tendered regions (Fig. 3.10). Users in the tendered regions pay approximately 10% less than those in the privatized and state-owned distribution areas, on average. Note that some companies won bids with 0 cent bids. In some occasions, even connection fees were bid as low as $5 per customer. With such low bids that are fixed for 8 years and significant investment requirements in the beginning of the franchise period, it is very difficult for most of these companies to recover their investments and generate a decent rate of return in a short period of time. There are additional fees these LDCs collect, including about $700 per certificate to equipment installers, which have to pay about $70 renewal fee per year and $10 installation inspection and approval. These fees are occasional and limited in number. It appears that these companies are interested in long-term steady returns that such regulated utilities offer all around the world. When we look closer at the current structure of end-user prices, it appears that the main component of natural gas prices is the cost of gas purchase from BOTAŞ (between 68 and 81% of the total price) and taxes (18%) (Erdoğdu 2011).

The firm that obtains a license from EPDK is obligated to construct natural gas network and supply natural gas to its own users in its predetermined distribution area. Accordingly, the firm needs to begin investment within six months, the supply of gas to consumers within 18 months, and to provide access to all users, who want to be connected, within five years. Customers consuming more than 15 mcm per year are free to choose supplier during the first five years. The threshold amount is supposed to decline per EU regulations in later years.

In this scope, 56 tenders have been carried out by EPDK as of September 2011 (Fig. 3.11). Sixty-seven distribution regions have been connected to natural gas

Fig. 3.11 Cities connected to natural gas supply lines. *Source* EPDK 2010

supply lines for both industrial and residential users, as of September 2011, compared to only six cities that were connected to a distribution network before 2001. However, although seven regions were awarded licenses natural gas has not yet been supplied to these cities. On the other hand, there are 14 cities that have not yet obtained a distribution license. All remaining cities are planned for natural gas supply in the near future (EPDK 2010: 39).

6.3 *Transmission Developments: The Role of BOTAŞ as a Natural Monopoly*

Third-party access to transmission grid is a crucial element of institutionalizing competition in the natural gas market. According to the NGML, the transmission company is obliged to connect demanding legal users to the 'most appropriate' grid in one year. Accordingly, EPDK and BOTAŞ will decide together how network access and usage tariffs are regulated. EPDK has the dispute resolution authority with respect to transmission issues. According to the 2001 law, existing, planned, and under construction parts of the national transmission grid remain under BOTAŞ ownership. As a transmission company, BOTAŞ provides transportation services to importers, wholesalers, producers, and exporters. It also enters into delivery contracts with producers, free consumers, storage companies, and other transmission companies. BOTAŞ signed eight long-term (from 15 to 30 years) purchase contracts with six gas exporting countries (Russia, Iran, Turkmenistan, Azerbaijan, Algeria, and Nigeria) between 1986 and 2001 (Table 3.5).

Table 3.5 Turkey's natural gas sale and purchase projects signed by BOTAŞ (2006)

Agreements	Volume (during the plateau period) (bcm per year)	Date of signature	Start	Duration (Years)	Status
Russian Fed. (Westward)	6	14 February 1986	1987	25	In operation
Algeria (LNG)	4	14 April 1988	1994	20	In operation
Nigeria (LNG)	1.2	9 November 1995	1999	22	In operation
Iran	10	8 August 1996	2001	25	In operation
Russian Fed. (Black Sea)	16	15 December 1997	2002	25	In operation
Russian Fed. (Westward)	8	18 February 1998	1998	23	In operation
Turkmenistan	16	21 May 1999	–	30	–
Azerbaijan	6.6	12 March 2001	2007	15	In operation

Source The data is retrieved on 9 Sept 2011 from http://www.BOTAŞ.gov.tr/index.asp

In 1984 the government of Turkey signed an intergovernmental agreement with the former Soviet Union. According to this agreement, in 1986, BOTAŞ for the first time signed a natural gas sale and purchase agreement for a 25-year period. Construction of the 842-kilometer Russian Federation–Turkey Natural Gas Main Transmission Line (Western line) began on October 26, 1986, and reached Hamitabat on June 23, 1987. Turkey started consuming natural gas in 1987. Natural gas imported via this pipeline has been used for electricity generation at the Trakya Combined Cycle Power Plant in Hamitabat. The pipeline reached Ankara in August 1988. Residential and commercial users in Ankara started to use gas in October 1988. Natural gas imported by this agreement reached to six bcm per year in 1993 (Mazzanti and Biancardi 2005, p 210). In 1996, this pipeline was extended to the western Black Sea region via the Izmit-Karadeniz Ereğli line. Currently, this line enters Turkey at Malkoclar at the Bulgarian Border and then follows Hamitabat, İstanbul, İzmit, Bursa, Eskişehir route to reach Ankara (BOTAŞ 2009). This line was extended to Çan for the purpose of supplying natural gas for Çanakkale Ceramic Factory in Çan via the Bursa-Çan Natural Gas Transmission Line that was completed in 1996. In 2000, this line was expanded from Çan to Çanakkale as the Çan-Çanakkale Natural Gas Transmission Line.

The first import contract from the Western pipeline expired at the end of 2011. This contract has not been renewed for several reasons. First, Turkey, because it has bought the most expensive gas via this contract and Russia reduced the price of natural gas it sold to Italy (Edison company) in July 2011, asked for a decrease in the price of natural gas as a precondition to renew the contract but Russia did not accept.[7] Second, according to the natural gas market law of 2001, BOTAŞ cannot sign a new natural gas purchase contract as an importer with any supplier until its market share declines to 20%. Third, according to a decision of EPDK that has

[7] Today's Zaman, "Turkey Cancels Natural Gas Contract with Russia http://www.todayszaman.com/news-258670-turkey-cancels-natural-gas-contract-with-russia.html, 10.02.2011.

been published in the Official Gazette on 28 November, 2011, private companies rather than BOTAŞ would renew this contract with Russia. EPDK assessed the offers for imports by the private companies in November 2011.

In 1998, BOTAŞ signed another agreement with Russia to import 8 bcm per year of natural gas from the Western line via TURUSGAZ-BOTAŞ, Gazprom (Russia), and GAMA (Turkey, civil contractor) joint venture. Another agreement was signed with Russia on December 15, 1997 to import 16 bcm of gas per year through the *Blue Stream* pipeline beneath the Black Sea (Fig. 3.12). In order to construct Blue Stream pipeline, a joint venture was established by Gazprom and ENI (Italy). On December 2002, natural gas started flowing from Russia to Turkey via the Blue Stream pipeline.

In August 1996, Turkey signed a 25-year natural gas sale and purchase agreement with Iran to import three bcm per year initially, increasing to 10 bcm per year in 2007. The Eastern Anatolia Natural Gas Main Transmission Line was completed at the end of 2001 between Doğubeyazıt and Ankara/Seydişehir. Natural gas from Iran through this pipeline began flowing in December 2001. In April 2002, the Karacabey-İzmir Natural Gas Transmission Line, an extension of the Eastern Anatolia Line, became operational.

In 1999, BOTAŞ signed a purchase contract of 16 bcm of natural gas per year for 30 years with Turkmenistan. The envisioned pipeline would have crossed the Caspian Sea and followed a path parallel to Baku–Tblisi–Ceyhan crude oil pipeline and connect to the Eastern Anatolia Line near Erzurum (Mazzanti and Biancardi 2005, p. 210). This pipeline was never realized due to disagreements between Azerbaijan and Turkmenistan related to delineation of offshore boundaries, as well as the high cost of the pipeline. Perhaps more importantly, Turkey did not need the gas from Turkmenistan after all the volumes included in the above-mentioned contracts. Turkmenistan gas may yet flow through Turkey if the Nabucco pipeline ever becomes a reality and Turkmenistan still has any gas left after contracts it signed with Gazprom, China, and Iran.

Table 3.6 and Fig. 3.12 show the existing pipelines as well as those under construction or planned. As of 2010, the total length of domestic transmission network in Turkey reached 11,332 km.

6.4 Import and Export

With a license from EPDK, importers can sell natural gas to wholesale market, free consumers, or exporters. The 2001 law stipulates that annual natural gas imported by each import company cannot exceed 20% of the national gas consumption projection of that year. Companies that obtain an import license can perform wholesale activity without a wholesaler license. Accordingly, importers can sell the domestic production of natural gas as well. Export companies can export the gas produced in the country or transported from abroad to international

Table 3.6 Natural gas pipelines in Turkey

Pipelines	Length (kms)	Diameter (inches)	Date of operation
Pazarcık-Kdz. Eregli	210	16–24	May 1996
Bursa-Can	213	8–12–16	December 1996
Malkoclar, Onerler-Istanbul, Hersek	160	24–36	September 1998
Can-Canakkale	116	12	July 2000
Eastern Anatolia main line (Dogubeyazit-Konya, Seydisehir)	1,490	48–40–16	June 2001
Eskisehir-Bozoyuk	75	40	January 2002
Mihallicik-Eskisehir	76	40	January 2002
Bozoyuk-Adapazari (Phase 1)	63	36	January 2002
Karacabey-Izmir	240	36	May 2002
Bozoyuk-Adapazari (Phase 2)	63	36	June 2002
Samsun-Ankara 1	501	48	October 2002
Kirklareli-Onerler, Bursa Karcabey	99, 75	36	July 2003
Gaziantep-Osmaniye-Adana-Mersin	287	16–24–40	April 2005
Malatya-Gaziantep	240	16–24–40	May 2005
Konya-Isparta	258	16–40	May 2005
Sivas-Malatya	195	24–40	August 2005
Isparta-Nazilli	363	16–24–40	November 2005
Ordu-Giresun (Ph. 1-2)	158	10–14	July 2007
Adiyaman-Urfa-Elazig-Diyarbakir (Ph. 1-2-3)	123—130—170	(12–40)	May 2007
		(18–40)	June 2007
		(40–14)	July 2007
Nazilli-Izmir (Ph.1-2-3-4)	57.2—76.5—57.2—53.2	40	February 2007
		12–40	August 2007
		40	March 2007
		10–40	April 2007
Edirne-Tekirdag	79	14–12	November 2007
Van	165	14	January 2008
Sungurlu-Cankiri-Kastamonu	264	24–10	March 2008
Bozoyuk-Seckoy	140	36–24–20	January 2008
Amasya-Tokat-Merzifon-Erzincan	252	14–10–8	August 2008
Eastern Black Sea Region (Ph.1-2-3)	306	12–16–18–24	September 2008
Cankiri-Korgun-Kizilcahamam-Aktaskurtlar	158	24–8	October 2008
Aktaskurtlar Line valve Gerede-Bolu-Duzce NGPL	145	24	November 2008
Nevsehir-Ilgin-Aksehir	91	12–10–8	February 2009
Gonen	17	10	April 2009
Eskipazar-Karabuk and Zonguldak-Caycuma-Bartin	170	16–4–2	July 2009
Igdir	38	10	December 2009

Source IEA 2005; BOTAS 2009

Fig. 3.12 Turkey's natural gas infrastructure. *Source* IEA 2011b

markets by using transmission pipelines and obtaining an exporter license. Moreover, in order to liberalize both spot and long-term imports of LNG, Law No 5784 enacted in 2008 as a secondary legislation allows BOTAŞ and private companies with license to have contracts with countries including those with which BOTAŞ already has contracts (OECD 2010).

Turkey imports natural gas via pipelines from three different countries (Russia via multiple contracts and two pipelines, Iran, and Azerbaijan) and via LNG from two countries (Algeria and Nigeria) and occasional spot LNG cargoes. Although this portfolio is diversified, Russian gas still accounted for 46% of total imports in 2010. Still, this share represents a significant decline relative to 2005 when Russia supplied 66% of total imports with the same volume of 17.5 bcm. The share fell because total imported gas increased from 26.571 bcm in 2005 to 38.037 bcm in 2010 (Table 3.7).

Russia was followed by Iran (21%), Azerbaijan (12%), Algeria (10%), and Nigeria (3%). As seen in Fig. 3.13 imports from Azerbaijan began in 2007 and rapidly reached 4.9 bcm in 2009 and 4.5 bcm in 2010. Domestic gas production is small, around one bcm per year, and as of spring 2009, remaining recoverable gas reserves were close to six bcm. In recent years, TPAO, the state-owned oil and gas company, has intensified its gas exploration efforts (IEA 2009b, p 67) and major international companies such as ExxonMobil and Petrobras in addition to smaller companies have been exploring across the country but especially in the Thrace

Table 3.7 Natural gas import (2005–2010) (bcm)

Year	Russia	Iran	Azerbaijan	Algeria	Nigeria	Spot	Total
2005	17.524	4.248	0	3.786	1.013	0	26.571
2006	19.316	5.594	0	4.132	1.100	0.079	30.221
2007	22.762	6.054	1.258	4.205	1.396	0.167	35.842
2008	23.159	4.113	4.580	4.148	1.017	0.333	37.350
2009	19.473	5.252	4.960	4.487	903	0.781	35.856
2010	17.526	7.765	4.521	3.906	1.189	3.079	38.037

Source EPDK 2010, p 24

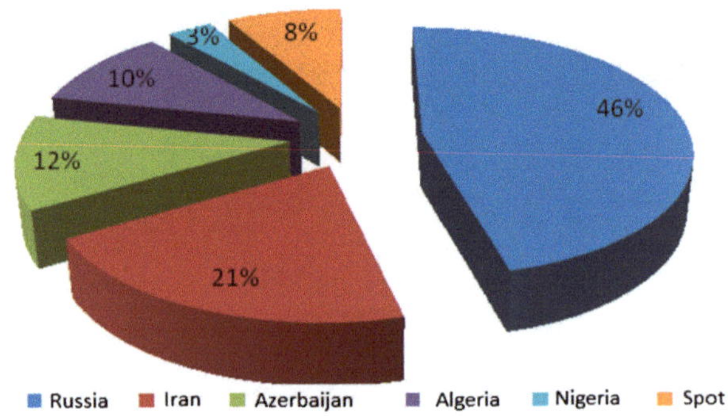

Fig. 3.13 The shares of gas imported countries in imports (2010). *Source* EPDK 2010, p 24

Basin and offshore Black Sea. Although some of these companies are primarily interested in oil discoveries, which is easily marketed across the globe and sells at a significant premium to gas (as long as gas prices are not indexed to oil prices), gas discoveries either in associated or non-associated form are still possible.

An important part of natural gas imported in Turkey comes from Algeria, Nigeria, and spot markets via LNG shipments. The global economic crisis in 2009 caused a decrease in natural gas prices; but in Turkey, whose economy fared better than most, many companies applied to obtain a license for spot LNG imports. As of the end of 2010, there were 22 companies with an import license for spot LNG, enhancing source diversity and hence energy security. As a result, 21% of natural gas in 2010 was imported via LNG shipment (EPDK 2010). While only BOTAŞ imported LNG in 2008, as of the end of 2010, BOTAŞ imported 62.7% the total LNG and the remaining 37.3% was imported by EgeGaz accounting for 8.2% of the total consumption (EPDK 2010).

In Turkey, natural gas exports by BOTAŞ began with 31 mcm in 2007. This rate reached 435 mcm in 2008 and 708 mcm in 2009, and declined to 649 mcm in 2010. In the first quarter of 2011, exported natural gas from Turkey was 183 mcm (IEA 2011c). As of 2010, in addition to BOTAŞ, three private companies obtained export licenses. Whereas SETGAZ has a license to export natural gas to Bulgaria for 30 years after 2010, Liquefied Natural Gas Company and EgeGaz have licenses to export natural gas to Greece for 30 years after 2010. However, these companies did not export any natural gas in 2010 (EPDK, 2010).

Table 3.8 Import amounts by importer companies (as of the end of 2010)

Company	Amount (bcm/year)	Market share (%)
BOTAŞ	32.2	84.1
EgeGaz	3.1	8.1
Enerco Energy	1.9	4.8
Bosphorus Gas	0.6	1.5
Avrasya Gas	0.4	1
Shell Gas	0.2	0.5
Total	38.3	100

Source EPDK 2010

6.5 Wholesale

Wholesalers must satisfy regulations on storage capacity, transportation conditions, and origins of buying. Wholesale companies can sign gas sale contracts with distributors, importers, exporters, and free users. Wholesale companies must obtain an import license for gas imports. Wholesale and import companies must store 10% of the imported gas within five years of obtaining the license. The law of 2001 aimed to limit the share of any wholesaler or BOTAŞ in the domestic market to 20% by 2009.

As discussed in Sect. 5, efforts to transfer contracts or volumes from BOTAŞ to private importers have not made much progress as of the end of 2011. BOTAŞ still continues to dominate the imports of natural gas although its share started to decline as discussed in the previous section. As shown in Table 3.8, BOTAŞ's share in the total imports was 84.1% in 2010, followed by EgeGaz with 8.1%, Enerco Energy with 4.8%. Overall, the current structure of the wholesale market is not the market structure aimed by the natural gas market law of 2001.

6.6 Eligible Consumers and Market Opening

In the pre-2001 market structure, eligible consumers such as gas-fired power generators and large industrial users, which consume more than one mcm gas annually, had the right to choose their own gas suppliers. In the new distribution regions, the eligibility threshold has been at one mcm in the first five years of the license term. In 2009, EPDK, with the aim of gradually opening the market for all customers, decided to decrease the eligibility threshold to 0.8 mcm for the new distribution areas after the first five years of the license term. The new threshold rate gave rise to a 2.8% increase in the total gas consumption for eligible consumers. These consumers have the right to sign a contract with production, import, distribution, and wholesale firms (EPDK 2010). Accordingly, in total, eligible customers account for around 80% of total gas consumption (EPDK 2010; IEA 2009b). This rate is on average 78% for EU countries (Mazzanti and Biancardi 2005).

Table 3.9 Storage facilities

Company	License term	Operation year	Storage facility	Maximum storage capacity (bcm per year)
BOTAŞ (LNG)	10 years after 4 April 2003	1994	Marmara Ereğlisi/ Tekirdağ	8.2
EgeGaz A.Ş. (LNG)	30 years after 4 April 2003	2006	Aliağa/İzmir	6.0
TPAO (Natural gas)	30 years after 18 April 2003	2007	Silivri/İstanbul	2.1
BOTAŞ (Natural Gas)		2015	Tuz Gölü/Konya-Aksaray	1

Source EPDK 2010; IEA 2009b

However, although they have the right to purchase natural gas from national and international producers, storage facilities, importers, and wholesale companies, the current market structure forces them to deal with BOTAŞ. They can bid for the tenders to be issued by BOTAŞ. Only after the tenders are realized new suppliers will be allowed to enter the market and consumers will have the opportunity to change their suppliers. As an important component of a competitive natural gas market, although eligible consumers have the right to choose their suppliers, they cannot currently implement this right due to the large market share of BOTAŞ.

6.7 Storage

According to the 2001 law, private storage facilities can obtain a license and sell natural gas to distribution companies and eligible consumers. Currently, Turkey has two LNG regasification terminals and one natural gas storage facility. Also, the construction of an underground facility, Salt Lake (Tuz Gölü) project, by a Chinese firm, China Tianchen Engineering Corporation, was under way as of the end of 2011. The storage consists of 12 caverns, initially providing around one bcm, but with potential for up to five bcm (IEA 2009b). It has a maximum send-out capacity of 40 mcm per day. It is aimed that the project will be completed in 2015. One of the existing facilities is owned by TPAO in Silivri, Marmara. This facility includes 2.1 bcm of underground storage at two depleted gas fields, with an injection capacity of 14 mcm per day and withdrawal capacity of 17 mcm per day (Table 3.9).

The Marmara Ereğlisi LNG terminal owned by BOTAŞ can operate with a maximum annual capacity of 8.2 bcm and a maximum send-out capacity of 22.05 mcm per day. The facility performs at full capacity in winter and at 60% capacity in summer, sending gas to the Turkish market via the Western pipeline (IEA 2009b).

The only private LNG import and storage facility of Turkey in operation is the Aliağa terminal owned by EgeGaz. The terminal was completed in 2006 but was not issued an import license for several years. Its value as a storage facility and spot LNG import point was later realized. Spot cargoes, readily available due to excess supply in the LNG market at the time, added to source diversity at a lower cost than oil-indexed contracts. It has an annual capacity of 6.0 bcm and a maximum send-out capacity of 16.4 mcm per day.

7 Price Regulation of Natural Gas

According to the NGML, gas prices and network access tariffs are regulated by EPDK, which applies the price-cap method in price regulation of storage, wholesale, and transmission facilities, and determines the unit service and depreciation charges (USDC) for the supply of natural gas in existing distribution zones. As discussed in Sect. 6.2, the USDC for distribution is based on the bids received during the tender process (Çetin 2010). Turkey has preferred uniform-ceiling rates and a 'fair' rate of return. However, although gas prices are regulated by EPDK according to the law of 2001, a new pricing system as in electricity, the automatic price-setting mechanism, has been in force in the price regulation of natural gas as well since July 1, 2008. Under this system, while retail gas prices for both industrial and residential consumers are regulated on a monthly basis by EPDK, wholesale prices are freely determined between the buyer and the seller. According to this regulatory structure, the price for non-eligible users is composed of the wholesale price and USDC. Eligible users pay for natural gas the wholesale price plus a transmission charge set by EPDK.

Although uniform-ceiling pricing in the price regulation of natural gas is an attempt to close the difference between household and industrial prices, it does not eliminate cross-subsidies fully. In Turkey, natural gas prices for household consumers have been higher than prices for industry users such as electricity generators and manufacturers (Fig. 3.14). Until the early 2000s, price increases were reflected mostly on industrial consumers rather than residential consumers, as a political choice (Çetin and Oğuz 2007a).

Following global oil and gas prices, Turkish retail gas prices increased dramatically in 2008, as the government moved to liberalize prices after holding rates constant from 2002 to 2007. The government justified the price increases by citing higher gas import prices and the need to improve BOTAŞ's financial position after years of holding prices for domestic consumers at below-market rates. The government also argued that higher prices would help prepare the sector for privatization by making the gas market more attractive to investors. However, the decline in natural gas demand, the increase of gas supply via low priced spot LNG imports, and the fall in oil prices in the second half of 2008 led to lower gas import prices for Turkey in 2009, prompting BOTAŞ to bring prices down for end-users in line with the automatic price-setting mechanism (OECD2010; Erdoğdu 2011).

On the other hand, as depicted in Fig. 3.15, gas prices for Turkish industrial consumers are above the average in other IEA countries and the prices for Turkish household users are below the IEA average (Fig. 3.16). These two figures strongly suggest that Turkey pursues a typical cross-subsidy policy whereby industrial users subsidize residential users.

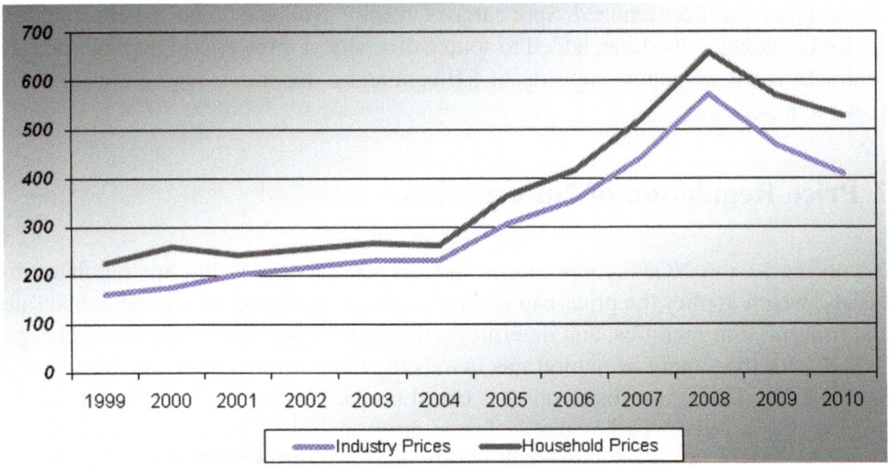

Fig. 3.14 Natural gas prices for industrial and residential users by years

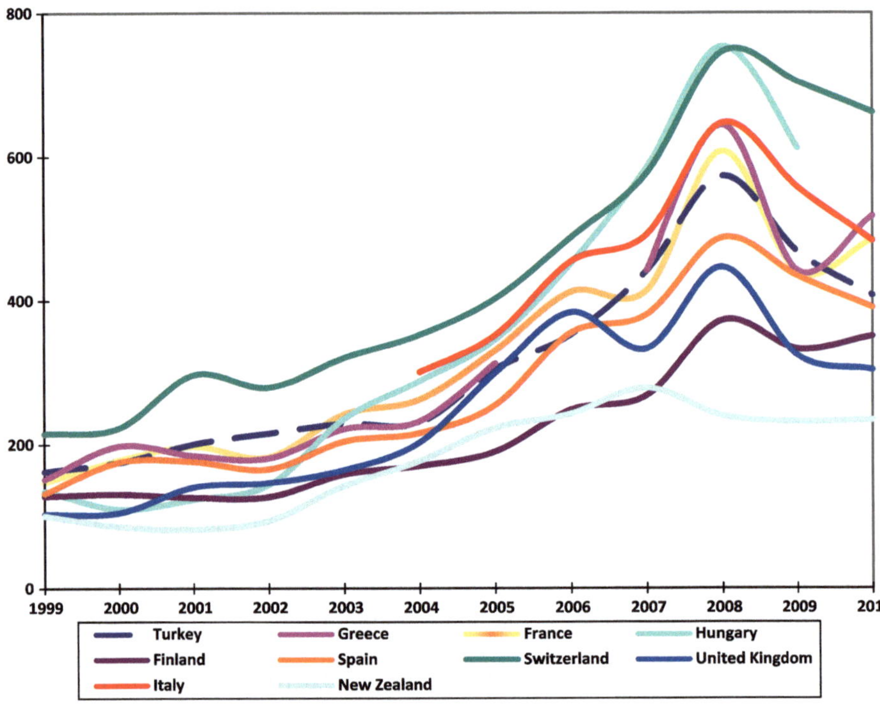

Fig. 3.15 Natural gas prices* for industrial users in US dollars. *Source* IEA 2011b. * Average price per 10^7 kcal on a gross calorific value basis. *Note* Data concerning the prices in 2006 and 2010 are not available for Greece and Hungary, respectively

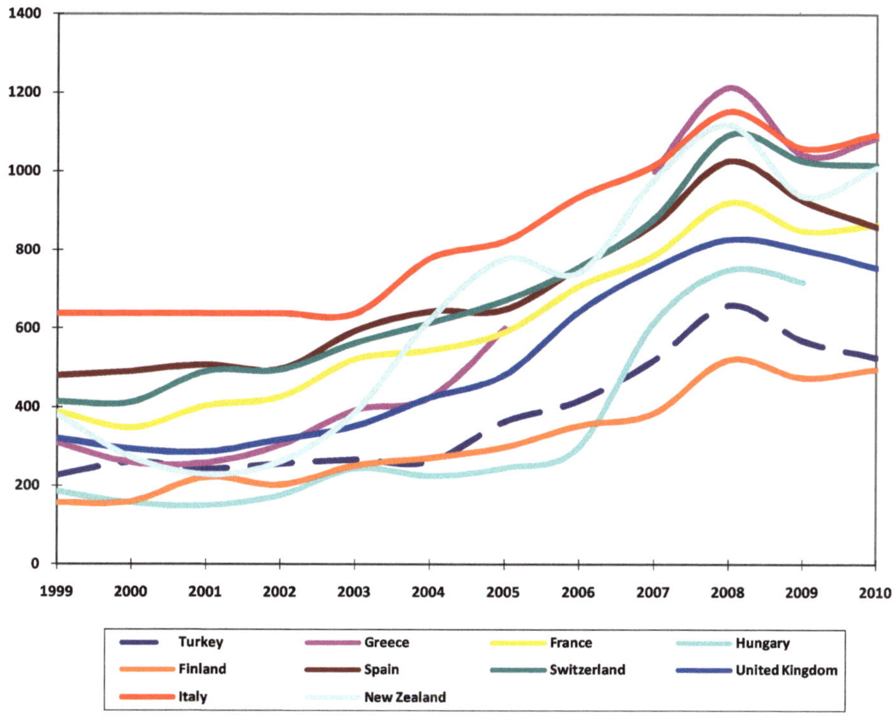

Fig. 3.16 Natural gas prices* for household users in US dollars. *Source* IEA 2011b. * Average price per 10^7 kcal on a gross calorific value basis. *Note* Data concerning the prices in 2006 and 2010 are not available for Greece and Hungary, respectively

Gas prices for industrial users closely follow the heavy fuel oil price since most gas import contracts includes a formula that ties the price of gas to that of oil or its products. End-user prices continue to increase due to current high wholesale prices. In addition, value-added tax (VAT) is applicable to households and non-commercial usage at a rate of 18%. A fixed excise tax (Fuel Consumption Tax) of 22.9 new Turkish lira per 10^7 kilocalories gross calorific value (GCV) applies to natural gas for industry or electricity generation. As seen in Fig. 3.17, in comparison to other IEA countries, tax rates in natural gas prices for Turkish industry users are considerably higher than tax rates in other countries, whereas taxes in prices for Turkish households are relatively lower, implying another form of cross-subsidy in favor of the households.

8 The Role of Turkey as a Conduit of Natural Gas

Turkey is located close to major gas sources of the world in Russia, Iran, Iraq, Egypt, Azerbaijan, and Turkmenistan. LNG supplies are potentially available, as a near 50% increase in global LNG output is anticipated in the near future

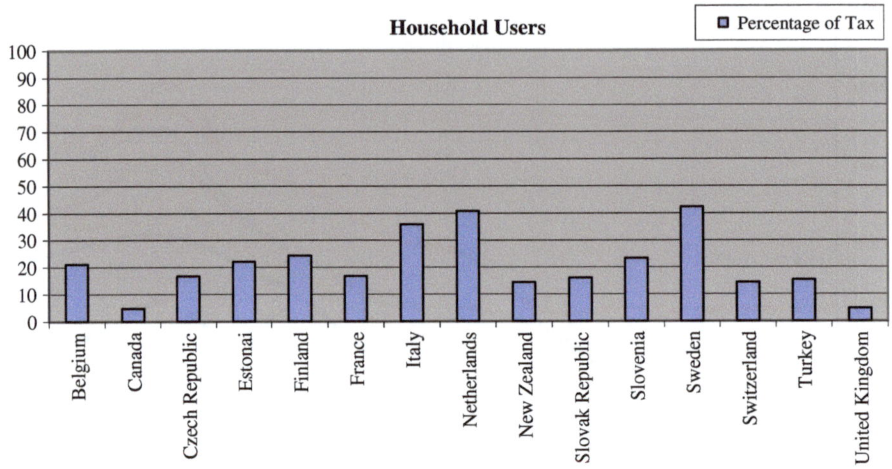

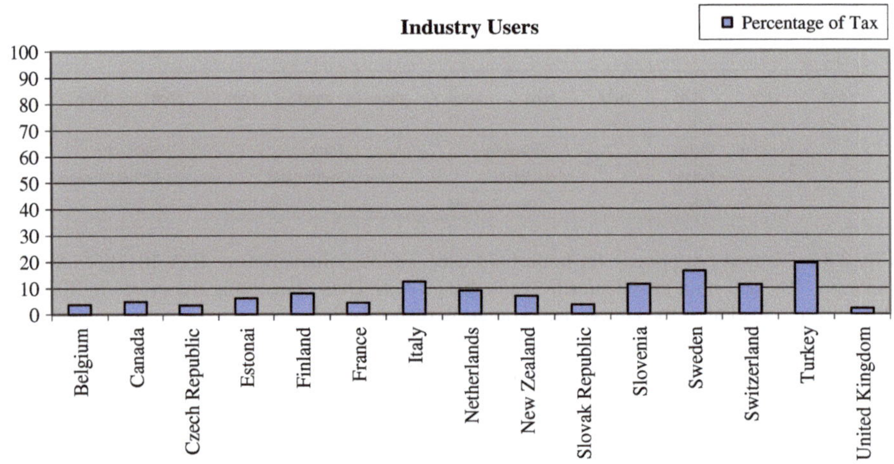

Fig. 3.17 Percentage of taxes in natural gas prices for selected countries (2011). *Source* IEA 2011d. *Note* Because there is information of tax shares only for the industry users of these countries, the same countries are also used for the tax shares of natural gas prices of household users

(IEA 2009b). Turkey currently imports natural gas from Russia, Iran, and Azerbaijan via pipeline and LNG from Algeria and Nigeria and aims to import natural gas from Turkmenistan, Egypt, and Iraq and later to transport it to Europe (Fig. 3.18). Turkey is keen to establish new gas supply routes, to increase co-operation among neighboring countries and to stimulate the integration of Turkish and European gas markets (IEA 2007a, p 227).

Despite the apparent logic of a direct link between the gas-rich regions and the European gas markets, the southern corridor for gas supply to Europe through Turkey has been slow to develop (IEA 2009c).

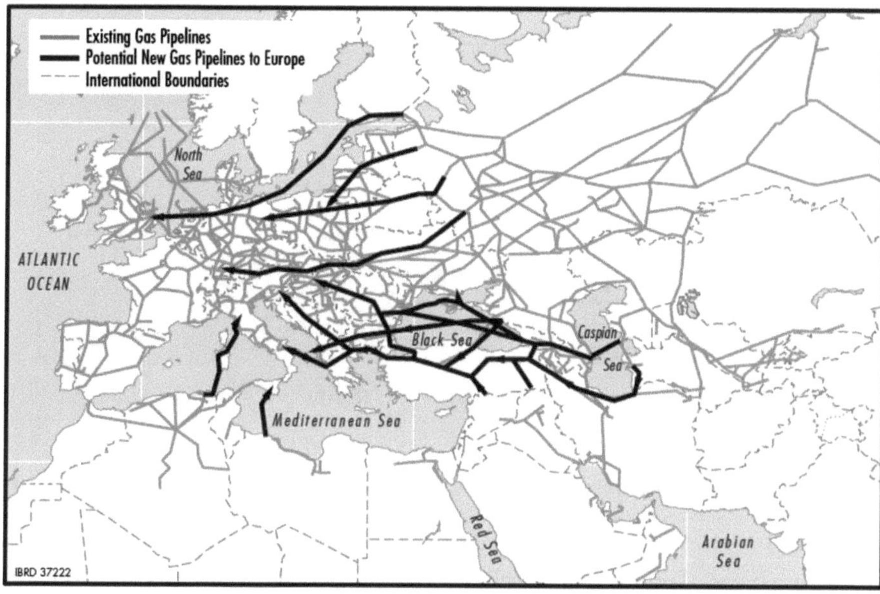

Fig. 3.18 Turkey between energy-rich countries and Europe. *Source* World Bank 2010

8.1 Current and Planned Projects

There are several existing and planned projects that can increase the volume of natural gas flowing through Turkey to consumers in Europe. They are designed to provide access to resources in different regions via different routes but some of the planned projects seem to compete with others or existing infrastructure.

8.1.1 The South Caucasus Project (The Baku–Tbilisi–Erzurum pipeline or Shah Sea Project)

The South Caucasus or Shah Sea Project, including the Baku–Tbilisi–Erzurum natural gas pipeline with a capacity of 11 bcm per annum, is designed to carry gas from Azerbaijan's Shah Sea field to Turkey, where it is linked to the Turkish gas distribution system at the city of Erzurum (Fig. 3.19). Turkey (BOTAŞ) signed an agreement with Azerbaijan (SOCAR) on March 12, 2001 for this project. The construction of the pipeline was initiated in 2004 and completed by the end of 2006. It has been in operation since July 2007.

The South Caucasus pipeline follows the route of the Baku-Tbilisi-Ceyhan crude oil pipeline through Azerbaijan and Georgia to Erzurum in Turkey. Its length is 692 km. According to the agreement, natural gas supply for the first 15 years will be two bcm per year and reach to 6.6 bcm during the plateau period (Çetin 2008). As of 2010, the supplied gas via this pipeline was 14 mcm per day, or over

Fig. 3.19 The South Caucasus pipeline. *Source* http://www.socar-germany.de/eng/socar/scp.html

five bcm a year. Turkey will purchase 91 bcm of gas over 15 years from this pipeline as per the agreement. It is expected that Kazakhstan will connect to this pipeline in the future and transport its natural gas to Europe, filling the rest of the pipeline's 11-bcm capacity. Eventually, gas may be supplied to the Nabucco project, discussed in further detail below, from the Erzurum connection (Fig. 3.20).

8.1.2 The Southern Europe Gas Ring Project (Turkey–Greece–Italy Natural Gas Project)

The Southern Europe Gas Ring Project has been developed to transport natural gas from the Caspian Basin, Russia, the Middle East, Southern Mediterranean countries, and other probable international sources through Turkey and Greece within the scope of the Interstate Oil and Gas Transport to Europe (INOGATE) initiative of the EU Commission. The total length of the Turkey–Greece interconnection will be 296 km. While 211 km of the pipeline lies within Turkey, its 85 km is within Greece. The part of the project within Turkey territory starts from existing Karacabey Pig Station and ends in Ipsala/Kipi.

The Intergovernmental Agreement between two countries and related natural gas sale and purchase agreement between BOTAŞ and the Greek counterpart, DEPA, were signed in 2003. It was envisaged that natural gas supply would start in 2006 at 250 mcm per year and then increase to 750 mcm per year. The construction of the South European Gas Ring Project started on July 2005 and the pipeline has been in operation since November 2007.

Later, the Turkey–Greece–Italy natural gas pipeline was designed to extend the Turkey–Greece pipeline from Greece to Italy beneath the Adriatic Sea. A feasibility study for linking the Interconnector with Italy via a pipeline crossing the

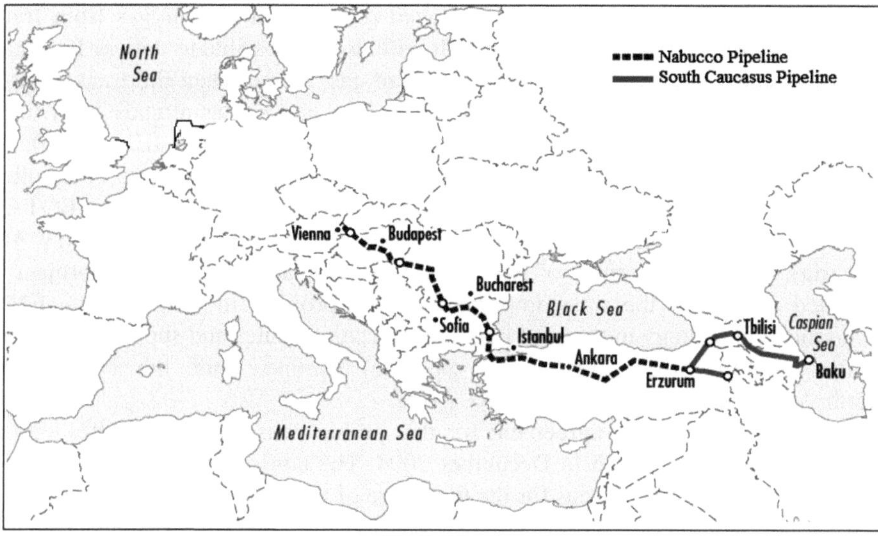

Fig. 3.20 A link between the Nabucco and the South Caucasus pipelines. *Source* WB 2010

Adriatic Sea was completed by the end of 2004. In October, 2009, a "Joint Declaration" was signed between Turkey and Italy to extend the pipeline to Italy. Both countries reiterated their political support for the project (Yazar 2011). This project is currently being promoted by Edison of Italy (in collaboration with DEPA of Greece and BOTAŞ of Turkey) to bring gas for power generation into southern Italy. According to the Project, the volume of natural gas to be transported to Italy by this pipeline will be approximately 13 bcm per annum. About 3.6 bcm of this volume will be supplied to Greece and the remaining will be transported to Italy. It is expected that the project will be in operation in 2012.

8.1.3 Bypassing Russia: The Nabucco Project

The Nabucco Project aims to construct a pipeline from Turkey to Austria via Bulgaria, Romania, and Hungary with a capacity of 31 bcm and is planned to become operational by 2015 (IEA 2011b) although this start date has been postponed several times before; most recently, the first gas flow date was given as 2017.[8] At 3,400 km in length, it is a south-to-north route to Central and Western Europe, terminating at OMV's (Austria gas company) Baumgarten hub in Austria. The primary aim of the project is to deliver Caspian gas from the potentially large offshore Shah Deniz complex in Azerbaijan to Europe, bypassing Russia.

---

[8] According to the company web site: http://www.nabucco-pipeline.com/portal/page/portal/en/pipeline/timeline_steps.

Additionally, it is planned that the Nabucco project will deliver gas from Iran, or possibly from Turkmenistan via Iran. It will also be possible to deliver Iraqi gas along the same route and potentially Egyptian gas, if and when the transmission pipeline infrastructure is in place (WB 2010). The project has already been fully supported by signing intergovernmental agreement in July 2009 (IEA 2011b).

The Nabucco project is being undertaken by a consortium of gas companies from each of the six countries through which the project would pass: BOTAŞ (Turkey), Bulgargaz (Bulgaria), Transgaz (Romania), MOL (Hungary), OMV AG (Austria), and RWE (Germany)[9] with equal share for each. The Nabucco project is designed as one of the most important energy projects in scope of the EU's diversification strategy in terms of both transportation routes and suppliers. It is the fourth supply corridor for natural gas into Europe, after the North Sea, North Africa, and Russia (IEA 2009b, p 76).

The first co-operation agreement for this project was signed in 2002, with a feasibility study completed in December 2004. The consortium initially regarded Iran as a primary source of gas for the first stage of the project and Tehran signed a Memorandum of Understanding with OMV in January 2004 to assess what role the National Iranian Gas ExportCo (NIGEC) could play in the pipeline. However, Iran's exports to Turkey have been much lower than those stipulated in the contract and sometimes been interrupted, as noted above. The Nabucco project sponsors have reoriented their supply priorities over the years, first in favor of the Caspian, in particular Azerbaijan (IEA 2007a) and more recently Iraq. However, Turkmenistan remains a desired option and Kazakhstan, Iran, Egypt, and Russia are also alternative gas sources, although it is not expected that Russia and Iran will be major contributors of the project at least in the early stages. In short, first gas for Nabucco is expected to be transported either from northern Iraq or from the second phase of the Shah Sea field in Azerbaijan[10] (IEA 2009b, p 76).

8.1.4 Transcaspian Turkmenistan–Turkey–Europe Natural Gas Pipeline Project

A Trans-Caspian pipeline to transport Turkmen gas from the Caspian Sea to Europe via Turkey has been pursued since the 1990s but, for a variety of reasons, has never materialized. Although Turkmenistan signed deals with Gazprom to export more gas via Russia and with China via a new pipeline, the country remains of interest to developers of Nabucco among other projects, primarily because the Trans-Caspian pipeline project is the most direct route to transport Turkmen gas to

[9] RWE is the largest electricity producer in Germany. RWE participated in the Nabucco consortium with an agreement signed in Vienna in 2008. Additionally, German–Austrian Bayerngas Company seeks to join the consortium as a seventh partner in 2012.

[10] However, there are other projects that count on the Shah Sea gas, including the ITGI discussed earlier and a new project, the Trans-Anatolia, discussed below. Additionally, increasing natural gas demand in Azerbaijan, Georgia, and Turkey is dependent on this gas (IEA 2009b).

Europe (WB 2010). Turkey and Turkmenistan signed a Framework Agreement on October 29, 1998 for realization of the project. By this Agreement, it was aimed that 30 bcm per annum of Turkmen gas will be transported via this pipeline, with 16 bcm to Turkey and the remaining to Europe. Later, BOTAŞ of Turkey and the Competent Body of Turkmenistan signed a Natural Gas Sale and Purchase Agreement valid for 30 years in May 1999. Accordingly, 16 bcm per annum of Turkmen gas would be delivered to Turkey.[11]

Turkmen gas would be purchased at Turkey–Georgia border and Turkmenistan would take all the responsibility for the construction and operation of the pipeline section between Turkmenistan and Georgia.

However, the project has not yet been implemented because the slow-paced and non-transparent decision-making process in Turkmenistan led to the withdrawal of most major Western firms. Turkmen authorities have not extended a mandate letter to the consortium that would construct the Turkmen section of the pipeline and these companies withdrew from the consortium. Although various protocols and memorandum of understandings were signed since then, no development has occurred yet (İpek 2006). Also, the conflict between Azerbaijan and Turkmenistan regarding the offshore boundary between the two countries hampered negotiations. There are potentially valuable oil and gas resources under the Caspian, claimed by both countries. Finally, Azerbaijan always desired to send its own gas via any pipeline that would pass through its territory. With some of the newer projects (e.g., the Trans-Anatolia project discussed below), Azerbaijan can probably ship all its available gas, opening the way for accepting Turkmen gas.

8.2 New Developments

Although there are many existing and planned projects as we discussed, new ideas continue to materialize as some of the planned projects get delayed for various reasons. More importantly, demand for gas in Turkey and in Europe remains strong despite recent economic slowdown because many countries want to phase out coal due to climate change concerns and nuclear due to safety concerns. At the same time, many countries such as Iraq, are seeking markets for their gas resources.

8.2.1 Trans-Anatolia Project

Turkey and Azerbaijan signed a memorandum of understanding on the construction of the Trans-Anatolia Natural Gas Pipeline in 2007. Later, an intergovernmental contract was signed on 26 December 2011. It is planned that the Trans-Anatolia Gas Pipeline will transport via Turkey natural gas produced in Shah Sea 2 field of

---

[11] Received from http://www.botas.gov.tr/index.asp, 27 Nov 2011.

Azerbaijan. The consortium of SOCAR, BOTAŞ, and TPAO will start to construct the pipeline in 2012 in order to complete it by the end of 2017. The shares are split 20-80 between Turkey and Azerbaijan. Third party international oil and natural gas companies are expected to join the consortium during the construction phase of the project.

The volume of natural gas to be transported in this pipeline will be 16 bcm per annum for the first phase. Whereas six bcm of gas will be delivered to Turkey, 10 bcm will be transported to Europe. The amount of natural gas to be supplied from Azerbaijan will be increased to 24 bcm per annum in the future. This increase will particularly be important for Azerbaijan that aims to increase its gas production from 25.3 bcm for this year to 50 bcm per annum by 2025.

This project appears to undermine the Nabucco project, which also counts on the Shah Sea gas as one of its anchors. In September 2011, BP, the operator of the Shah Deniz project proposed the South-East Europe Pipeline (SEEP). The proposal envisions using existing pipeline capacity in Turkey and Europe and building only about 800 miles of new pipeline, or about a third of the total distance between Shah Deniz and customers in Europe. If the amount of gas available from Azerbaijan remains limited and is primarily used to meet internal demand in Turkey and/or to supply SEEP and ITGI, the Nabucco project may indeed lose out. If, on the other hand, gas production in Azerbaijan increases significantly as expected and/or the Trans-Caspian can be realized, possibly taking advantage of the Trans-Anatolia rights-of-way, the Nabucco project can benefit. It is also possible that the Trans-Anatolia and SEEP projects may reduce the cost of the Nabucco project by delivering the gas to it at the Bulgarian border rather than the Georgian border or Erzurum. It is important to remember that the Nabucco project has all the groundwork done with respect to regulatory permitting in EU and transit countries in Europe. At the end of the day, though, it is the availability of gas supplies and the ability to finance will determine which pipelines will get built and when.

8.2.2 Egypt–Turkey Natural Gas Pipeline Project

The Egypt-Turkey natural gas pipeline project was designed to transport Egyptian gas from Turkey via Jordan, Lebanon, and Syria to Europe. The pipeline is under construction and it has already reached Homs in Syria. Accordingly, natural gas started to be delivered from this pipeline to Jordan, Lebanon, and Syria. The remaining part of the pipeline between and Syria (Homs) and Turkey (Türkoğlu) has not yet been constructed because of commitment insufficiencies regarding the supply of natural gas from the Egyptian side (Yazar 2011).

Although Turkey and Syria signed two Memorandums of Understanding in 2009 in order to complete the remaining parts of the pipeline on both sides of the border until 2011, construction of the pipeline has not yet been completed. The signed memorandums include gas sales to Syria from Turkey, gas transportation from Iran and Azerbaijan to Syria and other Arab countries via Turkey, and transportation of Egyptian and Syrian gas to Turkey in the next years

(Yazar 2011). This project was impacted by the "Arab Spring" movement and the resulting change of government in Egypt, which is going through a period of political uncertainty. The conditions in Syria are much more dire and uncertain at the time of writing. But, it is clear that the unrest in Syria has postponed any chance of pipeline completion indefinitely.

8.2.3 Iraq–Turkey Natural Gas Pipeline Project

The project was developed to transport Iraqi gas to Europe via Turkey. With this project, Turkey aims to import 10 bcm of natural gas from the gas fields to be developed in Iraq. The related ministers of Iraq and Turkey signed a Framework Agreement in December 1996 and the companies in Turkish Side of the Agreement have been signing contracts with international energy companies. BOTAŞ, TPAO, and TEKFEN, signed a Memorandum of Understanding in July 2005 and Workings Groups were established. This integrated project includes field development, production, and processing and pipeline transportation of gas from the northwest region of Iraq. The project has been delayed due to the sanctions imposed on Iraq by the United Nations and ongoing political uncertainties in Iraq. However, taking into consideration the developments in Iraq and increasing gas demand in Europe, the companies and Turkey continue to take the necessary initiatives in order to improve the project's chances. The Ministry of Energy and Natural Resources of Turkey and the Iraqi Oil Minister signed a Memorandum of Understanding in Ankara On August 7, 2007. The ultimate aim of these studies is firstly to transport Iraqi gas to Turkey and later to Europe via Turkey.[12] In fact, gas from Iraq is of highest priority for the Nabucco pipeline to have enough volumes to justify investment. However, the central government in Baghdad and the regional Kurdish authorities in northern Iraq have to reach an agreement in terms of the legality of contracts signed by the Kurdish authorities either for exploration and production or export of hydrocarbons without the approval of the central government in Baghdad.

9 Conclusion

Turkey has been reshaping its natural gas sector by implementing the various requirements of the NGML, which was enacted in 2001. The main aim of the law was to establish competition in the market by unbundling BOTAŞ and encouraging private participation in import, wholesale, storage and distribution of natural gas. However, BOTAŞ continues to play a dominant role in the market place primarily due to its large share in legacy import contracts and participation in some large

[12] Received from http://www.botas.gov.tr/index.asp, 27 Nov 2011.

distribution regions and storage facilities. More importantly, the government too continues to take actions contrary to the spirit of the NGML if not its letter. For example, only private companies were supposed to sign new import contracts after receiving a license from EPDK, but the government signed a new contract with Egypt in 2008 by changing the law of 2001 and transferred the responsibility of the contract to BOTAŞ, adding to state company's import share despite the fact that the NGML required the company to reduce its market share to 20% by 2009. Although there have been efforts to transfer contracts or volumes via the gas release program, these have failed. The main reason seems to be unwillingness of suppliers such as Gazprom to deal with new, private parties rather than BOTAŞ, which is understandable given the favorable price formulas and Treasury guarantees included in their legacy contracts. Accordingly it is not surprising that EPDK has not fined BOTAŞ for not complying with NGML's requirements although the law gives the regulator such authority.

According to the NGML, eligible consumers have the right to choose their suppliers and the third-party access right to transmission, distribution, and storage facilities under non-discriminatory conditions. However, they can face difficulties in practice due to cross-subsidies and the large market share of BOTAŞ, which still dominates 90% of the wholesale market and 84.1% of the total imports.

Although Turkey is a natural energy bridge between Europe and the energy-rich countries, it has little underground storage capacity that could help the country to realize its aim to be a major transit corridor for gas supplies. But the storage deficiency also hampers the development of a competitive internal gas market as envisioned by the reform process. There are several developments that helps with the storage situation. The private LNG terminal built on the Aegean coast in 2002 was finally allowed to receive LNG cargoes; spot cargoes imported by numerous companies are helping Turkish market not only to diversify its import sources but also to add some storage flexibility. The underground storage facility under construction at Tuz Gölü should also help greatly market players in balancing domestic demand, imports and exports as well as seasonal fluctuations in each.

Despite legacy contracts of BOTAŞ, Turkey started to reduce its dependence on imports from Russia and Iran by diversifying the sources of gas supply. It has not renewed Turkey's first gas import contract, the 25-year agreement signed in 1986 with the Soviet Union at the time and expired in December 2011, because Russia did not accept a decrease in the contracted gas prices. Several private companies with import licenses from EPDK have been negotiating with Gazprom and possibly other gas suppliers in Russia to import gas via the Western pipeline, replacing BOTAŞ. At the time of writing, there were no new deals between any of these companies and suppliers. Given the possibility of shortage in the winter months, the government signed a short-term deal with Russia for a limited volume of gas at reportedly lower prices than those commonly seen in existing contracts. Going forward, though, private companies have to succeed in importing gas preferably from a diversified group of suppliers and at prices that are not linked to prices of oil or its products; otherwise, the reform process will be handicapped. The EgeGaz LNG terminal has started playing an important role in both diversifying Turkey's gas sources and lowering the cost of gas as private companies import spot LNG cargoes at prices that are not tied to oil. Allowing companies to sign long-term LNG import contracts rather than spot cargoes and construction of new LNG import terminals should be encouraged by EPDK and ETKB as well as gas consumers in Turkey. The conditions in the LNG market offer opportunities to sign long-term deals at non-oil indexed prices. Given the apparent structural shift in global oil and gas markets, gas prices are likely to be lower than oil prices for some time to come. Increased volumes of LNG imports will also put pressure on prices of new pipeline imports.

Lastly, Turkey has been pursuing important international pipeline projects to transport natural gas from the energy-rich regions to Europe. In particular, the Nabucco and the South Caucasus projects are notable to meet gas demand of Europe, bypassing Russia, to increase co-operation among neighboring countries, and to ensure the integration of Turkish and European gas markets. The natural gas pipeline projects that were signed with Egypt and Iraq would be useful to diversify sources in terms of both Turkey and Europe. Overall, although the Turkish strategy to pursue multiple pipelines and sources may seem reasonable in terms of enhancing energy security, some of the country's actions appear contradictory. In particular, the recent decisions to allow Russian alternative to Nabucco, South Stream, rights of way under Turkish waters of the Black Sea and the Trans-Anatolia pipeline agreement with Azerbaijan are commonly seen as major blows to the Nabucco project. BP's SEEP project offers another alternative. It is possible that, in the long-term, all of these options will materialize perhaps in a merged fashion as demand for gas in Turkey and Europe continues to grow but it is clear that the Nabucco project, the start date of which has been repeatedly postponed, appears to be falling behind in the near term. Nevertheless, Turkey's role as a natural gas bridge is poised to solidify. Increased supplies of natural gas via pipelines and as LNG from numerous sources will also help Turkey develop a liquid and competitive internal gas market.

References

Akçollu, Y. (2006); "Major Challenges to the Liberalization of the Turkish Natural Gas Market", Oxford Institute for Energy Studies, NG 16, November 2006.

Atiyas, I. and M. Dutz (2005); "Competition and Regulatory Reform in Turkey's Electricity Industry", in (eds.) Hoekman, Bernard M. and Subidey Togan, *Turkey: Economic Reform and Accession to the European Union*. Herndon, VA, USA: World Bank, The, 187–208.

BOTAŞ (2009); *Annual Report*, BOTAŞ, Ankara.

BOTAŞ (2010); Sector Report, BOTAŞ, Bilkent-Ankara.

Çetin, T. (2010); "Institutional Change in the Turkish Energy Industry", in (eds.) T. Çetin and F. Yılmaz; *Understanding the Process of Economic Change in Turkey: An Institutional Approach,* NOVA Science Publishers, NY, 2010, USA, 275–318.

Çetin, T. (2008); "Competition, Regulatory Reform and Probable Clashes during the Restructuring Process of Turkey's Natural Gas Market", in (Eds.) N. David and T. Michel (2008), *Natural Gas Research Progress,* Ch.14, Nova Publishers, NY, USA, 2008, 467–496.

Çetin, T. and F. Oğuz (2007a); "Reform in the Turkish Natural Gas Market: A Critical Evaluation" *Energy Policy,* Vol.35, No.7, July 2007, 3856–3867.

Çetin, T. and F. Oğuz (2007b); "The Politics of Regulation in the Turkish Electricity Market", *Energy Policy,* Vol.35, No.3, March 2007, 1761–1770.

Doane, M., and Spulber, D., (1994); "Open access and the evolution of the US spot market for natural gas", *Journal of Law and Economics,* Vol.37, No.2, 477–517.

EPDK, 2010. Annual Report, EPDK, Ankara.

EPDK, 2004. Annual Report, EPDK, Ankara.

Erdoğdu, E. (2011); "The Regulation of Natural Gas Industry in Turkey", in (eds.) T. Çetin and F. Oğuz *The political Economy of Regulation in Turkey,* Springer, NY,145–176.

Gallick, E.C. (1993); *Competition in the Natural Gas Pipeline Industry*, Praeger Publishers, WestPort, CT.

IEA (2005). Energy Policies of IEA Countries, Turkey-2005 Review, IEA/OECD Paris.

IEA (2007a); Natural Gas Market Review 2007, IEA/OECD Paris.

IEA (2007b); Natural Gas Information 2007, IEA/OECD Paris.

IEA (2009a); Natural Gas Information 2009, IEA/OECD Paris.

IEA (2009b); Energy Policies of OECD Countries: Turkey 2009 Review, IEA/OECD, Paris.

IEA (2009c); Natural Gas Market Review 2009, IEA/OECD Paris.

IEA (2011a); Energy Balances of OECD Countries, IEA/OECD, Paris.

IEA (2011b); Natural Gas Information 2011, IEA/OECD Paris.

IEA (2011c); Oil, Gas, Coal and Electricity: Quarterly Statistics, First Quarter, IEA/OECD, Paris.

IEA (2011d); Energy Prices and Taxes: Quarterly Statistics, Second Quarter, IEA/OECD, Paris.

İpek, P. (2006); "The Aftermath of Baku-Tbilisi-Ceyhan Pipeline: Challenges Ahead for Turkey", *Perceptions,* Vol 11, Spring 2006, 1–17.

Intven, H. and Tetrault, M., (2000); "Price regulation", in. Intven, H., Tetrault, M. (Eds.), *Telecommunications Regulation Handbook,* World Bank.

Kılıç, A. M., (2006); "Turkey's Natural Gas Necessity, Consumption and Future Perspectives", *Energy Policy*, Vol.34, No.14, 1928–1934.

Mazzanti, M. R. and A. Biancardi (2005); "Institutional Endowment and Regulatory Reform in Turkey's Natural Gas Sector Reform", in (eds.) Hoekman, Bernard M. and Subidey Togan, *Turkey: Economic Reform and Accession to the European Union*. Herndon, VA, USA: World Bank, the, 209–220.

OECD (2010); OECD Economic Surveys: Turkey-2010, OECD, Paris.

Tunç, M., U. Camdalib, and C. Parmaksızoğlu, (2006); "Comparison of Turkey's Electrical Energy Consumption and Production with Some European Countries and Optimization of Future Electrical Power Supply Investments in Turkey", *Energy Policy,* Vol.34, No.1, 50–59.

Yazar, Y. (2011); "The growing role of Turkey in the EU's security of energy supply", *European Energy Review,* January 2011,

WB (2010); The Future of the Natural Gas Market in Southeast Europe, The International Bank for Reconstruction and Development/The World Bank, WA, USA.

Chapter 4
Alternative Energy Options for Turkey

1 Introduction

Turkey, like many other countries, has been promoting renewable energy technologies and energy efficiency programs, but the country had a later start than most to initiate a legal and regulatory framework and to develop targeted support programs. A definition of renewables was introduced via an amendment of the electricity law in 2003 but the Renewables Law was not passed until 2005. Significant new wind capacity was added between 2009 and 2011. As of the end of 2011, more than 1,600 MW of installed wind capacity was reported.[1] Now, the country has a goal to generate 30% of electricity from renewables in 2023.[2] This is not necessarily an aggressive goal given that large-scale hydro has always been an important part of the generation portfolio in Turkey, accounting for more than 40% of generation in the early 1990s but down to the 17–24% range in 2008–2010. More striking is the goal of 20,000 MW of wind power capacity, requiring more than a 10-fold increase in 12 years.

In addition, there is renewed interest in building the country's first nuclear facility at the Akkuyu site. A bidding round in 2008 seemed rushed with only one company, a state-owned Russian company, entering and winning. The requests of other interested bidders to postpone the due date of bids were denied, raising questions about the fairness and transparency of the process. A high court annulled the award in late 2009 but an intergovernmental agreement between Russia and Turkey in early 2010 cleared the path for the Akkuyu plant. The government also seems to ignore opposition by nuclear experts and local residents. There have been efforts to build a nuclear power plant since 1976 when the first license was issued for the Akkuyu site, which is now condemned by some experts as too seismically

---

[1] ETKB (2011). The amount of installed capacity at the end of 2010 has been reported at 800, 1,300, 1,400, or 1,500 MW by various sources. The discrepancy may be due to increased construction activity since 2009 with wind farms coming online frequently.

[2] DPT (2009).

I. Atiyas et al., *Reforming Turkish Energy Markets*,
DOI: 10.1007/978-1-4614-0290-9_4,

active. Given that renewables are still costlier than conventional technologies and system operators have to deal with intermittency and low capacity factor, like any rapidly growing country without significant hydrocarbon resources, Turkey's desire to diversify its energy portfolio is understandable. Yet, nuclear energy remains expensive with costs increasing more than any other technology in the last decade. Most importantly, as reminded by the Fukushima Daiichi accident, nuclear power plants can be dangerous if they are not managed well and regulated properly beginning with the site selection process and following through with safety inspections during construction and operation.[3]

The drivers for increasing interest in these alternative technologies are, as in most other places, reducing dependence on imported fuels (especially natural gas and oil)—hence enhancing energy security; increasing local job creation and economic activity (by use of domestic resources and local technology development and production); cutting long-run energy costs; and reducing local pollution as well as greenhouse gas (GHG) emissions.

The Turkish Renewable Energy Law has many of the standard clauses found in similar laws elsewhere, requiring load serving entities but also other suppliers to provide a certain percentage of their electricity from renewable resources, providing price support, ease of access to rights of way for interconnection, and the like. In particular, in its path to joining the European Union (EU), Turkey has been trying to harmonize its legal frameworks with EU laws and regulations in the energy sector as well as other sectors of the economy.

But, every country is different in terms of their resource endowment, physical infrastructure, existing generation portfolio, stage of economic development, and social pricing policies among others. For example, Turkey's economy is growing faster than most EU member countries (especially those in Western Europe) since the country is still behind those countries in terms of economic development.[4] Accordingly, the ability of Turkish citizens to afford higher electricity prices and Turkish government's ability to subsidize prices for renewables are more limited. In fact, Europe has been realizing the limits of how much of these subsidies Europeans can afford. Since late 2008, economic recession and associated financial difficulties forced many countries, including celebrated champions of renewables

---

[3] It is worth noting, however, that the safety record of the nuclear industry remains a stellar one when measured by the number of major accidents or fatalities per kWh generated. The challenge faced by the industry is one of risk perceptions and psychology: although the probability of a major accident is minuscule, the impact can be large and dispersed over time in terms of illnesses caused by radiation, invisibility of which is a psychological factor of fear. A "safety culture" must be in place in oversight bodies for public to feel confidence in regulators and operators following safety procedures unfailingly. This kind of confidence existed in Japan but the Fukushima Daiichi accident, coming after a series of mishaps by TEPCO, might have eroded it. The non-transparent relationship between utilities such as TEPCO and the Japanese government is now under scrutiny.

[4] 2010 Gross National Income (GNI) per capita was $9,500 in Turkey and $38,500 in the Euro area in current US$ (data.worldbank.org). The gap narrows but remains large when purchasing power parity figures are compared: $15,170 in Turkey and $34,111 in the Euro area.

such as Spain and Germany, to cut back on their support, endangering viability of many existing projects and certainly eliminating some planned projects going forward. The policies, laws, and, particularly, implementing regulations in Turkey have to take these kinds of conditions peculiar to Turkey into consideration.

The Turkish public seems to be paying increasing attention to pros and cons of different options. Challenges from local communities against the Akkuyu nuclear facility as well as some renewable facilities such as the small run-of-the-river hydro facilities are worth considering when evaluating the future prospects of these technologies in the Turkish energy sector. At the same time, there is a growing lobbying effort by investors who are positioning themselves to take advantage of subsidies and local production incentives. Although a laudable goal, promoting domestic manufacturing of equipment can lead to many unintended consequences, including lower quality production, bottlenecks in the supply chain, and shortages of parts. It is also important to remember that most EU countries justify their own support for renewables on the grounds of exporting technology to countries like Turkey. Both EU and Turkey, however, should be aware that China and India have been investing heavily in wind and solar technologies and already started capturing global market share from established manufacturers of Europe and the United States. Many more countries are being added to the list of renewable technology manufacturers and exporters, rendering this sector globally competitive.

Turkey is the only Annex-I country to the Kyoto treaty without a target of GHG reduction. Emissions have been increasing as the country has continued to grow fast although energy intensity has been relatively stable. Most of the increased demand has been met by electricity generated in modern, efficient combined cycle plants by burning natural gas, which burns much cleaner than coal. The increasing share of wind and relative renaissance of hydro will also help Turkey grow with relatively less GHG emissions. The addition of nuclear power, if and when it happens, will help the country further reduce its emissions per dollar of economic output. Turkey also has a young but aggressive energy efficiency policy, which, if implemented successfully, will keep demand growth in check. Overall, the country is well placed to follow a growth path that is less energy (hence less emission) intensive than paths followed in the past or the one China has been pursuing in recent years.[5]

Finally, it is important to underline a potentially significant challenge. Fitting renewables, energy efficiency, and nuclear energy into the competitive market structure poses a set of particular challenges. All of these technologies tend to be more expensive than the currently prevailing wholesale prices. The intermittency of

---

[5] Canada, Japan, and Russia withdrew from the Kyoto Protocol and will not sign up for further commitments. Canada has not been able to meet its previous commitments. With the US already out of the picture, EU is not likely to carry any additional burden in controlling emissions, especially when the Euro crisis is straining the economies of member countries. But, even without an extended Kyoto Protocol, Turkey has economic reasons to pursue a less energy-intensive strategy, which will help to keep GHG emissions in check.

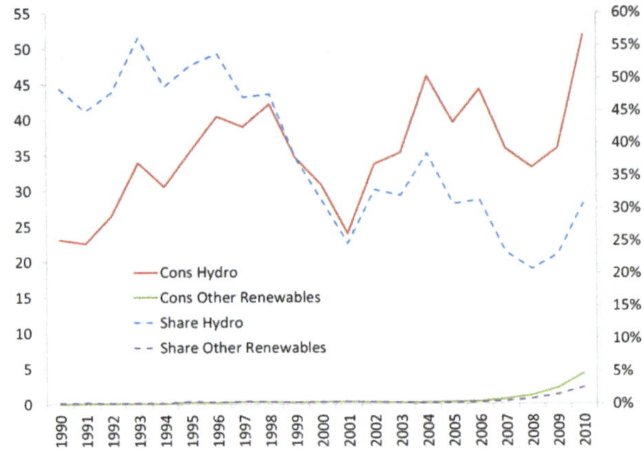

Fig. 4.1 Hydroelectric and other renewables consumption (TWh) and share in net consumption. *Source* Data from BP (2011) and Energy Information Administration International Statistics (www.eia.gov)

renewables not only challenge grid operations (from frequency control to real-time balancing of load and generation) but may also force thermal plants to cycle, i.e., ramp up and down to accommodate variability in intermittent generators, impacting their economics and emissions. Already, special support incentives offered for renewables and nuclear facilities raise questions about the viability of the competitive market model. Although energy efficiency investments are often considered the 'low-hanging fruits' in terms of yielding higher benefit-to-cost ratios, all are not created equal.[6] The return on efficiency investment is not always readily visible, especially in the absence of price signals (e.g., dynamic or much simpler peak time pricing). These issues are discussed further in following sections.

2 Renewable Energy

Technical assessment studies indicate that Turkey has large wind, solar, hydro, and geothermal resources, especially relative to its energy needs but the estimates cover a wide range. Hence, a cautious approach to these resource estimates is warranted, especially given the fact that these resources have not been used much with the exception of hydro (Fig. 4.1). As recently as the early 1990s, more than 40% of electricity consumed in Turkey was from hydroelectric facilities, mostly large dams in the eastern part of the country on major rivers such as Fırat (Euphrates).

---

[6] For example, see McKinsey & Company (2010). Research by McKinsey & Company over the last several years and across several jurisdictions consistently ranked many energy efficiency strategies (e.g., building efficiency improvements, increased mileage for vehicles, more efficient home appliances, switching lighting from incandescent to CFL and LED) as some of the lowest cost GHG abatement options. In fact, many of them have a negative cost; i.e., it actually pays back to pursue these efficiency strategies.

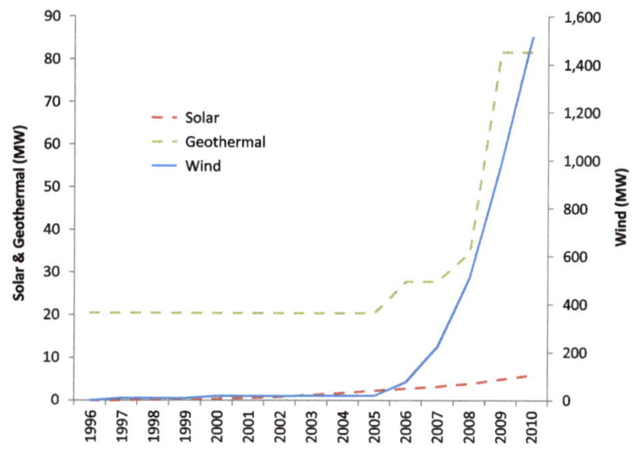

Fig. 4.2 Installed generation capacity of renewables (MW). *Source* Data from BP (2011)

Generation from hydro facilities and their share dropped in the late 1990s as new gas-fired generation came online. These facilities were mostly combined cycle plants and were built via build-operate-transfer (BOT) or build-operate (BO) mechanisms with long-term power purchase agreements that included take-or-pay and international arbitration clauses backed by the Turkish government. Accordingly these plants get dispatched before other facilities as much as possible, reducing contribution of hydro and coal plants at times.

Rapidly growing Turkish economy of the 2000s raised demand for electricity; hydro generation increased, albeit not constantly, to help meet rising demand in the country while at the same time continuing to lose its market share. Hydro accounted for 46% of total generation in 1993 while it accounted for only 17% in 2008 although hydro generation was about the same in both years (34 terawatt-hours, or TWh, in 1993 and 33.3 TWh in 2008). In 2010, with demand growth high (especially high peak load in summer for air conditioning), almost 52 TWh were generated by hydro facilities, setting a new record. This record level accounted for only about 25% of total generation.

Historically, renewables other than hydro have not played a significant role in electricity supply (Fig. 4.1). Only in the second half of the 2000s, one can notice their contribution to the system. In 2010, consumption of other renewables (wind, geothermal, and solar) was estimated at more than four TWh, which represented only 2.5% of net consumption in the country. There has been a little over 20 MW of geothermal capacity since the early 1990s but three times more capacity has been added since 2005 reaching about 82 MW in 2010, which represented only 0.16% of total installed capacity in the country (49,562 MW). Wind capacity was about 20 MW in the early 2000s but expanded exponentially after 2005, reaching almost 1,700 MW by the end of 2011, representing about 3% of country's total installed capacity. Although solar installations also expanded after 2005, installed solar capacity remains low at about six MW (Fig. 4.2).

Table 4.1 Renewable energy resources in Turkey

	Theoretical	Technical	Economic
Hydro	433 TWh	216 TWh	125 TWh
Wind	88 GW	83 GW	10 GW
Geothermal	4.5 GW	2 GW	22 TWh
Solar	102 TWh	102 TWh	1.5 TWh
Biomass	197 TWh		197 TWh

Source Balat (2010) referencing Kumbaroğlu et al. (2004)

Although resources are technically large, only a small percentage of these resources can be expected to be brought online on a commercially viable basis. How much renewable generation can eventually be developed will depend on availability of sustainable policies that (1) provide adequate financial support to most cost disadvantaged technologies; (2) can be maintained long term (regardless of political or economic changes); (3) do not hamper grid reliability; and (4) do not unduly hurt existing fuels and technologies in a way that would translate into higher prices to consumers, negatively impacting economic activity.

2.1 Resources

Natural capacity of most renewable resources is reportedly quite high in Turkey but what is technically harvestable is significantly less and economic potential is even smaller. There are discrepancies (sometimes quite significant) in figures reported in different sources, reflecting the challenges associated with estimating the potential of these resources that have not been previously exploited at any significant scale with the exception of hydro. Differentiating between theoretical capacity and technical or economic capacity requires the incorporation of different technologies' cost structures, state of development, economic incentive structures, and electric market conditions, complicating the analysis. In Table 4.1, estimates reported in Balat (2010) are provided.

Erdem (2010), referencing Evrendilek and Ertekin (2003), concurs with the economic estimates of some resources as provided in Table 4.1: 125 TWh of hydro, 197 TWh of biomass, and 22 TWh of geothermal. But, the economic solar estimate of Erdem (2010) at 102 TWh is much larger than the economic potential but same as technical potential in Table 4.1. In contrast, Kaygusuz (2011) and Tunç (2010) provide significantly larger estimates for economic solar potential at more than 300 TWh. Estimates of Kaygusuz (2011) for theoretical (or natural) and technical solar capacities are even more aggressive at 977,000 TWh and 6,105 TWh, respectively.

Kaygusuz (2011) is less optimistic than others when it comes to geothermal (1.4 TWh). The technical and economic estimates provided in Table 4.1 are inconsistent. Assuming an aggressive capacity factor of 95%, two GW of technical capacity can produce 16.6 TWh ($0.002 \times 8{,}760 \times 0.95$), which is significantly less than 22 TWh provided in Table 4.1. The General Directorate of Mineral Research and Exploration (Maden Tetkik ve Arama, MTA) estimates economic generation potential at one GW, which would generate about 8.3 TWh at 95% capacity factor.[7]

Kaygusuz (2011), and Evrendilek and Ertekin (2003) reported 50 TWh of economic wind capacity, which is higher than the economic generation that can be expected from 10 GW reported in Table 4.1—about 44 TWh even at the relatively high capacity factor of 50% (a more likely estimate would be about 31 TWh at 35% capacity factor). İlkılıç (2012) provides the most optimistic assessment of technical wind potential at 132 GW onshore and 17 GW offshore.

Overall, the estimates for hydro, the resource that is best known probably because it has been developed for decades, are most consistent across different sources. The only different estimate for economic hydro potential is provided by EMO (2011) and Erdoğdu (2011), based on General Directorate of State Hydraulic Works (DSİ, Devlet Su İşleri) figures, at 140 TWh as compared to the consensus figure of 125 TWh. For everything else, there is a wide range of estimates that clearly depend on technological, cost and economic incentive assumptions. The solar estimates show the largest variation across sources. It is advisable to be conservative and treat lowest estimates for each category as most likely.

2.1.1 Hydro

Turkey has been generating significant amounts of electricity from water resources for decades, especially through large dams on Fırat and Ceyhan rivers in the southeast, and on Kızılırmak and Yeşilırmak in the north central and northeast. There are 27 hydroelectric dams in Turkey with a total capacity of almost 11 GW. Three more large facilities of 2.2 GW are under construction. Twenty small facilities of 314 MW are also in operation. There are many more projects of various sizes but mostly smaller facilities in various stages of development.[8] Altogether close to 16 GW of installed capacity is in operation as of the end of 2011.

Six of the large dams accounting for roughly 6.5 GW are on the Fırat river. Most of this capacity was built as part of the Southeast Anatolia Project (GAP, Güneydoğu Anadolu Projesi), which, in the 1970s, identified the Fırat-Dicle Basin as the target of a total of 13 projects for irrigation and power generation to fuel economic development of the region. As part of GAP, 22 dams and 19 associated hydroelectric plants to generate 27 TWh of electricity per year, and irrigation of 1.82 million hectares of land were envisioned.[9]

---

[7] For more information, please visit http://www.mta.gov.tr/v2.0/daire-baskanliklari/enerji/index.php?id=jeotermal_potansiyel (last accessed on November 6, 2011).

[8] The full list of hydro projects can be found at http://www.eie.gov.tr/HES/index.aspx in a searchable database format (last accessed on October 30, 2011).

[9] For more information, please visit http://www.gap.gov.tr/ (last accessed on December 20, 2011).

Still the new record of 52 TWh of hydro generation set in 2010 represents only about 40% of the economic potential of 125 TWh. However, the Renewables Law defined hydro facilities with less than 15 km^2 of reservoir area[10] as eligible for renewable support and license applications for hydro facilities have increased significantly. Since the passage of the Renewables Law in May 2005, 720 HES licenses have been issued by EPDK for roughly 18 GW of power generation capacity.[11] A small percentage of them (159) with 3.7 GW capacity started operating but most of the rest (561) representing close to 14 GW of capacity were under construction as of the end of 2011. Among those that started operations, 71 (about 45%) are facilities with larger than 10 MW nameplate capacity, totaling about 3.3 GW. Similarly, almost half of the facilities under construction (271) are facilities larger than 10 MW of capacity, totaling about 12.4 GW. Another 86 HES applications were under consideration by EPDK; with a total of 888 MW; these are mostly small hydro facilities.[12]

2.1.2 Wind

More optimistic estimates of onshore wind potential are 400 TWh theoretical (natural), 110 TWh technical, and 50 TWh of economic output.[13] These estimates are significantly higher than the generation levels implied by the capacity figures provided in Table 4.1 at 35% capacity factor (270 TWh theoretical and 31 TWh economic). Best locations in Turkey (Fig. 4.3) may reach a capacity factor of 50% at 50 meters but 35% is the capacity factor that can be expected from average quality sites that are more readily available than best locations, especially onshore where it is cheaper to build wind farms and connect them to the grid. There has been a lot more interest in building wind facilities than solar plants so far due to lower cost of wind and more market-ready state of the wind technology.

Since 2002, developers pursued licenses to build wind farms—more than a thousand. In November 2007, 725 applications for more than 70 GW were filed with the Energy Market Regulatory Authority (EPDK, Enerji Piyasası Düzenleme Kurumu). Many of these applications were for the same locations; it was not possible to connect all of these to the grid. According to the Turkish Transmission Company (TEİAŞ, Türkiye Elektrik İletim Anonim Şirketi), the grid could handle

---

[10] This area and the generation capacity that can be built based on this area are larger than 10 MW, which is a common threshold used to define small hydro facilities eligible for renewable support not just in EU (http://www.energy.eu/) but also worldwide (http://www.small-hydro.com/).

[11] All licensing data are made available by EPDK at http://www2.epdk.org.tr/lisans/elektrik/lisansdatabase/verilentesistipi.asp (last accessed December 22, 2011). Most licenses are for 49 years but there are some as short as 30 years.

[12] License applications are made available by EPDK at http://www2.epdk.org.tr/lisans/elektrik/lisansdatabase/uygunuretim.asp (last accessed December 22, 2011).

[13] For example, see Kaygusuz (2011).

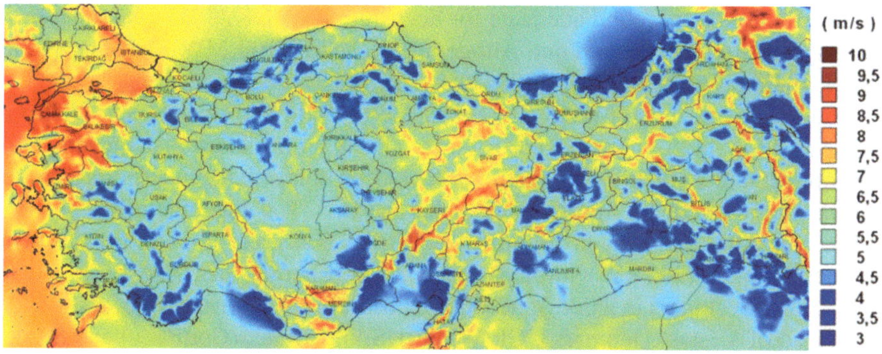

Fig. 4.3 Wind atlas of Turkey at 80 m. *Source* ETKB (2011). Wind potential by city can be obtained at http://www.eie.gov.tr/duyurular/YEK/YEKrepa/REPA-duyuru_01.html

up to seven GW.[14] Moreover, the total installed capacity in Turkey was about 40 GW at the time; together with previously filed applications, a total of 86 GW of wind capacity was in different stages of the licensing process. Clearly, an untenable situation; most of these facilities are never intended to be built but rather applications are made to secure licenses that can be later sold for a profit to legitimate companies committed to build wind farms.

The process is new and has been improving. Nowadays, there are two more steps before EPDK decision on a license. The General Directorate of Electrical Power Resources Survey and Development Administration (EİE, Elektrik İşleri Etüt İdaresi Genel Müdürlüğü) conducts a technical review of the applications. The EİE identifies overlapping applications and evaluates feasibility of proposed facilities. Then, TEİAŞ holds a tender for locations with multiple applications; the highest bidder is granted the license. The bid criterion is the annual 'wind power plant contribution' fee the winner will pay to TEİAŞ as their contribution to system costs for 20 years. The fees ranged from 0.01 to 6.5 kr per kWh with an average of about 1.75 kr/kWh, or roughly one cent per kWh at the market exchange rate of late 2011.

Since the passage of the Renewables Law in May 2005, 184 renewable energy source (RES) licenses have been issued by EPDK for roughly 6.4 GW of power generation capacity.[15] A small percentage of them (20) with 869 MW capacity started operating but most of the rest (129) representing about 4.5 GW of capacity were under construction as of the end of 2011. Another 42 RES applications with a

---

[14] Price Waterhouse Coopers (2009).

[15] All licensing data are made available by EPDK at http://www2.epdk.org.tr/lisans/elektrik/lisansdatabase/verilentesistipi.asp (last accessed December 22, 2011). Most licenses are for 49 years but there are some as short as 20 years.

total of 1.8 GW were found adequate for licensing by EPDK.[16] The overhang from 2007 appears to have cleared out. Altogether, close to 1,700 MW of wind capacity was operational as of the end of 2011.

Wind facilities remain relatively expensive to build and operate, especially in the absence of high enough feed-in tariffs. There is no additional incentive for offshore wind in Turkey. Some facilities have been delayed due to a shortage in the global supply chain for turbines and other parts.[17] The manufacturing of wind turbines or other parts has been limited in Turkey. Enercon of Germany has been producing small (800 kW) turbines since 2005. Enercon has also been selling turbines to developers in Turkey, accounting for more than one-third of the market and ahead of Vestas (Denmark), GE Wind (USA), Nordex (Germany) and Suzlon (India). Enercon and Vestas have accounted for half of the market in 2009 according to Erdem (2010) followed by GE Wind with 20% of the market, Nordex with 16%, and Suzlon with 4%.

With the new incentives for domestic equipment (Table 4.2), more Turkish companies could become interested in the manufacturing of windmill parts as well as other technologies to supply the renewables industry. Already, Soyut Enerji and Model Enerji produce wind turbines and other parts. Soyut Enerji has a line of battery-supported small systems of 1–30 kW for remote applications as well as a line of grid-ready turbines of 50 kW to 1.65 MW. Model Enerji has partnered with Windtec, a subsidiary of American Superconductor, and started production of 1.65-MW turbines.

However, a note of caution is necessary. This strategy of promoting domestic industries is implemented almost universally around the world as more countries join the ranks of manufacturers of parts and equipment from wind blades to solar panels. Some take the form of local content requirements; others consist of subsidies or import tariffs. The Turkish local content approach is in the form of bonus payments for parts manufactured in Turkey; it does not require but encourages the use of locally manufactured parts via bonus payments (Table 4.2). But, it can still deter cheaper, or worse higher quality, parts from coming to Turkey. See more on the renewables-based economic development strategies and relevance for the Turkish renewables policy in Sect. 2.4.

2.1.3 Solar

The estimates for solar potential cover a wide range, especially for theoretical capacity and also for economic capacity, which has a range of 1.5–360 TWh. Solar also offers significant thermal potential at 25 million tons of oil equivalent (mtoe) economic, which is equal to a little less than a quarter of total primary energy

---

[16] License applications are made available by EPDK at http://www2.epdk.org.tr/lisans/elektrik/lisansdatabase/uygunuretim.asp (last accessed December 22, 2011).

[17] Price Waterhouse Coopers (2009).

Table 4.2 Renewable incentives (Euro cent/kWh)

	January 2011	2009 proposal
Renewable tariffs for first 10 years		
Onshore wind	5.6 (EU: 5-30)	8
Offshore wind	na (EU: 5-58)	12
Hydro	5.6 (EU: 4-22)	7
Geothermal	8	9
Solar PV	10.2 (EU: 5-58)	25 (20 for the second 10 years)
Concentrated solar power (CSP)		20 (18 for the second 10 years)
Biomass/Landfill gas	10.2 (EU:3.9-30)	14
Tidal		16
Bonus payments for components manufactured in Turkey		
Wind		
Blades	0.6	0.6
Generator and power electronics	0.8	0.8
Tower	0.5	0.5
All other mechanical components	1	
Hydro		
Turbine	1	1
Generator and power electronics	0.8	0.8
Geothermal		
Steam or gas turbine	1	1
Generator and power electronics	0.53	0.5
Steam injector or gas compressor	0.53	0.5
Solar PV		
PV panel integration	0.6	0.6
Modules	1	1
Module cells	2.7	3
Inverter	0.5	1
Tracking system	0.4	0.4
Solar CST		
Radiation collection tube	1.8	3
Mirrors	0.5	
Tracking System	0.5	0.5
Mechanical components of heat storage	1	1
Mechanical components of heat collection	1.8	2
Stirling engine	1	0.5
Panel integration and mechanical construction	0.46	0.5
Biomass/Landfill gas		
Fluidized bed steam boiler	0.6	0.6
Liquid or gas fueled steam boiler	0.3	0.3
Gasification and gas cleaning components	0.5	0.8
Steam or gas turbine	1.5	1.5
ICE or Stirling engine	0.7	0.7
Generator and power electronics	0.4	0.4
Cogeneration system	0.3	0.3

Source Law No. 6094 for 2011; Price Waterhouse Coopers (2009) for 2009; http://www.energy.eu/ for EU FITs

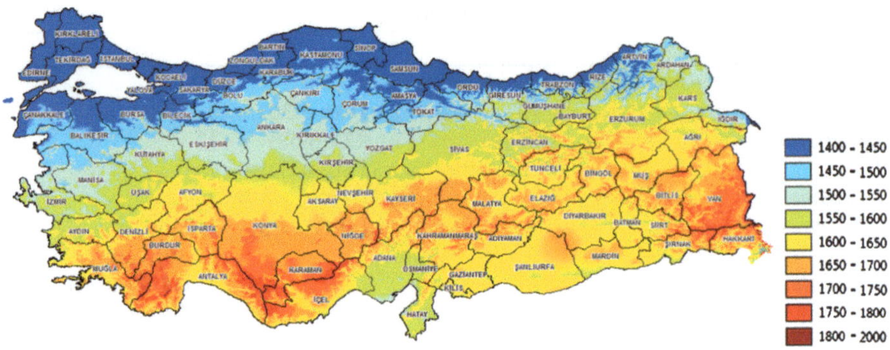

Fig. 4.4 Solar radiation map of Turkey (annual kWh/m^2). *Source* EİE http://www.eie.gov.tr/MyCalculator/Default.aspx (Accessed on December 19, 2011)

consumption in Turkey in 2010 (111 mtoe).[18] Although passive solar has been used in Turkey for decades for water heating especially in the southern coastline (some of the reddest areas in Fig. 4.4), there is no other significant solar power application in the country. Only six MW was installed as of 2010 mostly by public entities such as fire-watch towers in forests, meteorological stations, highway emergency phones, communications towers, and research institutions. There are no licenses provided by EPDK for solar facilities yet. The delay in expansion of solar power is primarily due to high capital (installation) cost and low tariff support. The new feed-in tariffs remain quite low compared to FITs provided by most EU countries (Table 4.2); but with the help of bonus payments for locally produced parts, new Turkish FITs may induce further investment on solar capacity.

Concentrated solar power (CSP) systems require a fairly flat (slope of less than 5°) land area of 10,000–30,000 m^2 per megawatt of electricity produced. This large piece of land should preferably be otherwise not used for economically productive activities (say for agriculture), and not ecologically sensitive. Access to water is also important for steam generation, mirror cleaning, and, in particular, wet cooling at the CSP facilities regardless of whether they are trough or tower designs. Water consumed for wet cooling in CSP facilities is higher than the water used for conventional thermal facilities fueled by coal, natural gas, or uranium; such CSP facilities require more than 750 gallons of water per megawatthour (MWh) generated as compared to 180 gallons by gas-fired and 200 gallons by coal-fired plants.[19] Alternative cooling solutions exist but are either not technologically ready to scale up or too costly. As a result, water is becoming a serious issue for locating CSP facilities, for example, in southwest US where the solar radiation is most attractive. As discussed in Sect. 2.4, Turkey too has occasional severe water shortages, especially in certain locations, which should be considered when siting CSPs.

---

[18] Kaygusuz (2011).

[19] For example, see Table 4.1 in Carter and Campbell (2009).

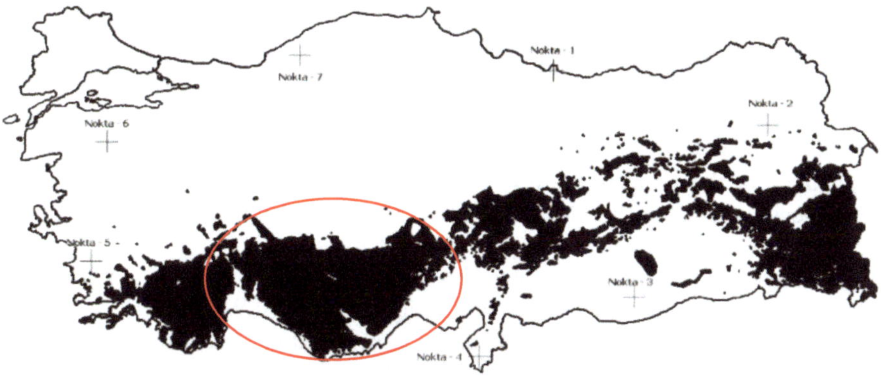

Fig. 4.5 ETKB guidelines on eligible solar regions

Kaygusuz (2011) reports that solar thermal systems are economic only for locations with direct normal irradiance greater than 1,800 kilowatthours (kWh) per m^2 per year. According to the ETKB guidelines published after the January 2011 amendments, only the applications for areas with 1,650 kWh per m^2 per annum or higher will be considered. Note that shaded areas in Fig. 4.5 overlap with those shaded as highest radiation in Fig. 4.4. There are regional limits totaling 600 MW, the nationwide limit set by the 2010 amendment to the Renewables Law (to be installed by the end of 2013). This limit, which was challenged by the potential solar developers, still leaves large areas of Turkey from the Western Mediterranean toward East and Southeast eligible. However, some regions have larger shares. Konya leads with 92 MW, followed by the Van-Ağrı region with 77 MW and Antalya with 58 MW. Overall, the Central Mediterranean region (area circled in Fig. 4.5) dominates with about half of total MW limit for the whole country. In February 2012, ETKB decided to remove these limits; the only requirement is a minimum irradiance of 1,620 kWh per m^2 per annum. Since the map in Fig. 4.5 already captures some of the best areas as indicated in Fig. 4.4 it is not clear that this new decision will lead to increased activity in the solar arena.

According to Kaygusuz (2011), Turkey has more than 240,000 km^2 of wasteland, i.e., unsuitable for agricultural and other uses, that can be used for siting solar facilities. This estimate translates into one-third of the country's overall land area and must be ignoring ecologically, historically, culturally, and archeologically sensitive areas, forests, and other natural resources. Nevertheless, as Kaygusuz (2011) suggests, even if only 1% of this "wasteland" (2,400 km^2) was allocated to solar thermal plants, anywhere from 60 to 120 GW of generation capacity could be built. According to Tunç (2010), the amount of land otherwise not qualified but usable for building solar facilities is about 11,350 km^2, which would indicate close to 550 GW of capacity assuming 20,000 m^2 as average land requirement. According to Tunç (2010) 363 TWh can be generated from these facilities.

At the same time, Tunç (2010) warns about the risk of lack of planning and oversight; as with the wind licensing process where many opportunists applied for licenses for the same location, often the most convenient and easily identified location, there is a risk that productive agricultural lands can be licensed for renewable energy projects. Turkey should not squander valuable farming lands while trying to increase its renewables generation with a licensing process tainted by cronyism and simple mentality of trading licenses. New regulations require applicants for the same location to compete under TEİAŞ supervision, similar to the process applied to wind developers.[20] If the land owner applies for a solar license, no other developer can apply for that location.[21]

Although the potential solar amounts are larger than total installed generation capacity in the country at the time of writing (about 50 GW in 2011), only 15–30 GW of the potential (60–120 GW) can be considered dispatchable because intermittent nature of solar allows a capacity factor of about 25%. More importantly, each MW of these facilities cost significantly more than other technologies, which makes financing a challenge (see discussion below on costs). Also of importance is the location of these appropriate sites relative to the grid; the need to build additional transmission lines increases the cost of electricity from these plants to end users.

According to Tunç (2010) the cost of solar energy in Turkey should be at least 15 cents per kWh for CSP and closer to 20 cents for photovoltaic (PV) systems. However, it is worth noting that the financial viability of projects under these prices depends on how projects are financed (debt-equity ratios, return expectations), the terms of power purchase agreements, or PPAs, versus sale to market, and availability of incentives (investment credits, tax credits, renewable energy credits, local content bonuses). The solar PV FITs provided by Italy and Spain, two countries in the same solar radiation band as Turkey, are greater than 30 €cent (36–44 in Italy and 32–34 in Spain). In fact, most countries in the EU offer a FIT greater than 27 €cent except for Estonia (5.1) and Hungary (9.7).[22]

Nevertheless, costs for both PV and CSP technologies have been coming down, more so for PV than CSP, partially thanks to Chinese government subsidies to the PV manufacturing sector. Even in the US some expect that the levelized cost of electricity from utility-scale CSP can decline to as low as 10–12 cents per kWh within this decade. Still, grid integration of intermittent resources remains as a challenge. With electricity storage, both solar and wind can overcome their intermittency problem but there are numerous storage technologies with different capacity ranges and discharge times, only some of which can help with large-scale storage necessary for wind and power support (e.g., pumped storage or compressed air energy storage, or CAES).[23] Overall, though, technologies remain expensive and small scale.

---

[20] The specifics of this tender process have not been published in regulations at the time of writing; but they will likely be similar to those of the wind tender.

[21] Boden and Gümüş 2011.

[22] Energy prices and tariffs can be found at http://www.energy.eu/.

[23] For example, see the comparison of different technologies at http://www.eia.gov/todayinenergy/detail.cfm?id=4310 (last accessed on December 28, 2011).

A new approach, hybrid systems of wind-solar, gas-solar, or gas-wind-solar, offers hope; storage can be added to any of these systems. Turkey is at the forefront of testing these integrated systems; in mid-2011, MetCap Energy Investments, a Turkish company, agreed with GE to build the first of its kind integrated renewable combined cycle (IRCC) plant, combining gas, solar and wind.[24] The 530-MW plant will be using gas turbines supplemented by 50 MW of solar-generated steam and 22 MW of wind turbines, and is expected to achieve 69% efficiency for gas burn at the proposed location in Turkey, much higher than any other generation facility in common use today. Such a plant may require flexibility in gas supply; due to variable availability of wind or solar, gas units may have to ramp down or up depending on the time of the day and season, and plant's dispatch obligations (e.g., based on day-ahead submissions to the grid operator). The natural gas market should be liquid enough to provide such flexibility and operators should be financially ready to manage variability in revenues.

2.1.4 Geothermal

Turkey has rich geothermal resources with 276 geothermal occurrences. Based on MTA data, Başel et al. (2010) report that at least one well was drilled in 110 fields with surface temperatures ranging from 22.5 to 220°C. Total identified thermal capacity is about 4,500 MWt (based on a reference temperature of 20°C). Accordingly, about three quarters of these fields have a capacity less than five MWt. Başel et al. (2010) evaluated 55 fields, out of which 17 fields with high temperatures (over 100°C) were found suitable for electric power generation with a capacity to generate 710–1,032 MW of energy and 20,313–32,246 MW of heat.

Note that the generation potential from the suitable fields is estimated at a maximum 1,032 MW, or roughly one GW as compared to two GW reported in Table 4.1 as technical potential. Even if all of 1,032 MW of capacity was installed and used to generate electricity, at most eight TWh would be produced at about 90% capacity factor. Although not insignificant, this amount represents only a small portion of 210 TWh consumed in 2010. As the consumption continues to rise, eight TWh will become less significant. Still, this could save about 1.5 bcm of gas imports, worth $400–600 million depending on the oil price since almost all gas import contracts are tied to the price of oil. In addition, geothermal facilities are expected to supply heat to about 500,000 residences, 7,500 acres of greenhouse farming and about 400 thermal spas. Altogether, it is estimated that 6–7 billion dollars of value can be generated for the Turkish economy.

Since 2005 when installed capacity was only 20 MW (same since the early 1990s), Turkey has been following a strategy to develop its geothermal resources as quickly as possible to fuel local economies especially in greenhouse farming

---

[24] For example, see http://www.bloomberg.com/news/2011-06-07/ge-chosen-by-metcap-for-combined-cycle-power-plant-s-technology.html (last accessed on October 2, 2011).

and tourism in addition to power generation. MTA auctioned geothermal fields for 30 years with the option of 10-year extensions. As of the end of 2011, 18 geothermal facilities had an electricity production license from EPDK. Seven stations with an installed capacity of 114 MW are in operation and 11 facilities with an installed capacity of 315 MW were under construction.[25] The official target is 600 MW by 2023 although EİE forecasted 550 MW by 2013 in some reports. When the facilities under construction are finished, total installed capacity will be close to 430 MW. Given that geothermal facilities take several years to come online fully, the EİE estimate seems slightly optimistic; but the 2023 target is certainly within reach and can be surpassed. With the near quintupling of installed capacity since 2005, the industry has been gaining experience in project development and reservoir management, which may lead to faster development moving forward.

2.1.5 Biomass and Biofuels

Biomass from landfill gas and agricultural waste can be used for power generation but it is one of the most expensive options. The cost is location and source specific but it ranges from 12 to 26 cents per kWh (see Fig. 4.6 and associated discussion in the next section); the tariff support for biomass is only about 13 cents per kWh (Table 4.2). The potential for biomass is probably the most limited in Turkey. As of the end of 2011, there are 21 facilities with a production license and six more facilities with autoproducer licenses. Total capacity of these facilities is 146 MW, 88 MW of which was under operation and 58 MW was under construction at the time of writing.[26] There was one application for a six-MW facility found appropriate by EPDK in mid-2011 but not licensed by the end of 2011.[27]

Although most of the renewables discussion so far focused on power generation, biofuels can have a significant role in the transportation sector. There are reportedly three ethanol plants (using sugar cane as feedstock) with about 150 million liters of capacity but production has been much less at 40 million liters in 2010. According to Balat (2010), 28 million hectares of land is cultivable in Turkey but only 4–5% of it is used for growing biofuels crops. Installed biodiesel production capacity of 1.5 million tons per annum is the second largest in Europe after Germany but production is low (60,000 tons). If Turkey follows EU policies

---

[25] All licensing data are made available by EPDK at http://www2.epdk.org.tr/lisans/elektrik/lisansdatabase/verilentesistipi.asp (last accessed December 22, 2011). Most licenses are for 29 years but there are some licenses as long as 45 years.

[26] All licensing data are made available by EPDK at http://www2.epdk.org.tr/lisans/elektrik/lisansdatabase/verilentesistipi.asp (last accessed December 22, 2011). License durations are most variable for biomass facilities; there are some for 49 years but others are for 10, 15, 20, 23, 24 or 30 years.

[27] License applications are made available by EPDK at http://www2.epdk.org.tr/lisans/elektrik/lisansdatabase/uygunuretim.asp (last accessed December 22, 2011).

of 5–6% blending with diesel, 851,000 tons of biodiesel will be needed. Recycling of used cooking oil can be sufficient to meet this requirement. Mandates to use ethanol and biodiesel have been recently introduced: 2% in 2013 and 3% in 2014 for ethanol and 1% in 2013, 2% in 2014, and 3% in 2015 for biodiesel.

2.2 Legal and Regulatory Framework for Renewables

Turkey did not establish any particular policy for promoting renewables until the early 2000s. The law that restructured the electricity market passed in 2001 although private sector participation in generation started in the 1980s via build-operate-transfer (BOT) and build-operate (BO) models. Most of these projects focused on natural gas, which was becoming increasingly available via multiple pipelines and as liquefied natural gas, or LNG. The country needed cost-competitive, large-scale, reliable base load generation to fuel its growing economy. As such, renewables other than large hydro did not attract much attention. State-owned DSİ has built and operated large hydro facilities for decades. Since the market restructuring, EÜAŞ has been operating existing hydroelectric facilities and generation units of any new dams DSİ builds. Private companies interested in building hydro facilities have to obtain the right to use the water from DSİ, which collects the per kWh fee bid in the auction by the winners once they develop their facility and start generating. DSİ also supervises feasibility and construction of these facilities. In addition to hydro, passive solar has been widely used in the southern coastline since the 1980s for water heating purposes primarily and a small amount of geothermal potential has been used primarily for heating purposes (greenhouses, district heating and thermal spas).

2.2.1 Chronology of Renewables Support in Turkey

In the early 2000s, Turkey started developing support mechanisms for renewables. This trend was at least partially fueled by the country's enhanced focus on joining the EU, which had, and still has much more aggressive goals for increasing the share of renewables. Later in the decade, supply scares resulting from Russia cutting natural gas to Ukraine and rising oil prices also contributed to the policy of diversification of energy sources. There have been a series of important laws, regulations, and related programs since 2001 (Fig. 4.6).

In 2001, the Electricity Market Law No. 4628 (EML) was adopted which aimed at restructuring the Turkish electricity market, unbundling generation, transmission and distribution activities, privatizing some of the state assets, and introducing retail competition (see discussion in Chap. 2). Although the Law tasked EPDK with encouraging renewables it did not provide a clear definition of technologies or resources that counted as "renewable generation" and did not assign any particular incentives.

Year	Hydro	Wind	Solar	Geothermal	
2001	11,673	19	0.6	20.4	Electricity Market Law No. 4628 – EPDK to encourage renewables;
2002	12,241	19	0.9	20.4	
2003	12,579	20	1.3	20.4	Amendment of Electricity Market Licensing Regulation: updated definition of renewable s; licensing fee 1% of regular; exemption from annual license fee first 8 years; grid connection priority.
2004	12,645	20	1.8	20.4	Strategy Paper by the High Planning Council: liberalization roadmap with the responsibility of promoting renewables
2005	12,906	20	2.3	20.4	**Law on Utilization of Renewable Energy Resources for Electricity Production No. 5346** (FIT of €cent 5-5.5/kWh if younger than 10 years; can sell at market prices or via bilateral contracts; retail providers' obligation to procure renewables at least equal to their market share in previous year; 85% reduction in fees related to land use)
2006	13,063	76	2.8	27.8	Amendment to Environment Law No. 2872: allow carbon trading, obligatory standards, tax credits, exemptions from various fees and emission penalties to promote renewable and clean energy technologies.
2007	13,395	225	3.3	27.8	• Geothermal Resources and Mineral Waters Law No. 5686 • Energy Efficiency Law No. 5627 • Amendment to EML: exemption from licensing & company establishment requirements if less than 500 kW • Feed-in-tariff implementation
2008	13,829	512	4.0	34.6	• State as a last resort to build capacity • Penalties for non-compliance with construction plans • TEİAŞ to launch tenders for wind applications for the same grid.
2009	14,553	984	5.0	81.6	
2010	15,525	1512	6.0	81.6	Law No. 6094 – Amendments to the Renewables Law.
2011	15,776	1,600		114	Renewable Energy Support Mechanism: feed-in-tariffs and "made in Turkey" premiums

Fig. 4.6 Legal and regulatory timeline for renewables. *Sources* BP (2011) for wind, solar and geothermal (2001–2010); TETAŞ (2011) for hydro (2001–2010). 2011 data is from EPDK (http://www2.epdk.org.tr/lisans/elektrik/lisansdatabase/verilentesistipi.asp)

The definition of renewables was introduced in the Electricity Market Licensing Regulation but revised in 2003, 2005, and 2011. The final definition included wind, solar, geothermal, biomass, biogas (municipal waste included), wave, tidal, pumped storage, run-of-the-river hydro, and hydroelectric dams with a reservoir area of less than 15 km^2.

Some incentives were provided in 2003 in an amendment to the Electricity Market Licensing Regulation. The initial licensing fee for renewable facilities was reduced to 1% of the regular fee applied to conventional generation facilities; renewable facilities were exempted from annual renewal fees for the first eight years of their operation. Grid connection priority was to be given to developers using domestic natural and renewable resources. Retail providers had to purchase renewable generation to serve non-eligible customers as long as there was no cheaper alternative.

The 2004 Strategy Paper by the High Planning Council laid down the liberalization roadmap, assigning the responsibility of promoting renewables to the State Planning Organization (DPT, Devlet Planlama Teşkilâtı) and the Ministry of Energy and Mineral Resources (ETKB, Enerji ve Tabii Kaynaklar Bakanlığı).

A significant milestone was reached in 2005 with the passage of the Law on Utilization of Renewable Energy Resources for Electricity Production No. 5346 (also known as the Renewables Law). The law was mostly in line with similar legislation in EU countries, introducing feed-in-tariffs (FITs) and obligation to purchase by load serving entities (retail providers serving eligible customers and distribution companies with captive customers). FITs were set fairly low at €cent 5-5.5 per kWh and were to be implemented starting in 2007 for facilities younger than 10 years. To qualify, companies needed to obtain a renewable generation license and Renewable Energy Source, or RES, certificate from EPDK. Renewable generators, could, however, sell in the spot market or via bilateral contracts at higher rates. Load serving entities had to purchase renewable generation equivalent to their share in the market in the previous year. Renewable facilities were also granted many exemptions from land use fees and 85% discount in state lands for the first 10 years of operation—the Ministry of Environment and Forestry and the Ministry of Finance govern the access to state properties. Renewable facilities are also exempt from reserve capacity requirements that apply to all generation facilities greater than 50 MW based on the Electricity Market Ancillary Services Protocols. In 2007, amendments of the EML exempted facilities smaller than 500 kW from licensing altogether. Although these entities could only generate to meet own needs, they could transfer any excess generation to local distribution license holders at the national tariff.

Between 2006 and 2008, there were several laws that could also help promote renewable (or green/clean) technologies. In 2006 the Environment Law No. 2872 was amended to allow carbon trading, obligatory standards, tax credits, exemptions from various fees and emission penalties to promote renewable and clean energy technologies. In 2007, Geothermal Resources and Mineral Waters Law No. 5686 was passed to regulate exploration, development, ownership rights and economic use of geothermal resources. In 2007, the Energy Efficiency Law

No. 5627 was passed. The provisions of the law has been put into implementation fairly quickly; as in many other countries, energy efficiency investments in Turkey are seen as low-hanging fruits in terms of conserving energy and reducing negative environmental impacts of energy production, delivery, and consumption. The implementation of the energy efficiency programs are discussed in further detail in Sect. 3.

In 2008, the EML was amended in important ways. For example, a capacity market was proposed; and the state was declared as the last resort for building additional generation capacity in response to resource adequacy concerns. Given their intermittent nature, renewables may not benefit from the capacity market as much as thermal facilities that can offer time-independent firm capacity. Still, to the extent generation forecasting can be improved in accuracy and generation is peak coincident or at least partially load-following, renewables can collect additional revenues from the capacity market. No capacity market has been established at the time of writing, but TEİAŞ is empowered to procure new generation capacity or rent existing generation capacity via ancillary services.

Mainly in response to multiple license applications for the same wind farm locations in 2007, stricter penalties were introduced for noncompliance with facility construction schedules after receiving license. These penalties included nullification of the license and cashing in of guarantee bonds by EPDK.[28] In addition, TEİAŞ was tasked with launching tenders for further competition among the parties who applied for the same wind farm locations.

The 2009 update of the Electricity Market Strategy Paper introduced the 30-percent target for renewables (including large-scale hydro) by 2023, the hundredth anniversary of the Republic of Turkey. Given that renewables accounted for almost 27% of total generation in 2010, the 30-percent target is not ambitious but rather realistic. It can basically be met by increasing large-scale hydro generation, which accounted for close to 25 out of 27% of total renewables share in 2010. It is worth noting, however, that the share of renewables was less than 20% during 2007–2009. While the hydro generation capacity is installed, its availability has been subject to water levels in the dams, water need for irrigation purposes and, perhaps most importantly, priority dispatching of thermal units (especially gas-fired BOT or BOO plants with take-or-pay PPAs). With electricity demand rapidly increasing in the country, hydro facilities will likely be called upon more than in recent years.

The most ambitious vision of the Strategy Paper is the 20-GW target for installed wind capacity. As of the end of 2011, close to 1,700 MW of wind capacity was installed in Turkey; more than 12-fold increase by 2023 is a tall order in terms of investment requirements as well as system integration challenges. If 20 GW of wind capacity is installed by 2023, the generation from these wind farms can be expected to be around 60 TWh assuming an average capacity factor of 35%; but wind generation would still account for 10–15% of projected consumption in 2023. Significantly higher levels of wind generation may displace hydro generation rather

[28] An extension can be granted in force majeure situations.

than thermal plants since coal plants perform better when run as base load; most gas plants have long-term PPAs; and gas supply contract terms and constraints in gas storage systems may not allow for flexible use of the fuel to cycle. If hydro is displaced by wind, total share of renewables would be undermined.

Also in 2009 new feed-in-tariffs (FITs) and domestic production premiums were proposed but not approved after some debate. Instead, a newer version of these FITs and premiums were passed by the parliament in late December 2010 as Law No. 6094 amending the Renewables Law of 2005. These tariffs are applicable to facilities that started operation after May 18, 2005 or will start operating by December 31, 2015; and they are valid for the first 10 years of operation for each facility.[29] Local content premiums are valid for five years.[30] The new law also expanded the requirement to purchase renewables from load serving entities to all suppliers, including generators and wholesalers.

The two versions of renewables incentives are compared in Table 4.2; FITs approved in 2010 are in general much lower than those proposed in 2009, especially for solar and wind. There are no separate FITs for offshore wind and CSP. Local content premiums are either the same as or lower than those proposed in 2009. Turkish FITs are consistently at the lower end of the range of FITs seen in the EU countries. There are only a few countries that offer lower FITs than Turkey. Many countries (11) do not offer FITs for solar but among those who offer a solar PV FIT (16), only Estonia and Hungary offer a lower FIT than Turkey; the next lowest FIT is 27 €cent/kWh as compared to 10.2 €cent/kWh in Turkey. Given the difficulties faced by some of the highest FIT countries such as Spain, Germany, and Italy since the financial crisis of 2008, Turkish FITs may be more reasonable at least from the perspective of long-term sustainability. The subjugation of renewables incentives to political changes is one of the biggest risks faced by investors in these technologies worldwide. Although perpetual support of technologies that can never survive in a competitive environment is not warranted, a predictable incentive structure for a reasonable period until full commercialization is often necessary.

Although FITs do not seem to be high enough to encourage large-scale investment in renewables, especially solar, offshore wind, and biomass, there are other electricity market conditions that can help renewables. For example, one concern for investors, especially international ones, is the ability to collect payments in a timely and secure manner. The fact that settlements for the Market Financial Settlement Center (Piyasa Mali Uzlaştırma Merkezi, PMUM) will be executed via the banks holding collateral from both public and private market participants commensurate with their default risk offers a certain level of comfort.

A pool managed by PMUM will collect FITs from energy suppliers, obligated to buy renewable generation, and redistribute to RES producers. RES producers do not carry any real-time market risk in the case of a mismatch between their predicted

---

[29] Boden and Gümüş (2011).

[30] Boden Law Office (2011b).

generation and real-time generation. The National Load Dispatch Center provides the day-ahead supply predictions for renewable sources to PMUM to be sold at the market price; any discrepancies are handled via ancillary services. This mechanism started operating along with the day-ahead market on December 1, 2011.

All renewables generators have the freedom to sell directly to eligible customers (large users) via bilateral contracts. This creates an opportunity for signing long-term contracts that would instill confidence in lenders in terms of revenue generation; revenues based on these bilateral contracts will be more predictable than revenues subject to volatility in the spot market. In particular, the distribution companies could help increase contract volumes.

Despite low FITs, there has been international interest in renewable projects in Turkey. The support from international finance institutions such as the German Development Bank (KfW Bankengruppe), World Bank (WB), International Bank of Restructuring and Development (IBRD), Council of Europe Development Bank (CEDB), Agence Française de Développement (AFD), and Japan Bank for International Cooperation and International Finance Corporation (JBIC) has been encouraging for domestic lenders as well. Although the interest has been present despite financial crises since 2008, most recent difficulties in Europe, which led to cancelation of many support programs for renewables in countries such as Germany and Spain, will likely curtail international lending for renewables projects in Turkey as well.

For the implementing regulation, approved in June 2011, there are certain requirements in order to qualify for the local content bonus payment. First, the supplier of locally manufactured eligible parts has to produce a Manufacture Status Document showing that the part or the equipment is manufactured in Turkey. This document has to be prepared by a certified public accountant and certified by the Chamber of Commerce (or Industry), to which the manufacturer belongs. This document is valid for five years from the date of issue. Second, a Manufacture Certificate showing compatibility with the international or national standards is required. The certificate must be prepared by an internationally accredited agency.[31] In order to benefit from bonus payments, the developer of the renewable facility is responsible for collecting these documents from parts and equipment suppliers and submitting them to ETKB or an agent of ETKB. Upon acceptance of the documents, EPDK will be informed of the bonus tariff that can be paid to the developer.

Also approved in June 2011 were regulations governing solar facilities and standards for parts and equipment, which directly relates to the bonus payments. EİE will be responsible for supervising solar generation facilities, collecting data related to their operations, including total annual generation. EİE has the right to inspect facilities to confirm the validity of the data submitted. EİE will also inform PMUM of the amount of electricity generated from solar energy for each invoice term.[32] The 2010 amendment to the Renewables Law (Law No. 6094)

[31] Boden Law Office (2011b).

[32] Boden Law Office (2011b).

limits the solar capacity that can be installed and connected to the grid by the end of 2013 to 600 MW. Given that there was only six MW of solar capacity at the end of 2010, this restriction should not be a major handicap. The limit is presumably to prevent an increase in electricity prices due to high FIT on solar and to avoid an onrush of license applications similar to what was experienced with wind in 2007.

More surprising is the designation of the Council of Ministers as the entity that will determine the future limits on solar capacity rather than expert entities such as TEİAŞ, EİE, or EPDK.[33]

2.3 Technologies, Costs, and Implications

The biggest challenges faced by most renewable technologies in Turkey are the same as elsewhere: the higher cost per unit of electricity generated, intermittency of generation, grid integration challenges due to frequency control, accuracy of load forecasting and other factors, and small scale of individual units. As the discussion in previous section shows, most developers were expecting higher FITs to overcome the cost hurdle.

The cost of generation from any type of facility using any type of resource depends on multiple factors including availability and cost of the resource, location of the facility, cost of parts and equipment, acquisition of rights of way, front end engineering and design, labor costs, and various fees associated with licensing. As such, there will be variations across jurisdictions but it is still useful to get a general sense of how the cost of electricity ranks across different generation options.

The costs for most generation technologies have increased in recent years. These upward trends are particularly significant for coal and nuclear facilities but also observed for gas and even wind construction. The increase in costs is primarily caused by the general inflation in global markets for raw materials and other major inputs, especially steel, for large capital-intensive projects caused by demand from rapidly emerging economies of the world. There are, however, increasing costs associated with tougher requirements for siting facilities, extended regulatory approval processes, and increased safety standards especially for nuclear facilities.

In Fig. 4.7, cost estimates from three different sources are provided: (1) *The Cost of Generating Electricity* prepared by PB Power for the Royal Academy of Engineering in March 2004. The study considers capital, operating, and fuel

[33] Also, the Turkish government challenged the independence of regulators such as EPDK by subjecting them to audits by the relevant ministry (by issuing the decree having the force of law No. 649 in August 2011). Independent energy regulators have been promoted as the linchpin of success for restructuring energy markets as they would insulate the market against the capriciousness of politicians. In reality, their independence has always been challenged by politicians all over the world since energy, especially electricity, remains a 'political' commodity. The Turkish government seems to be explicit about this oversight but this action still raises concerns about the future of the Turkish electricity market.

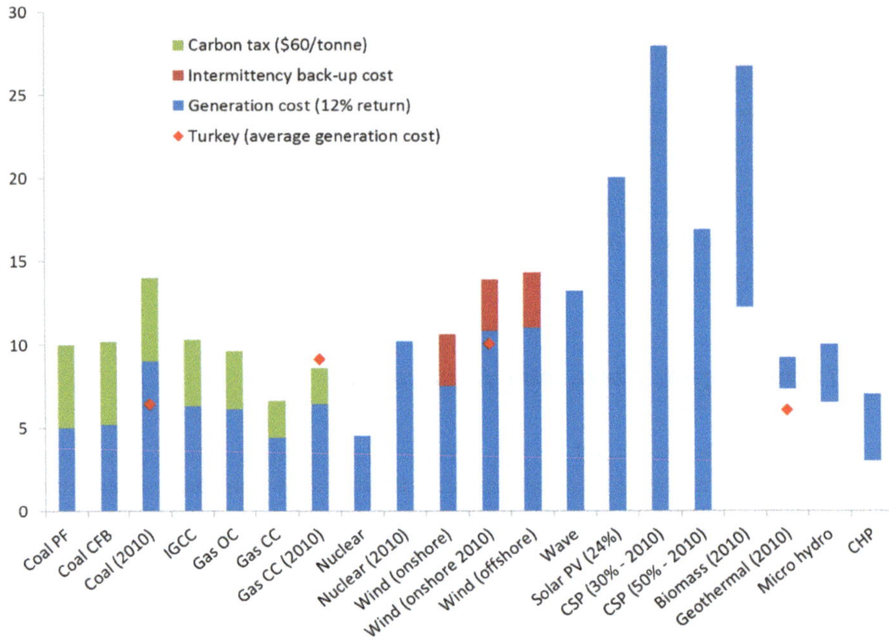

Fig. 4.7 Cost estimates for different generation options (cents per kWh). *PF* pulverized fuel, *CFB* circulating fluidized bed, *IGCC* integrated gasification combined cycle, *OC* open cycle, *CC* combined cycle, *PV* photovoltaic, *CSP* concentrated solar power, *CHP* combined heat and power

expenses for 20–40 years of operation depending on the plant type and assuming a discount rate of 7.5%; (2) *Projected Costs of Generating Electricity* prepared by the International Energy Agency (IEA) and Nuclear Energy Agency (NEA) in 2005. This report is based on actual cost data from more than 130 power plants built in IEA member countries, including 27 coal, 23 natural gas, 13 nuclear, 19 wind, 6 solar, and 24 combined heat and power (CHP) facilities. The study considers capital, operating, and fuel expenses for 30–40 years of operation depending on the plant type and assumes a discount rate of 10%; (3) Modeling done by the Center for Energy Economics, Bureau of Economic Geology, University of Texas at Austin, based on the capital and operating cost data provided by the US Energy Information Administration in November 2010[34] for 25–30 years of operation depending on the plant type and assuming a discount rate of 10%. Plants are equally financed via debt and equity; no tax credits, investment grants, or other incentive program revenues are considered. Prices are calculated to yield a 12% return on the investment.

All 2010 estimates provided in Fig. 4.7 are from the Center for Energy Economics. Only the estimates for solar, micro hydro, and CHP are taken from the

[34] US Energy Information Administration (2010).

IEA–NEA report; all else are from the study by PB Power because all the estimates by PB Power (excluding carbon tax) fall in the range of estimates provided in the report by IEA and NEA: 3.5–6 cents/kWh for coal; 4–6.3 cent/kWh for natural gas plants assuming a gas price of 3.5–4.5 $/MMBtu; 3–5 cents/kWh for nuclear; and 4.5–14 cents/kWh for wind.

Note that the wind cost has the widest range. There are locations where wind will be competitive with coal and nuclear facilities and even cheaper at locations where it can be produced for as low as 4.5 cents per kWh according to the report by the IEA and NEA. Since wind is intermittent, the system operator will have to secure back-up generation through ancillary services.[35] The cost of securing these back-up services can undermine wind's competitiveness but a carbon tax of $60 per tonne would compensate for these costs (Fig. 4.7).

Biomass has a wide range from 12 to 26 cents per kWh but overall it is one of the most expensive options. Micro hydro and CHP are relatively inexpensive with costs ranging from 6.5 to 10 cents per kWh for hydro and 3 to 7 cents per kWh for CHP. CHP offers the additional benefit of increased efficiency in terms of capturing more of the heat content of fuels used. Solar remains expensive, especially concentrated solar power, or CSP.

2.3.1 Generation Costs in Turkey

Using the data provided in Erdoğdu (2011)[36] for economic life, capacity utilization, efficiency, fuel cost, and total capital cost, prices were calculated to reflect at least some of the conditions in Turkey. Natural gas plants are most sensitive to fuel cost because Turkey imports almost all of its natural gas via oil-indexed pricing. As such, in 2008, natural gas price supplied to electricity generators reached $14 per million Btus (IEA 2010b). If that was the prevailing price level for the lifetime of a plant, a gas-fired generator would need at least 11 cents per kWh to earn a 12% return. Luckily, oil prices did not stay at the level of 2008 peak. Still, even at the more common $8–10 per million Btus, gas generators in Turkey require more than 8 cents per kWh, which is higher than the representative cost in Fig. 4.7. The higher cost in Turkey is a result of rising oil prices and tying gas prices to oil prices. Turkey should move away from such contracts as global supplies of natural gas via LNG have been becoming increasingly competitive. Turkey imported spot LNG cargoes in 2010 at much lower prices (see discussion in Chap. 3).

Coal plant capital costs provided in Erdoğdu (2011) are significantly lower than the most recent figures from the EIA. For example, using $1,443 per kW provided for an imported coal plant, $2.7 per million Btus fuel cost (based on fuel heat content provided), a coal-fired plant would only need 6.2 cents per kWh to make a 12% return. However, carbon cost would push this up to 11–12 cents range.

[35] Back-up needs are discussed further later in this section.

[36] Table 6 on page 693.

Although a lignite-fired plant costs more to build ($1,820 per kW) and is less efficient (34 vs. 41%), fuel is much cheaper: domestically produced lignite at $1.9 per million Btus (despite much lower heat content). Accordingly, the price necessary to earn a 12-percent return is not much different at 6.6 cents per kWh.

Although the capital cost of wind at $1,400 is significantly less than the estimates of the EIA ($2,500), since Erdoğdu (2011) assumes only 25% capacity utilization, the price the wind developer needs for a 12-percent return is still more than 10 cents per kWh.

Clearly, much more detailed calculations are necessary for any type of facility that will be built in Turkey based on the specific data associated with the particular site, technology, fuel supply terms, and regulations. But, the cost comparisons depicted in Fig. 4.7 appear to be generally valid for Turkey with the exception of gas plants that generate electricity more expensively than a representative plant due to higher cost of oil-indexed gas imports.

2.3.2 System Impacts

It is often misleading to look at the cost of electricity generated by a particular technology in isolation from system impacts. These system benefits and costs are not taken into account in typical levelized cost of electricity (LCOE) calculations. In Fig. 4.7, only the intermittency back-up costs for wind are shown. Accordingly, the LCOE is a useful first screen to evaluate our generation options but can be misleading in the absence of full system impacts.

Some of the challenges with integrating intermittent resources such as wind into large grids that cannot be captured in a straightforward cost comparison include the need to build new transmission lines, frequency control, ability to forecast wind generation accurately for system reliability, and impact on dispatch order and hence market efficiency. For example, wind dispatching has been causing negative prices in West Texas, where the largest concentration of wind farms exists, as wind generators bid negative prices in order to get dispatched and collect their production tax credits and revenues from the sale of renewable energy certificates (RECs). These artificially lowered prices weaken the signal to developers to add sufficient capacity in a timely manner risking resource adequacy. Texas decided to spend about $6 billion to build new transmission lines to the new wind facilities; and the system operator has been developing new protocols to manage frequency fluctuations due to wind generation variability, to improve wind forecasting accuracy, and to secure enough back-up generation. As in Texas, often wind, solar, and geothermal resources are not near load centers; their development necessitates additional investment in transmission lines. In most systems, the cost of transmission expansion is socialized. In Turkey, too, TEİAŞ is responsible for building new lines but in practice developers may end up paying for some of the interconnecting lines. They recover this investment over 10 years as a reduction in their system usage fees. Bülbül (2011) demonstrates that similar problems are likely to occur in the northern Aegean and Marmara Sea regions, where many wind farms are coming online or are under construction; these regions have some of the best wind resources in Turkey as demonstrated in the wind atlas of the country (Fig. 4.3) but do not have the transmission capacity and grid management protocols in place to accommodate all the wind.

Utilities worldwide followed the strategy of integrated resource planning, or IRP, for years because generation units do not operate independently of other units. For example, using a combined cycle unit at higher capacity factor would imply savings in fuel and emissions from less efficient units replaced by it. Utilities and system operators (not to mention regulators) also value resource adequacy because it helps to avoid brownouts or, worse, blackouts; hence they care about ramping capability and life of the resource option. Since wind does not blow and the sun does not shine all the time, wind and solar facilities' electricity generation fluctuates throughout the day and sometimes unpredictably. In most jurisdictions, the outputs of these facilities are mandated to be dispatched. As such, they need back-up. When they come online, other facilities have to ramp down to accommodate the intermittent output; and when their output is reduced, other facilities have to ramp up. Facilities that are most able to "cycle" (i.e., ramp up and down in short notice) and provide this back-up service are simple or open cycle units and also combined cycle plants. Simple cycle units that burn natural gas or oil are least efficient and emit more pollutants per kWh generated. In some locations (e.g., Texas and Colorado) even coal units are cycled to accommodate wind, with higher emission rates during ramp-ups.

Turkey is planning to add 5–10 GW of nuclear capacity within the next 10 years (see Sect. 4). Nuclear units are not designed to provide cycling back-up for renewables. As such, a future vision of significantly increased nuclear and renewables may be difficult to manage without gas-fired units (simple or combined cycle) and possibly some coal units providing cycling support to intermittent renewables. Increased cycling undermines the economics of these plants unless they have PPAs in place that guarantee take-or-pay clauses. These clauses, however, will increase the overall cost to the system. On the other hand, Turkey may be able to use its large hydro generation capacity to match the fluctuations in renewables although this might mean suboptimal use of hydro capacity.

Overall, system impacts of wind and solar are likely to add to the cost of electricity to be supplied from these facilities. Most of these costs are socialized in most jurisdictions, hence the society should be aware of them. The emission reduction and energy security benefits may be high enough to justify these additional costs but the accounting of these costs and benefits have to be done transparently and accurately.

2.4 Assessment of Renewable Energy Developments in Turkey

Although a latecomer to the world of supporting renewables with formal mandates and incentives, Turkey has been making rapid progress, especially in wind and hydro. As discussed in detail in the previous section, wind but particularly solar and biomass face cost challenges but the higher cost of natural gas in Turkey (due to oil-indexed pricing of gas imports) may help although, as discussed in Chapter 4, Turkey should wean itself of the oil indexing of gas prices, which has been costing the country in foreign exchange outflows unnecessarily. The bigger hurdles to overcome will likely be associated with system integration in terms of building new transmission lines and managing intermittency. Since these issues were discussed in sufficient detail in the previous section, we will focus on some other risk considerations in this section.

2.4.1 Challenges Facing Hydro

The country has always generated large amounts of electricity from large hydro facilities but there is more potential in the country and an increasing focus on smaller facilities with many facilities under construction. Altogether, hydro has the potential to supply Turkey's goal of generating 30% of its electricity from renewables without the help of wind, solar or geothermal.

However, the expansion of hydroelectric capacity is facing some challenges. First, Turkey faces water problems, with occasional water shortages in large cities such as İstanbul and Ankara and water level reduction in lakes, rivers, and underground reservoirs. Changing rainfall patterns, likely due to climate change, increases uncertainty about availability of water for different uses. More than 70% of water is used in irrigation of agricultural fields in a very inefficient manner in arid locations to raise water-hungry crops such as cotton and sugar beet.[37] There are efforts to improve water use efficiency. For example, the World Wildlife Fund and ETİ, a manufacturer of foodstuff, started training farmers in Konya in drip-irrigation techniques to reduce water consumption by up to 50%.[38]

Second, there is increasing local opposition to hydro facilities, especially small facilities, for several reasons as voiced by the protesters and environmental and professional groups that observe these developments: forced migration and flooding of historical, cultural and archeological sites (for large hydro facilities), reduction in flow rates that impact downstream ecology negatively; unregulated construction practices whereby by-products are dumped into the streams or the nature; disregard to historically and culturally important locales. The challenge is not only the hydro facility itself but also the impact of constructing power lines to connect to the grid. The transfer of water use rights to private companies for 49 years is a particularly sore point among protesters, including professional associations such as the Chamber of Electrical Engineers (EMO, Elektrik

---

[37] The situation is akin, albeit at a smaller scale, to the extraordinary shrinking of the Aral Lake due to inefficient irrigation of cotton fields in Uzbekistan, a relic of misguided Soviet policy.

[38] "WWF and ETİ promote water conservation methods in Konya." *Hürriyet Daily News*, April 29, 2010. http://www.hurriyetdailynews.com/n.php?n=wwf-and-eti-promote-water-conservation-methods-2010-04-29 (last accessed November 6, 2011).

Mühendisleri Odası). EMO (2011) reports that more than 80 court cases have been filed against small hydro facilities in the eastern Black Sea region of Turkey, and 45 out of 46 concluded cases were in favor of the local protesters. Many incidences of local population protesting against construction and bloody altercations between the police, or the gendarmerie, and the protesters have been reported in the press.[39] Some banks announced that they will not finance hydro projects that harm the environment.[40]

There are some safeguards in place to prevent undue environmental impact of these hydro facilities. Developers have to sign an agreement with DSİ to determine water use rights, which governs the seasonally adjusted minimum, or environmental, flow rate. This level of flow is determined by DSİ as adequate for the existing fish population, wildlife, and water quality. Critiques point out that the flow rate is not based on a national (or international) standard that can be consistently applied across the country. For example, Erdoğdu (2011) points out that, unlike in Europe, there is no obligation to build passage ways for migrating fish.

Finally, geopolitical stress related to water shortages downstream can create conflicts in the region. Turkey's GAP project is important for economic development of the southeast region of the country but it has been seen as a threat by Syria and Iraq since its early days. Fırat (Euphrates) and Dicle (Tigris) rivers start in Turkey but supply almost all of freshwater needs in Syria and Iraq. In 1990, both Iraq and Syria were upset when Turkey cut water flows for about a month to finish the construction of the Atatürk Dam. In 2009, in response to water shortages, the Iraqi parliament blamed Turkey and asked for more water. There was a "water" summit among the three countries in late 2009 to discuss the water flow but no agreement was reached.

Going forward, increasing oil and gas production in Iraq requires larger amounts of water for field operations, so will new thermal generation plants and, in general, growing economy and population of Iraq. The immediate needs of oilfield operations will likely be met with seawater at least in the Basrah region; but pumping and piping seawater is expensive and cannot be expected to meet all of country's needs, let alone oil and gas operations in other parts of Iraq.

Climate change may influence water availability negatively in Turkey as well as downstream countries. Globally, sharing of water resources is expected to become more adversarial with the early signs being witnessed among the riparian countries sharing the Nile, Mekong, and Jordan rivers. In addition to bilateral solutions, United Nations and other multinational organizations are working on developing international standards, which can limit upstream countries' ability to generate

---

[39] There are too many reports to cite but the following articles should be sufficient to demonstrate the severity of the issue: http://www.setimes.com/cocoon/setimes/xhtml/en_GB/features/setimes/features/2011/06/04/feature-01; http://www.hurriyetdailynews.com/n.php?n=villagers-protest-hydro-dam-in-northern-turkey-2011-09-25; and http://enerjienstitusu.com/2011/09/22/trabzon-da-koylulerle-hes-calisanlari-birbirine-girdi-7-yarali/ (last accessed on September 25, 2011).

[40] http://enerjienstitusu.com/2011/09/24/cevreye-zarar-veren-hesin-kredisi-iptal-edilecek/ (last accessed on September 25, 2011).

power from major dams.[41] Although there are still many uncertainties regarding future climate change impacts and water availability in different regions, given the past conflicts among Turkey, Syria and Iraq, and the energy and water needs of growing populations and economies in the region, future conflicts cannot be ruled out.[42]

2.4.2 Fallacy of Renewables-Based Economic Development

Turkey is pursuing a strategy of using renewables as a way of economic development via local content programs. Gülen (2011a) points out that almost all of the countries or regions that implemented a policy of supporting alternative technologies did so with the explicit goal of exporting their products. Exports are often the only way to achieve the desired levels of jobs and economic activity since domestic markets are often too small. Similarly, Ladislaw and Goldberger (2010) observe that: "…each of the countries examined below see green stimulus as part of a larger strategic goal to be a leader in clean energy and climate-friendly technologies in the years to come."[43]

Although the Turkish local content approach is not based on mandates but rather on bonus payments for using locally produced parts, it is raising concerns among globally established suppliers. More importantly, renewables industry has become globally competitive in a fairly short period of time, at least partially in response to rich incentives available in Europe and the US[44] As in many other manufacturing operations, Chinese and Indian companies have a cost advantage. Their cost advantage will likely disappear or diminish as wages and costs increase in these countries but next several years could be difficult for emerging Turkish businesses despite the additional incentives. Those incentives can also be found against the World Trade Organization (WTO) and/or EU rules on fair trade. International trade implications of similar local content requirements are already being felt. In response to bankruptcies and factory closures by solar companies in the US, a group of US solar manufacturers petitioned the US International Trade

---

41 For example, http://www.unesco.org/water/wwap/.

42 For example, see the conflict scenario developed by Uppsala Model United Nations project, UMUN (2009), or the NATO scenario depicted in Lorenz and Erickson (1999).

43 Also see CEE-UT (2009) for the renewables programs in US states, many of which defined locally available resources as eligible for support and resisting regional or national trade of renewable energy certificates.

44 The following web site lists 129 wind turbine manufacturers in 31 countries and 17 US states: http://energy.sourceguides.com/businesses/byP/wRP/lwindturbine/byB/mfg/mfg.shtml. The number of main manufacturers is 130 at http://www.thewindpower.net/manufacturers.php but 34 companies have been acquired or do not exist any longer. These lists are not definitive in that companies self-report, some of the companies are subsidiaries of others and not all produce large scale turbines or supply only parts of a wind system; but the lists are also not complete and have been growing (both sites accessed on October 11, 2011). The solar industry is no different with many countries joining the ranks of solar manufacturers practically every day.

Commission to investigate China's support of its solar industry with respect to dumping and illegal subsidies.[45] China reportedly poured $30 billion of subsidies into its solar industry in 2010.[46] This action is one of the latest international trade battles caused by support programs for clean energy technologies across the globe.[47] The lesson from these industry observations and trends is that economic development promises based on locally produced and installed renewable energy technologies are difficult to defend.

The key point to remember for Turkey, or any other jurisdiction pursuing promotion of renewables, is that energy is a key input to the rest of the economy. Since energy supply is capital rather than labor intensive, the sector will not create as many jobs as many other sectors of the economy for the same dollar invested but reliable and affordable supply of energy will certainly increase economic activity and job creation in the rest of the economy.

2.4.3 Unintended Consequences of Biofuels

Biofuels for transportation is worth considering for Turkey that imports most of its transportation fuels or the crude oil feedstock for its refineries; but with a growing population, increasing loss of top-soil, water challenges discussed earlier, and uncertain impacts of climate change Turkey should be aware of the food versus fuel debate and other pitfalls of biofuels policies. For example, the US policy of supporting corn-based ethanol due to the strength of the agricultural lobby in Washington, D.C. is a costly mistake that does not help with reducing oil imports. Ethanol production capacity expanded quickly in response to generous subsidies from the federal government starting with the Energy Policy Act of 2005. Subsidies for ethanol created a market for corn production, which was artificially high due to generous farming subsidies since the 1970s. But the market for ethanol-only vehicles was, and remains, very small. An artificial market for ethanol has been created as an additive to gasoline replacing methyl tertiary butyl ether (MTBE), which has been used as an

---

45 "US Solar Panel Makers Petition Govt. to Investigate Chinese Solar Subsidies, Dumping." Power Magazine, October 19, 2011 http://www.powermag.com/POWERnews/4113.html (accessed on October 23, 2011).

46 Many companies in the US and Europe are said to shut down facilities or declare bankruptcy having failed to compete with Chinese solar manufacturers, which lowered the cost of PV panels at least partially due to generous subsidies from the Chinese government. See Gülen (2011b) for a more detailed discussion.

47 For example, in late 2010, the United Steelworkers filed a complaint accusing China of violating WTO rules by providing subsidies to its clean-energy sector and supporting it with local content policies (http://online.wsj.com/article/SB10001424052748704644404575481743747170692.html). In September 2010 Japan complained to WTO about Ontario's green energy program and its local content requirements (http://www.theglobeandmail.com/report-on-business/ontario-clean-power-subsidies-draw-wto-challenge-from-japan/article1705239/). Both sites last accessed on October 23, 2011.

oxygenate to reduce emission of pollutants since the 1970s. MTBE was pushed aside for its potential negative health impacts to create a quick market for rapidly expanding ethanol production although there is still no definitive scientific evidence.[48] The switching of fields to corn from other products, and using more corn for ethanol rather than food had additional inflationary impact on food prices.[49]

Biodiesel experience in Europe and sugarcane-based ethanol production history in Brazil offer better alternatives but there are similar unintended consequences. Like many of our energy options, biofuels offer both benefits and costs across multiple dimensions such as economics of resources and technologies, energy security and environmental improvement. Turkey should be careful in following policies to support biofuels to minimize negative consequences and to maximize benefits so that biofuels add net value to the economy. Most importantly, biofuels should not be used as an excuse to create additional subsidies for an inefficient agricultural sector.

3 Energy Efficiency

Similar to its renewable energy policy development, Turkey's focus on energy efficiency is also recent and mainly driven by its efforts to comply with EU standards. In 2004, an Energy Efficiency Strategy was formulated to harmonize Turkish energy efficiency laws and regulations with those in the EU. This strategy led to the 2007 Energy Efficiency Law, which, along with subsequent amendments, guides the energy efficiency policy in the country. Despite recent rapid growth in income, energy intensity remains fairly low in Turkey, especially when measured in purchasing power terms. The services sector has grown faster than industrial activity, keeping energy consumption growth in check but higher incomes induced increased consumption by individuals in terms of miles traveled, addition of air conditioning units and more electrical appliances at homes. As Turkey continues to grow, energy consumption will continue to increase but there are opportunities to keep energy intensity growth low or even turn it around if

---

[48] MTBE is considered a potential human carcinogen although "To date, independent expert review groups who have assessed MTBE inhalation health risks (e.g., Interagency Assessment of Oxygenated Fuels) have not concluded that the use of MTBE-oxygenated gasoline poses an imminent threat to public health…EPA's Office of Water has concluded that available data are not adequate to estimate potential health risks of MTBE at low exposure levels in drinking water but that the data support the conclusion that MTBE is a potential human carcinogen at high doses." (http://www.epa.gov/mtbe/water.htm last accessed on December 19, 2011). .

[49] It is also questionable whether corn-ethanol provides any net environmental benefits in terms of reducing emissions. For a more detailed assessment of the US corn-ethanol policy, see Gülen and Shenoy (2007).

appropriate policies and public awareness lead to adoption of technological and behavioral changes to lower energy consumption.

3.1 Current State of Energy Efficiency in Turkey

Although not a perfect indicator, energy intensity, measured as total primary energy consumption per dollar of GDP, is often used to track energy efficiency of an economy. The metric is not perfect because it does not adjust for the composition of economic activity and stage of development. Economic growth has been historically characterized by a transition from agriculture to industrial activity and then to services.[50] During the early stages of this transition, economies typically become more energy intensive since industries consume more energy to generate a dollar of output than agriculture. Even agricultural activities become more industrialized and mechanized during this transition, raising the energy consumption in this sector.

The Turkish industry increased its energy consumption by an average 4.5% per year between 1990 and 2007, which was faster than the increase in overall energy consumption.[51] Hence it is not surprising that energy intensity in Turkey increased in the 1980s but stabilized since the late 1990s. This is similar to what happened in South Korea, energy intensity of which started to decline after peaking in the late 1990s (Fig. 4.8). In 2010, South Korea's per capita income was twice as large as that of Turkey (roughly $20,000 versus $10,000); South Koreans first enjoyed the level of per capita income Turks enjoyed in 2010 in the mid-1990s.[52]

Energy intensity has been declining worldwide. This decline is visible in developed countries such as the UK and the US but even more striking in China and Eastern Europe. The key driver is the collapse of the communist system with its focus on energy-intensive industries that were run very inefficiently and transition to an economy, though still industrialized, that is more efficient and services oriented. Still, China's energy intensity (depicted on the right vertical axis in Fig. 4.8) is almost three times as high as that of South Korea, highest among the rest of the countries shown (roughly 26,700 versus 10,300).

However, when measured in purchasing power parity terms, which captures the stage of economic development to a certain degree, China and South Korea are much closer with 11,100 and 9,800, respectively. Similarly, Turkey's energy intensity measured in PPP terms was 5,300 in 2008, which puts the country at par with Europe and Japan. Measured in market exchange rate, with 7,900 energy intensity, Turkey is placed much higher than Europe and at par with the US.

---

[50] For example, see Medlock and Soligo (2001).

[51] ABB (2011).

[52] In current US$ based on the Atlas method used by the World Bank (data.worldbank.org).

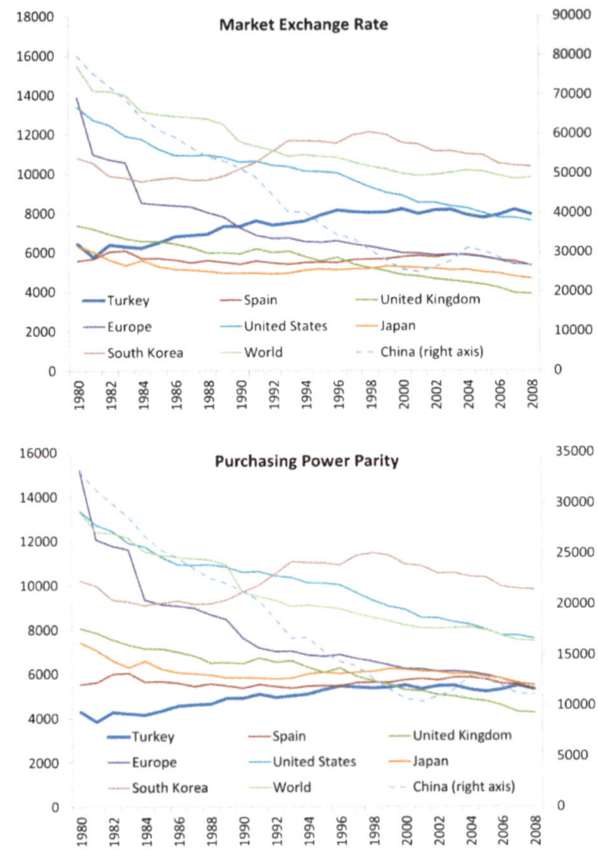

Fig. 4.8 2008 Total primary energy consumption per dollar of GDP (Btu per 2005 US$). Based on EIA International Statistics

Energy consumption in Turkey is low relative to most other OECD countries but its energy intensity is also low within similarly low per capita energy consumers such as China (Fig. 4.9). In fact, both Turks and Chinese consume less than the average citizen of the world but they are in the narrow range of 50–75 million Btus, much less than the European average of 143 million Btus or the US level of 332 million Btus.

However, Turkey can be considered "more efficient" than the Chinese or the world in general since the country achieves a higher per capita income with slightly less per capita energy consumption (first panel in Fig. 4.10). Energy intensity in Turkey is significantly less than that of China or the world but the country enjoys higher per capita income (second panel in Fig. 4.10). On the other hand, for roughly the same level of energy intensity as Turkey, Spain, Japan, and EU achieve much higher income levels. In short, although the country is much more efficient than many other rapidly growing economies, there is significant room for becoming more energy efficient while growing the economy. Achieving these goals will require a detailed energy efficiency policy that is centered on consumer education and awareness.

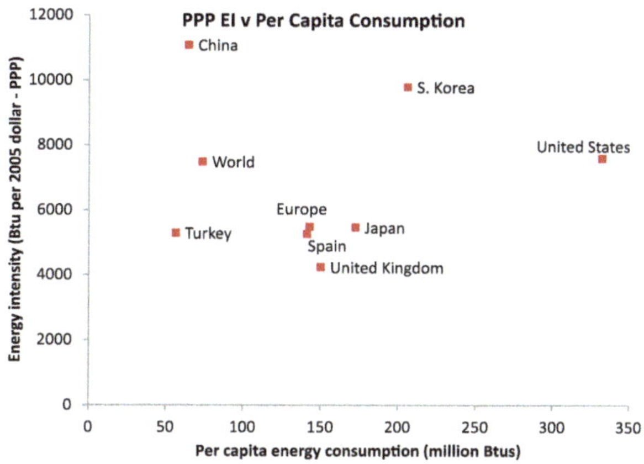

Fig. 4.9 Relationship of energy intensity and per capita energy consumption. Based on EIA International Statistics

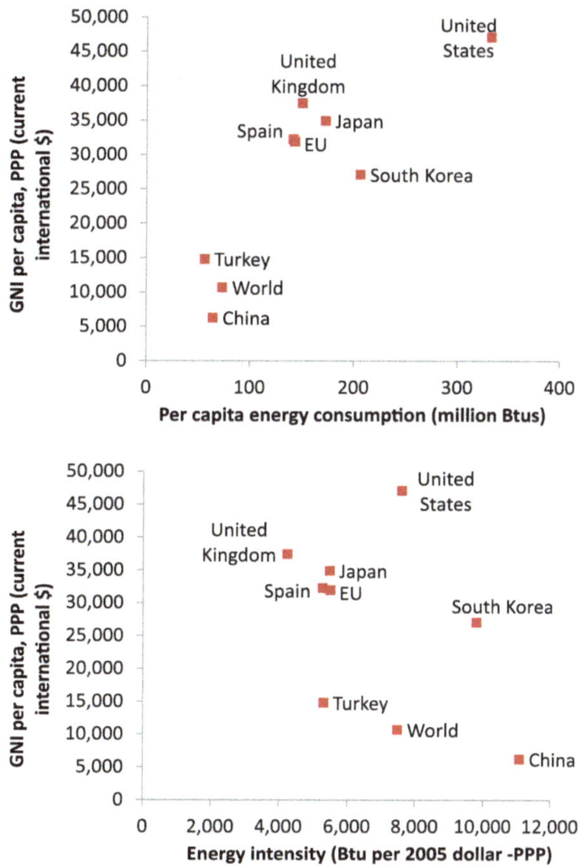

Fig. 4.10 Relationships of energy intensity and per capita energy consumption with per capita income. Based on EIA International Statistics and World Bank database

Large industrial users are more sensitive to energy prices, especially when exposed to global competition. Hence, it is not surprising that increasing fuel prices in the 2000s induced Turkish industries to become more aware of their energy consumption.

The single largest consumer of energy is the steel industry accounting for 20–25% (depending on the year) of the total consumption in the industrial sector. Chemical and non-metallic minerals (cement, ceramics, etc.) industries are other large consumers of energy with roughly 5–10% share each. Energy intensity has significantly improved in many of these energy-intensive facilities, falling more than 4% in the steel industry, 6% in the chemical industry, and more than 6% across the whole industrial sector between 2000 and 2008. High cost of oil in the 2000s was the key driver for these changes as it also impacts the cost of natural gas due to oil-indexed pricing of gas in import contracts.[53]

Overall, the industrial sector demand for energy increased on average 4.5% a year since 1990. The use of electricity surged from 20% of the sector's energy consumption in 1990 to 35% in 2009. Combined heat and power (CHP) represents 8% of industrial electricity consumption; its share, which has been rather stable since 2004, is above the world average (6%). The share of coal (including lignite), the second-largest energy source in the industrial sector, was relatively stable until 2007 at about 43%, but dropped to 33% in 2009. The share of natural gas increased significantly to more than 15% from less than 5% in 1990. High oil prices and availability of cleaner burning natural gas induced companies to reduce their use of oil to about 6% in 2009 from above 25% in 2000.[54]

Increasing the share of combined cycle gas generation in the Turkish electricity market led to a significant improvement in thermal generation efficiency from the low 30% range throughout the 1990s to 43% in 2009. Gas generation now accounts for 45% of the market although installed gas capacity is a little over one-third of the total installed capacity in the country. Technical and non-technical losses in the grid have been reduced somewhat since the beginning of 2000s, but are significantly higher than the world average of about 9%, and as of 2010 stand at 16–19% depending on which (TEİAŞ or TEDAŞ) data are sued (see Chap. 2). As discussed in Chap. 2, one of the reasons for privatizing electricity distribution networks was to reduce losses in the system. It is still too early to conclude on the performance of private distribution companies.

3.2 Legal and Regulatory Framework for Energy Efficiency

An Energy Efficiency Strategy was formulated in 2004 to harmonize Turkish energy efficiency laws and regulations with those in the EU. This strategy led to the 2007 Energy Efficiency Law (No. 5627), which along with subsequent

[53] The discussion in this paragraph is based on ABB (2011).

[54] The discussion in this paragraph is based on ABB (2011).

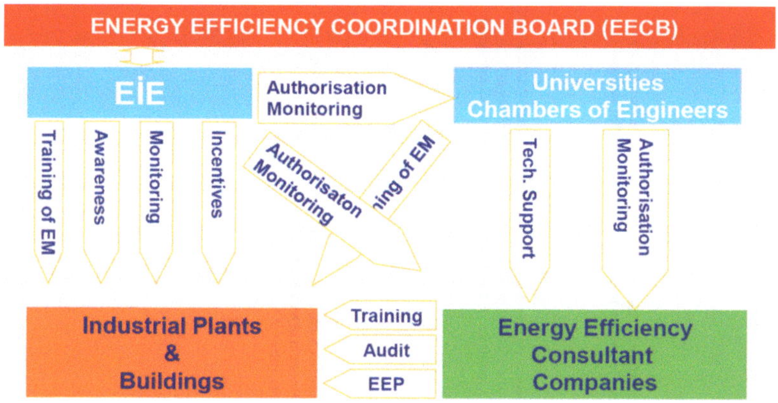

Fig. 4.11 Implementation of energy efficiency policies in Turkey. *Source* Çalıkoğlu (2010)

amendments and/or directives from implementing agencies guides the energy efficiency policy in the country. Under overall guidance of the Ministry of Energy and Natural Resources, EİE is responsible for the implementation of the policy. The 2007 law also instituted an Energy Efficiency Coordination Board (EVKK, Enerji Verimliliği Koordinasyon Kurulu). The Board is chaired by the ETKB; the assistant undersecretary of EİE acts as the secretary. The rest of the EVKK consists of one senior representative from each of the following: ETKB, DPT, EPDK, Ministry of Internal Affairs, Ministry of Finance, Ministry of Education, Ministry of Public Works and Housing, Ministry of Transport, Ministry of Industry and Commerce, Ministry of Environment and Forests, Treasury, Turkish Standards Institute, Turkish Scientific and Technological Research Institution, Turkish Union of Chambers and Commodity Markets, Turkish Union of Chambers of Engineers and Architects, and Turkish Association of Municipalities.

The Board has the following responsibilities: (1) updating of the national energy efficiency strategy; (2) preparation of implementation plans; (3) monitoring of implementation by responsible parties; (4) evaluation of plans' effectiveness; and (5) guiding EİE's studies. The Board will closely coordinate with the EİE, which will carry most of the responsibilities related to authorization and monitoring of energy efficiency implementation by industrial facilities and buildings. Universities and professional engineering societies and chambers will play a crucial role in providing technical support and training as well as working with consultants (Fig. 4.11).

The 2007 law does not specify a target in terms of benchmarks or deadlines. There is a general principle of reducing energy intensity by at least 10%. The 2011–2023 Energy Efficiency Strategy, EİE (2011), targets at least 20% reduction in 2023 energy intensity relative to the 2011 level. Previously, the target was set relative to the 2008 level. The law focuses on energy generation, transmission, distribution, and consumption phases at industrial establishments, buildings, power generation plants, transmission and distribution networks and transport. When it

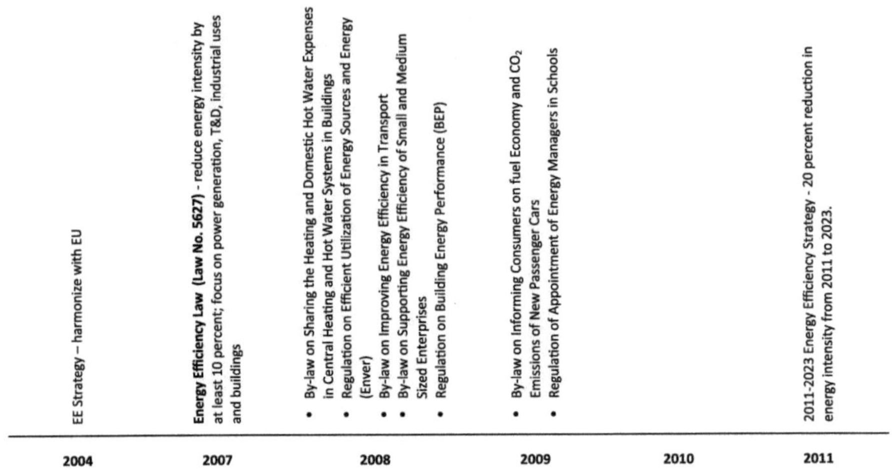

Fig. 4.12 Legal and regulatory timeline for energy efficiency

comes to general public, it envisions raising awareness about energy efficiency (Fig. 4.12).

The implementing framework was quickly promulgated and included the following key elements.[55]

- Bylaw on Sharing the Heating and Domestic Hot Water Expenses in Central Heating and Hot Water Systems in Building (April 2008) to be implemented by the Ministry of Public Works and Settlement.
- Bylaw on Improving Energy Efficiency in Transport (June 2008) to be implemented by the Ministry of Transport.
- Regulation on Support Program of KOSGEB (June 2008). KOSGEB, administration responsible for supporting small- and medium-sized enterprises (SMEs), covers up to 70% of the costs of energy efficiency training and consulting services procured by SMEs.
- Regulation on Efficient Utilization of Energy Resources and Energy (October 2008 with updates). This program, managed by EİE and known with its Turkish nickname, Enver, is a central piece of the energy efficiency awareness movement in Turkey.
- Regulation on Building Energy Performance (December 2008), prepared by the Ministry of Public Works and Settlement, covers existing or newly constructed

[55] Based on IEA (2010a) and Onaygil (2010). A complete list of documents that define the energy efficiency regulatory framework can be found at http://www.eie.gov.tr/duyurular/EV/mevzuat/EV_mevzuat.html (last accessed on November 22, 2011).

residential, commercial and governmental buildings with greater than 2,000 m^2 of usable area. An energy certificate is now necessary for all of these buildings.[56]

- Bylaw on Informing Consumers on fuel Economy and CO_2 Emissions of New Passenger Cars (January 2009) introduced vehicle labeling and a cash for clunkers program for pre-1979 heavy duty and passenger vehicles.
- Regulation of Appointment of Energy Managers in Schools (April 2009) to be implemented by the Ministry of Education.

The overall regulatory framework sets the administrative structure to develop and implement energy efficiency policies, penalties for non-compliance, incentives for encouraging energy efficiency and overall training and public awareness. Large consumers[57] are required to have a dedicated energy manager, who will be responsible for ensuring the implementation of efficiency programs and reporting to EİE annually the amount of energy consumed at each facility. Energy efficiency audits are required on insulation, heating, cooling, hot water, and lighting systems by the end of 2011.

EİE is quite active in raising public awareness about energy efficiency, distributing CFLs, organizing education campaigns, and an annual energy efficiency week every January. EİE also provides financial support for energy efficiency investments, covering 20% of capital costs up to a maximum of 500,000 Turkish Lira[58] if the company can commit to reducing its energy intensity by 10% over a period of three years. In 2009 and 2010, five million TL in each year was allocated to support the program. According to IEA (2010a), tens of companies applied; those approved by EVKK were granted funds to implement energy efficiency programs.

The local utilities are required to provide detailed information to their customers on their web sites including peak consumption level—absolute levels and relative to neighbors, cost of energy and other information that may help induce consumers to save energy. Ministries of Education and National Defense are expected to add curricula on energy efficiency.

All these requirements largely follow EU policies, including the Directive on the Energy Performance of Buildings (2002/91/EC). Appliance labeling on energy

[56] Certificates will be valid for 10 years with an initial period of three years to collect all data and measurements, inspections every two years. Engineers or architects designing new buildings will issue the certificates. For existing buildings, the local utilities will issue the certificate until 2017. They all need to be licensed by the Ministry of Public Works and Settlement.

[57] Commercial and service buildings having either 20,000 m^2 or more construction area or 1,000 ton oil equivalent (toe) or more total energy consumption annually; and governmental buildings with either 10,000 m^2 or more construction area or 250 toe or more total energy consumption annually. Those consuming more than 50,000 toe are required to establish an energy management unit, significantly larger undertaking than having an energy manager.

[58] Roughly $270,000 at the exchange rate of 0.54 US$/TL (November 22, 2011).

Table 4.3 Energy savings potential in Turkey

	Savings potential (%)		Savings potential (million toe/year)
	Electricity	Fuel	
Industry	25		8.0
Iron and Steel	21	19	1.4
Cement	25	29	1.1
Glass	10	34	0.3
Paper	22	21	0.2
Textile	57	30	1.1
Food	18	32	0.9
Chemical	18	64	2.3
Others	–	–	0.7
Building Sector	30		7.2
Residential	29	46	5.7
Public and Commercial	29	20	1.5
Total	27		15.2

Source Özdora (2010)

efficiency is also harmonized with EU directives; minimum energy efficiency standards for appliances are set to comply with EU Ecodesign Directive (2005/32/EC).[59]

3.3 Assessment of Energy Efficiency Developments in Turkey

There are opportunities for Turkey, as any other emerging and developing economy, to leap frog as its economy continues to grow. The World Bank estimated that Turkey can save up to 30% in buildings and 25% in the industrial sector (Table 4.3). There are technologies that can have a huge impact if used widely; these technologies cover design and production of efficient everyday appliances from washing machines to refrigerators to air conditioners as well as industrial furnaces and machinery. Increasing fuel mileage of cars manufactured can be as simple as focusing on clean diesel or multifuel vehicles rather than gasoline engines. Energy efficiency standards for residential and commercial buildings in terms of design and construction would help tremendously as urbanization continues leading to new construction, increasingly not only greenfield development but also quite often brownfield replacement or renovation of older buildings. Promotion of public transportation inter- and intracities, focusing on alternative fuels (CNG, LNG, electric, or biofuels) for fleet vehicles such as city buses and trains could also help reduce emissions in congested cities and the amount of imported fuels.

The transportation sector is not captured in Table 4.3. One of the main challenges is that, as in many other emerging economies, growing middle classes are

[59] IEA (2010a).

keen on owning a car. Private car ownership has increased significantly since the mid-1990s. According to the Ministry of Transport, private car traffic volume tripled between 1990 and 2007 while public transport increased only 8% and railway transport declined by 31%. Only 5% of freight are transported in railways; the rest are transported by trailer trucks in congested roads, causing air pollution, wear and tear on roads. Car ownership (92 out of 1,000) and road density (47 km per 100 km^2) remain much lower than the EU levels. The country has plans to expand the road network significantly, which may not be conducive to reducing energy intensity and dependence on imported fuels. The opportunity to pursue a different, more enlightened path of development is there for Turkey by focusing on smart urbanization and building an effective rail network for both passenger and freight traffic. But, people should be willing to use these public transportation options rather than private vehicles for their daily transportation needs; raising public awareness about benefits of energy efficiency is necessary.

3.3.1 International Funding

There is international support for energy efficiency projects in Turkey and Turkish banks are also financing such projects. For example, the European Bank for Reconstruction and Development (EBRD), which has been active globally in promoting energy efficiency and renewable energy projects, provided Vakıfbank in Turkey $100 million for such projects through EBRD's Mid-size Sustainable Energy Financing Facility (MidSEFF) launched in December 2010 and coordinated with the European Investment Bank (EIB).[60] Through MidSEFF, a total of about $550 million will be given to Turkish banks; other than Vakıfbank, Garanti Bankası and DenizBank also received funds.

Another Turkish bank, Şekerbank, received a credit line of €20 million from German institutions, Oesterreichische Entwicklungsbank AG and KfW Entwicklungsbank for the provision of energy efficiency loans to its clients.[61]

The United Nations Development Programme (UNDP) is supporting a program titled Market Transformation of Energy Efficient Appliances in Turkey. The program has a budget of $5.6 million and will run between 2010 and 2014. The mission of the UNDP project is "to demonstrate and enable companies in the industrial sector to adopt and use energy conservation measures and energy efficient technologies, so that energy efficiency in Turkish industry is improved." The project will focus on energy efficiency labeling for appliances. Key partners are EİE, Ministry of Industry and Trade, Turkish White Goods Manufacturers and

---

[60] http://www.ebrd.com/pages/news/press/2011/110513b.shtml (last accessed on November 19, 2011).

[61] http://www.oe-eb.at/en/projects/financing-projects/Pages/energy-efficiency-turkey.aspx (last accessed on November 19, 2011).

Arçelik A.Ş., a major producer of home appliances with a growing market share in Europe and the Middle East in addition to Turkey.[62]

4 Nuclear Energy

Turkey has a goal to generate 5% of total energy consumption from nuclear facilities by 2023. The country has been pursuing a nuclear power plant since the 1970s. For a variety of reasons, no plant has been built yet. Şirin (2010) argues that Turkey's failure to develop a nuclear plant was basically due to the lack of a long-term nuclear energy policy that captures social, economic, technical and political aspects of nuclear energy. But this policy should be built upon world-class laws and regulations developed and managed by expert technocrats. Nuclear science should guide development of this regulatory framework that will govern site selection, construction, operation and waste management according to strictest safety standards that should be revised based on the Fukushima and other accidents at nuclear facilities. Although the probability of a major accident has historically been low, the impacts can be quite large and psychologically difficult to handle for most of the populace. Transparency and public engagement are absolutely necessary from the bidding process forward.

In the late 2000s, Turkey passed a law to facilitate the construction of the first nuclear facility in the country. The tender held in 2008 led to only one bidder, Atomstroyexport, state-owned nuclear company from Russia. The award was canceled by the State Council in late 2009. An agreement between Russian and Turkish governments in early 2010 laid the new foundation for the Akkuyu nuclear facility to proceed. This is the most advanced nuclear project in Turkey but there are a number of challenges that are discussed later in this section.

Separately, in early 2010, EÜAŞ and KEPCO (Korea Electric Power Corporation) signed an agreement to study feasibility of a four-unit nuclear plant of about 5,800 MWe in Sinop. KEPCO is partially privatized but the state remains the majority shareholder via the government, which owns a little over 21% of KEPCO's shares, and the Korean Finance Corporation (KOFC), which owns close to 30% of the shares. KOFC is itself owned 100% by the government. KEPCO has been expanding globally and will build four units of APR-1400 design in the United Arab Emirates, two of which are under construction. The same design was considered for Turkey. In June 2010, Turkey and South Korea signed an MOU on nuclear cooperation with a goal of initial project agreement in September 2010. But the negotiations fell apart in November 2010 and Turkey has been pursuing alternative companies such as Toshiba from Japan, which, after the Fukushima accident, appears less likely. The Sinop site was identified in 1983.

---

[62] http://www.undp.org.tr/Gozlem2.aspx?WebSayfaNo=2228 (last accessed on November 19, 2011).

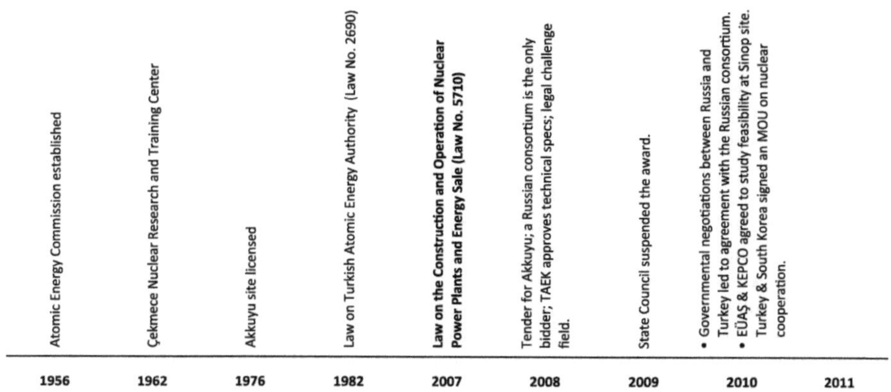

Fig. 4.13 Legal and regulatory timeline for nuclear energy

Uranium exploration has taken place since the 1950s but there is no significant production to date. ETİ-MADEN identified 9,000 tons of resources amenable to open-pit mining in late 2000s. Turkey also has an estimated 378,000 tons of thorium resources (third largest in the world after Australia and the US accounting for 13% of world total) according to the World Nuclear Association.[63] Although there is increasing excitement about using thorium to produce U-233, a much friendlier nuclear fuel than current fuels, there is no commercially operating nuclear power station in the world that uses thorium-based fuel. There have been many experiments, which were mostly successful but technology has so far proven economically prohibitive. India invested heavily to develop its own technology during the period of international sanctions but have not succeeded so far. With the recent lifting of most sanctions, India can import uranium fuels, which may reduce its appetite for investing more in commercialization of the thorium fuel cycle.

4.1 History of Nuclear Power in Turkey[64]

Turkey's nuclear saga started in 1956 with the establishment of the Atomic Energy Commission following the passage of the Atomic Energy Commission Law (Fig. 4.13). The following year, Turkey became a member of the International Atomic Energy Agency (IAEA). The first experimental reactor was commissioned in 1962. Soon after, plans for developing the country's first nuclear power plant were under way and were formalized in the Second Five-Year Economic

[63] http://www.world-nuclear.org/info/inf62.html (last accessed on November 20, 2011).

[64] This history is largely based on Şirin (2010) and Adalıoğlu (2009).

Table 4.4 International nuclear treaties

Title	Date in Force
Convention on the Cooperation in the Atomic Energy Field between the NATO Members and its Amendment	10 September 1956
Paris Convention on Third Party Liability in the Field of Nuclear Energy	13 May 1961
Protocol to Amend the Convention on Third Party Liability in the Field of Nuclear Energy of 29 July 1960	13 June 1967
Agreement on the Privileges and Immunities of the IAEA	26 June 1978
Revised Supplementary Agreement Concerning the Provision of Technical Assistance by the IAEA	11 November 1980
Agreement with IAEA on Application of Safeguards in Connection with the Treaty on the Non-Proliferation of Nuclear Weapons	1 September 1981
Protocol to Amend the Convention on Third Party Liability in the Field of Nuclear Energy of 29 July 1960, as Amended by the Additional Protocol of 28 January 1964	23 May 1986
Convention on the Physical Protection of Nuclear Material	8 February 1987
Convention on Early Notification of a Nuclear Accident	3 February 1991
Convention on Assistance in the Case of a Nuclear Accident or Radiological Emergency	3 February 1991
Convention on Nuclear Safety	24 October 1996
Additional Protocol to Agreement with IAEA on Application of Safeguards in Connection with the Treaty on the Non-Proliferation of Nuclear Weapons	17 July 2001
Joint Protocol Relating to the Application of the Vienna Convention and the Paris Convention	26 June 2007
Joint Convention on the Safety of Spent Fuel Management and on the Safety of Radioactive Waste Management	Ratification process under way

Source Gülay (2011). In addition, Turkey signed bilateral agreements on cooperation in the peaceful use of nuclear power with Canada, Argentina, South Korea, Germany, France, the United States, Ukraine, Russia, Jordan, Kazakhstan, Kyrgyzstan, and Azerbaijan. However, Turkey is not a signatory to the Vienna Convention on Civil Liability for Nuclear Damage, its Amendment Protocol and the Amendment to the Convention on the Physical Protection of Nuclear Material

Development Plan with a goal of having the first nuclear power plant built by 1977. The goal was not achieved and the Third Five-Year Economic Development Plan had the more modest goal of building an 80-MW prototype reactor, which was later abandoned in favor of a 600-MW plant.

In 1976, the Akkuyu site near Mersin in the Eastern Mediterranean Region of Turkey was selected and licensed.[65] The integrated state utility at the time started training its personnel and hired consultants to develop tender documents. The boiling water reactor (BWR) technology was selected and negotiations with a

[65] The site is within 200 km of Ceyhan, where a large oil terminal handles crude oil flowing from both Iraq and Azerbaijan. Ceyhan can become even a larger regional energy hub with more oil and gas from Iraq, the Caspian region and Russia flowing to its terminals in the future. Multiple projects including pipelines, refineries, and even LNG export terminals have been considered over the years to enlarge Ceyhan as an energy hub.

couple of suppliers were initiated in the late 1970s but failed due to Turkey's financial difficulties at the time. Erdoğdu (2007) reports that "the Swedish government's decision to withdraw a loan guarantee" was the key reason.

Turkey became a signatory to the Treaty on the Non-Proliferation of Nuclear Weapons in 1981 (Table 4.4). The Atomic Energy Commission was transformed into the Turkish Atomic Energy Authority (Türk Atom Enerjisi Kurumu, TAEK) in 1982 with a new law (No. 2690). Another site at Sinop on the Black Sea coast was identified in 1983 and companies were invited to submit proposals for both Akkuyu and Sinop sites. During the process, the government switched to the build-operate-transfer (BOT) model from a turnkey contract, which deterred some of the companies. Disagreement on some of the PPA terms, including the government purchase guarantee, led to withdrawal of the last remaining company in 1986, which was also the year of the Chernobyl accident. Following these events, the Department of Nuclear Power Plants within the state utility was closed and many experienced personnel in TAEK left. This period was the lowest point of nuclear ambitions in Turkey.

In the second half of the 1990s, another bidding round for the Akkuyu site attracted three companies but the tender was not finalized when the Council of Ministers canceled it in 2000 after multiple postponements. Turkey had 11 coalition governments in the 1990s—a lost decade in many ways. The nuclear tender was one of the victims of this period of political bickering and economic malaise.

In the early 2000s, the pursuit of Turkey's first nuclear power plant was reinvigorated with the plans of building 5,000-MW nuclear capacity at the Akkuyu site. The Law on Construction and Operation of Nuclear Power Plants and Energy Sale (Law No.5710) was enacted in 2007. By early 2008, preparations for a new tender process were ready. Atomstroyexport, Russian state-owned nuclear vendor, was the only bidder and was declared the winner. Although approvals were progressing, the State Council suspended the award in November 2009. A governmental agreement between Russia and Turkey was signed in May 2010 to proceed with the Akkuyu facility. This agreement was approved by the Turkish Parliament in July 2010 but the construction has not started as of the end of 2011.

Currently, there is a research and training reactor at Çekmece operated by TAEK and one pulse reactor operated by İstanbul Technical University. Recently, TAEK completed the construction of a proton accelerator facility at Sarayköy.[66]

4.2 Legal and Regulatory Framework for Nuclear

There are two laws that govern the nuclear sector in Turkey: the Turkish Atomic Energy Authority Law No. 2690 of 1982, which transformed the Atomic Energy

[66] Boden Law Office (2011a).

Commission established in 1956 into TAEK, and the 2007 Law on the Construction and Operation of Nuclear Power Plants and Energy Sale (Law No. 5710). These two laws are implemented via two bylaws, 21 directives, and 35 regulations.[67]

The 2007 Law was passed in November. By mid-December, TAEK, which is administratively under the Prime Minister's Office, developed and published criteria regarding nuclear safety, licensing, reactor types, power plant lifetimes, proven technology, and fuel technology among other issues outlined in the law. Few months later, in March 2008, implementing regulation was also published (Fig. 4.13).

Given the large capital cost of nuclear facilities, it is quite difficult for private firms to finance a nuclear plant and recover their cost in the competitive market, especially if the marginal fuel is natural gas and it is priced at less than $9-10 per million Btus. A 2008 amendment to the Electricity Market Law of 2001 allowed ETKB to pursue options to secure resource adequacy in the electricity grid in case of insufficient investment by private developers. The options include holding tenders for new capacity, EÜAŞ building new capacity or TEİAŞ renting capacity from existing facilities via ancillary services. Whether financing a 5,000-MW nuclear facility via these options fits the spirit of this amendment is debatable but it would be impossible to get a nuclear facility built otherwise.[68] TETAŞ is the state entity designated to purchase power from the nuclear facilities for 15 years.

The regulatory framework also calls for a National Radioactive Waste Account (NRWA) and Decommissioning Account (DA); the operator will pay 0.15 cent per kWh to each of these accounts. NRWA and DA have not been established yet. The Law No. 5710 stipulates that NRWA and DA will be established pursuant to secondary legislation derived by ETKB and the Treasury. Erdoğdu (2007) recommends private expert fund managers instead of government bureaucrats to manage these accounts. If decommissioning costs exceed the money collected in DA, the Treasury would cover up to 25% of the funds collected in DA. If there is still need for more funds, the operator will pay for those. The operator is also required to allocate 1% of its annual revenue for research and development. In case of a nuclear accident, the law calls for the Paris Convention on Nuclear Third Party Liability dated 1960 and additional amendments, and other national and international liability provisions.

In addition to TAEK, which is primarily responsible for licensing nuclear facilities, handling of nuclear materials, and radioactive waste and nuclear safety, ETKB, the Ministry of Health and the Ministry of the Environment and Forestry also have jurisdiction over various aspects of nuclear operations.

---

[67] Boden Law Office (2011a).

[68] Besides the opposition by local communities, the biggest challenge faced by nuclear plants in the US and some European countries is financing of large capital investment. This challenge is particularly difficult in competitive markets such as Turkey, Texas, PJM and the UK among others. Regulated markets can absorb the cost in their rate base if the regulators, and the society in general, are convinced of the need for nuclear power.

The existing framework is seen as unsatisfactory. In particular, the 2007 Law is very short with only five pages. For example, The Association for Energy Economics (Enerji Ekonomisi Derneği, EED) expressed its surprise to the rushed and short law with a press release. EED finds that the law with only nine substantive clauses falls very short of covering some key issues. In particular, EED points out the lack of details on prevention against accidents and radiation leaks; and the uncertainty associated with investor responsibility related to funds for waste management and decommissioning and site reclamation at the end of the plant's life—the Treasury can be called upon to meet some of these costs. According to IEA (2010a), there are no plans in the 2007 law for long-term waste management. EED also points out that the relatively high cost of nuclear and 15 years of purchase guarantee for 70% of first two units' output and 30% of generation from units three and four, and additional state subsidies are inconsistent with the market model. EED is not the sole professional group raising concerns about the brevity of the law and the ensuing licensing process. Especially after the Fukushima Daiichi accident in Japan, given the earthquake risk at the Akkuyu site and the absence of appropriate safe construction guidelines in the law and inexperience of energy institutions with nuclear energy there are many more concerned, not the least of whom are the local residents, who have opposed the Akkuyu facility for a long time.[69] Most worrying is the absence of an independent regulatory agency that would focus on safety.

In response to these concerns, there is reportedly new legislation under development. A new draft bill focuses on latest safety standards as guided by the IAEA may address some of the concerns mentioned above. Additional secondary legislation and regulations also seem to be under development at the time of writing.[70] In July 2011, two amendments impacted nuclear power plant licensing. First, nuclear developers have to submit the facility license to be obtained from TAEK to EPDK to apply for a generation license. Second, the capital requirement share for nuclear plants is reduced to 5% of the expected investment amount from the 20% that still applies to other forms of generation companies.[71]

---

[69] For example, "Building of Turkey's First Nuclear Plant, Sited on a Fault Line, Facing Fresh Questions," Reuters, March 25, 2011. http://www.reuters.com/article/2011/03/25/idUS196920289020110325 (last accessed on October 9, 2011).

[70] Boden Law Office (2011a).

[71] Boden Law Office (2011c).

4.3 Assessment of Nuclear Energy Developments in Turkey

The Akkuyu site was licensed in 1976 but that site is now seen inappropriate by some experts.[72] They claim that licensing criteria has changed significantly since 1976 under the light of accidents such as Chernobyl and Fukushima but also 35 years of operational history around the world. The site is within 25 km of the Ecemiş fault line, which was considered inactive in 1976 but is now accepted to be active. There have been demonstrations against the site by local communities since the late 1970s but in recent years these demonstrations have gained strength with the organizational help of international environmental groups. After the Fukushima Daiichi incident in Japan, a country considered by many to be technologically advanced, well organized, and proficiently regulated, the concerns of local communities as well as outside observers and stakeholders increased significantly. Uncharacteristically, the Japanese society is demanding more transparency and accountability from TEPCO and politicians, attesting to the societal earthquake caused by the nuclear accident. Turkish authorities should be learning from the Fukushima experience as they pursue the country's first nuclear plant and communicate with the Akkuyu residents.

In early 2008, ETKB invited bids for the Akkuyu site with a September 2008 deadline, leaving little time for interested companies to develop a bid, raising suspicions about the reasons behind such a short period to respond to a nuclear tender, with many technological, safety, environmental, and economic aspects to be developed by the project proposers and to be evaluated by TAEK and TETAŞ. The tender was managed by TETAŞ based on criteria set by TAEK in 2007.

Only one bid was submitted by the September 2008 deadline; requests of other interested parties for extension of deadline was denied. The financial crisis that hit the global economy in the second half of 2008 should have been reason enough to postpone the due date. Some firms asked for additional financial guarantees, presumably due to financial crisis (at least partially); these requests were also denied.

The sole bidder was a consortium led by Atomstroyexport, Russian state-owned nuclear vendor, with a proposal to build four 1,200-MWe units of AES2006 reactors (VVER, pressurized water reactor). TAEK approved technical specifications by December 19, 2008. By January 19, 2009 TETAŞ submitted the financial offer to the Council of Ministers. Before the Council of Ministers could make a decision, the State Council suspended the award in November 2009 following a legal challenge filed in 2008. Direct government talks between Russia and Turkey on broader energy and trade co-operations took over the Akkuyu project and an agreement was signed with the Russian consortium in May 2010 and approved by the parliament in July 2010.

---

[72] Professor Tolga Yarman, who has a Ph.D. in nuclear engineering from MIT and served in the committee that provided the initial license for the Akkuyu site in 1976, is now a staunch opponent of the site. One of the former directors of TAEK, Dr. Cengiz Yalçın, is concerned about the lack of transparency about some safety design elements. For details, see Güsten (2011) and Özbek (2011).

The project company is supposed to assume all financial and operational risks of the $20-billion project, starting construction in 2013 and operation of the first unit in 2019. TETAŞ will buy 70% of the electricity generated by the first two units and 30% of the electricity produced by units three and four for 15 years at a weighted average price of 12.35 cents per kWh. Another clause in the agreement allows for project company to charge up to 15.33 cents per kWh to ensure investment payback. Note, however, that these prices are nominal, i.e., the company will get paid 12.35 cents per kWh in 2019 prices. If discounted back to 2011, 12.35 cents translates into 5.8–8.4 cents per kWh, using a discount rate of 10% (annualized rate of increase of wholesale electricity prices in Turkey between 2003 and 2010)[73] and 5% (annualized rate of cost increase for power plants),[74] respectively. This price range is competitive when compared to prices seen in the day-ahead and balancing markets in Turkey, which fluctuated between 5 and 10 cents per kWh in 2011 in April and August, respectively.[75] The average wholesale price in 2010 was about 8 cents per kWh.[76] However, it is not likely for the investing company to recover its investment quickly and realize a decent rate of return at these prices; as discussed in Sect. 2.3, nuclear investments typically require a price higher than 10 cents per kWh to realize a rate of return of 12%. Although the contract with its low prices may seem like a good deal for Turkey, it raises concerns about financing of the project and, more importantly, about shortcuts that may be taken during the construction phase to reduce cost with direct implications on safe operation of the facility. As a state company, Atomstroyexport may not have the same financial return requirements but the support of the Russian state does not absolve the project from these concerns. It is worth remembering that one of the issues EÜAŞ and KEPCO, another state company, failed to resolve was the inability of KEPCO to offer a similarly attractive price for the Sinop location.

The pronounced goal of the country is 5% nuclear by 2020; but if both Akkuyu and Sinop facilities are built by that time, more than 10 GW of installed capacity will likely supply about 17–18% or more of Turkey's predicted electricity needs (about 420 TWh in high growth scenario), or about 13–15% of projected generation (about 520 TWh). Nuclear plants should operate as base load with 80–90% capacity factor and generate 70–80 TWh. The Akkuyu plant itself could account for 8–9% of total demand. This share is significant; it can deter investment in other generation facilities, gas or renewables, if the plant can indeed supply electricity at the low prices in the agreement. On the other hand, if the plant (all units) shuts down (say, for safety breaches), the reserve margin of the system can be dangerously low.

There are other important concerns. Although Turkey has been pursuing a nuclear power plant since the 1950s, the country does not yet have the human

---

[73] Electricity prices were taken from IEA (2011).

[74] Based on IHS CERA European Power Capital Costs Index, available at http://www.ihsindexes.com/ (last accessed on December 19, 2011). .

[75] EPDK (2011).

[76] EPDK (2010).

resources and institutional capacity to regulate and monitor the nuclear facilities as necessary (EDAM 2011). For example, there is no independent nuclear regulator and protocols for recycling and/or disposal of spent fuel are not developed. Nuclear facilities offer large potential benefits in the form of reliable, affordable, and emission-free electricity for a long period of time but they also pose a multitude of significant risks throughout their operations and the recycling of spent fuel. On the other hand, the recent government decree on auditing of independent regulators by relevant ministries raises many concerns about transparency and effectiveness of such a regulator, especially considering the fact that Akkuyu plant is based on an intergovernmental agreement between Russia and Turkey rather than resulting from a transparent bid process.

The proper management of these risks requires a certain "safety culture," which, unfortunately, does not seem to exist in Turkey. After the terrible İzmit earthquake in 1999, the authorities failed to punish contractors who did not comply with building standards and caused the deaths of thousands. Their failure was demonstrated once again in 2011, when many buildings in Van failed to stand even lower magnitude earthquakes. Similarly, the derailing of the fast train in 2004 did not lead to transparent investigations and penalizing of culpable parties except for some scapegoats. Many claimed the infrastructure was not up to standard. Fast trains continued to derail since 2004 along the same route. Examples can be increased but they all point to some fundamental challenges related to the fatalistic culture of the Turkish society but more importantly to the hierarchical structure of and the "culture of secrecy"[77] in state organizations even if they are supposedly independent regulatory bodies. Typically, instead of meritocracy, seniority governs promotion; no junior civil servant feels the need to offer ideas or braves to question his/her superiors. Appointment of cronies to key positions and hiring of unqualified cronies to technical positions further undermine the quality of performance. Nuclear industry regulation and operations, in contrast, require highly trained professionals who do not shy away from constant questioning of decisions and practices starting with the evaluation of project proposals and continuing through construction of the facilities, which can take up to 7-10 years, the operation of the facility, which can be up to 60 years, and the management of the spent fuel. There is no room for error or hierarchical bottlenecks in this process.

It is atypical for nuclear technology providers to also build and operate nuclear power plants. There is no operational experience with the proposed technology (VVER-1200) anywhere including Russia, where two plants are under construction but none are operational.[78] Although the technology is supposed to be an improvement on previous designs, the lack of operational experience is

[77] Erdoğdu (2007) underlines the necessity of eliminating this culture of secrecy when it comes to communicating transparently about the risks and benefits of nuclear power, and how the risks will be managed. Without the public trust, nuclear facilities cannot be built; or if they are forced, the public backlash can cost elections or high level positions as witnessed in Japan after the Fukushima Daiichi accident.

[78] EDAM (2011).

troublesome. Usually, it is better to use proven technology that can be duplicated at other locations in the future; this way, it will be easier for nuclear regulators and utility personnel to be well informed and educated about that technology. Universities can also benefit from perfecting their curriculum and laboratories to train their students on the standard technology to supply future human resources needs of the nuclear sector. France is the prime example of successful implementation of such a strategy.

Finally, many are concerned about increasing energy dependence on Russia. Turkey already imports a large percentage of its natural gas from Russia; using Russian nuclear technology and nuclear fuel would increase this dependence. Although Turkey would be diversifying its fuel portfolio, it would increase its source country dependence.

References

ABB (2011). *Turkey Energy Efficiency Report,* January 2011 update.

Adalıoğlu, U. (2009). Türkiye'de Nükleer EnerjininTarihçesi. Enerji 2023 Derneği, Ankara.

Balat, Mustafa (2010). "Security of energy supply in Turkey: challenges and solutions." *Energy Conversion and Management* 51, 1998-2011.

Başel, E. Didem Korkmaz, Ümran Serpen, Abdurrahman Satman (2010). "Turkey's Geothermal Energy Potential: Updated Results." *Proceedings,* Thirty-Fifth Workshop on Geothermal Reservoir Engineering, Stanford University, Stanford, California, February 1-3, 2010, SGP-TR-188.

Boden Akalın, Değer and Seda Gümüş (2011). Turkey Chapter in *Getting the Deal Through, Electricity Regulation in 28 Jurisdictions Worldwide.*

Boden Law Office (2011a). *Regulatory Report – Energy, March-April 2011.*

Boden Law Office (2011b). *Regulatory Report – Energy, May-June 2011.*

Boden Law Office (2011c). *Regulatory Report – Energy, July-August 2011.*

BP (2011). *Statistical Review of World Energy.*

Bülbül, İ. Kürşat (2011). *Çeşme Yarımadası Rüzgar Santrallerinin İletim Sistemine Bağlantısı.* İzmir Rüzgar Sempozyumu, December 23-24, 2011.

Carter, Nicole and Richard J. Campbell (2009). "Water Issues of Concentrating Solar Power (CSP) Electricity in the U.S. Southwest." *Congressional Research Service.*

Çalıkoğlu, Erdal (2010). "Energy Efficiency Policies and Programs in Turkey." Presentation at the International Consultation Workshop on Energy Efficiency Institutional Governance, The World Bank, Washington, D.C., June 1-2.

CEE-UT (2009). *Harmonization of Renewable Energy Credit (REC) Markets across the U.S.* Project report to State Energy Conservation Office (http://www.beg.utexas.edu/energyecon/transmission_forum/CEE_National_RECs_study.pdf).

DPT (2009). Electricity Market and Supply Security Strategy Paper. State Planning Organization (DPT, Devlet Planlama Teşkilâtı).

EDAM (2011). *Nükleer Enerjiye Geçişte Türkiye Modeli.* Edited by Sinan Ülgen, Ekonomi ve Dış Politika Araştırmalar Merkezi.

EİE (2011). *Enerji Verimliliği Strateji Belgesi, 2011-2023.*

EMO (2011). *Doğu Karadeniz Bölgesi HES Teknik Gezisi Raporu, 29-31 Ekim 2010.*

EPDK (2010). *2010 Elektrik Piyasası Raporu.*

EPDK (2011). "Overview of the Turkish Energy Market: Policies, Projections, Targets." Presentation at the World Energy Council Houston Business Forum, Houston, Texas, October 30 – November 2, 2011.

ETKB (2011). "Renewable Energy Opportunities for Investment." Presentation at the World Energy Council Houston Business Forum, Houston, Texas, October 30 – November 2, 2011.

Erdem, Z. Bengü (2010). "The contribution of renewable resources in meeting Turkey's energy-related challenges." *Renewable and Sustainable Energy Reviews* 14, 2710–2722.

Erdoğdu, Erkan (2007). "Nuclear power in open energy markets: A case study of Turkey." *Energy Policy* 35, 3061–3073.

Erdoğdu, Erkan (2011). "An analysis of Turkish hydropower policy." *Renewable and Sustainable Energy Reviews* 15, 689-696.

Evrendilek, F. and C. Ertekin (2003). "Assessing the potential of renewable energy sources in Turkey." *Renewable Energy* 28, 2303–2315.

Gülay, Kerem (2011). "Nuclear Power and Turkey: an Overview of Nuclear Legislation and Policy." http://www.mondaq.com/x/139810/Energy+Law/Nuclear+Power+And+Turkey+An+Overview+Of+Nuclear+Legislation+And+Policy (last accessed on December 19, 2011).

Gülen, Gürcan (2011a). *Defining, Measuring and Predicting Green Jobs.* Copenhagen Consensus Center. http://www.copenhagenconsensus.com/Default.aspx?ID=1542#7056.

Gülen, Gürcan (2011b). *Government support for energy technologies and green jobs.* CEE-UT Think Corner Research http://www.beg.utexas.edu/energyecon/thinkcorner/Think Corner - Government support for energy technologies.pdf.

Gülen, Gürcan and Bhamy Shenoy (2007). "Supporting Biofuels: A Case Study on the Law of Unintended Consequences?" Developing and Delivering Affordable Energy in the 21st Century, 27th USAEE/IAEE North American Conference, Houston, Texas.

Güsten, Susanne (2011). "Forging Ahead on Nuclear Energy in Turkey." The New York Times, March 23 http://www.nytimes.com/2011/03/24/world/middleeast/24iht-m24-turk-nuclear.html?_r=1&pagewanted=all (last accessed November 20, 2011).

IEA (2010a). *Energy Policies of IEA Countries: Turkey 2009 Review.*

IEA (2010b). *Natural Gas Information 2010.*

IEA (2011). *Energy Prices and Taxes*, Quarterly Statistics, Third Quarter 2011.

İlkılıç, Cumali (2012). "Wind energy and assessment of wind energy potential in Turkey." *Renewable and Sustainable Energy Reviews* 16, 1165-1173.

Kaygusuz, Kamil (2011). "Prospect of concentrating solar power in Turkey: The sustainable future." *Renewable and Sustainable Energy Reviews* 15, 808–814.

Kumbaroğlu G, N. Madlener, and M. Demirel (2004). "A real options evaluation model for the diffusion prospects of new renewable power generation technologies." In: 6th IAEE European conference, *Modeling in Energy Economics and Policy*, Zurich, Switzerland, September 2–3.

Ladislaw, Sarah O. and Nitzan Goldberger (2010). *Assessing the Global Green Stimulus*, Commentary, Center for Strategic and International Studies.

Lorenz, Frederick and Edward Erickson (1999). *The Euphrates Triangle: Security Implications of the Southeast Anatolia Project,* National Defense University Press, p. 47.

McKinsey & Company (2010). *Impact of the financial crisis on carbon economics: Version 2.1 of the global greenhouse gas abatement cost curve. Available at* http://www.mckinsey.com/Client_Service/Sustainability/Latest_thinking/Costcurves *(last accessed on December 21, 2011).*

Medlock Ken and Ron Soligo (2001). "Economic Development and End-Use Energy Demand." *The Energy Journal*, 22:2.

Onaygil, Sermin (2010). "Residential Energy Saving Opportunities." Presentation at the Energy Efficiency Conference, June 3-4, 2010, İstanbul, Turkey.

Özbek, Cengiz (2011). "Akkuyu, nükleer uzmanları ikiye böldü." Hürriyet, March 17 http://hurarsiv.hurriyet.com.tr/goster/printnews.aspx?DocID=17298417 (last accessed November 20, 2011).

Özdora, Gürhan A. (2010). "Getting the Legal/Regulatory Framework Right for a More Energy Efficient Future." Presentation at the Energy Efficiency Conference, June 3-4, 2010, İstanbul, Turkey.

Price Waterhouse Coopers (2009). *On the Sunny Side of the Street: Opportunities and Challenges in the Turkish Renewable Energy Market.*

Şirin, Selahattin Murat (2010). "An assessment of Turkey's nuclear energy policy in light of South Korea's nuclear experience." *Energy Policy* 38, 6145–6152.

TETAŞ (2011). *2010 Yılı Sektör Raporu.*

Tunç, Şenol (2010). "Güneş Enerjisi ile Elektrik Üretimi Yatırım Mevzuatı." Presentation at Solar Energy Technologies and Investment Frameworks Conference, USİAD and İstanbul Kültür Üniversitesi, İstanbul, February 18, 2010.

Türkyılmaz, Oğuz (2011). "Türkiye Enerjide Nereye Gidiyor?" *Mühendis ve Makina* 52:617, 40-46.

UMUN (2009). *The Water Conflict in the Euphrates and the Tigris: Scenario Background.* Uppsala Model United Nations. http://www.umun.se/upload/Scenario%202009.pdf (last accessed on December 22, 2011).

U.S. Energy Information Administration (2010), *Updated Capital Cost Estimates for Electricity Generation Plants*, November. http://www.eia.gov/oiaf/beck_plantcosts/index.html.

Chapter 5
Policy Recommendations for Turkish Energy Future

Turkey has been growing fairly rapidly since the 1980s; energy demand has increased accordingly, albeit at slower rates than in emerging economies such as China thanks to Turkey's lower energy intensity. Turkey does not have significant production of oil and gas; and most of domestic coal production is lignite, which has lower heat value. As such, the country's dependence on imported energy has increased over the years from just crude oil and oil products to natural gas since 1986 and coal more recently. As with all import-dependent countries, energy security has been a primary driver of Turkish energy strategies. But, energy security seems to have gained a renewed importance with the price of oil seemingly having reached a higher plateau since 2003–2004. The higher price of oil hits Turkey in two ways: first, the country's oil imports have increased in the last 10 years due to increased miles traveled by individuals and businesses and increased industrial use; and second, cost of gas imports increased along with the price of oil due to oil-indexed pricing in gas import contracts. As discussed in Chap. 1, the impact of the increased cost of energy imports has been quite visible in Turkey's trade and current account balance, with 22% of total import expenditures being spent on energy imports in 2011 as compared to 12% in 2002.

Accordingly, Turkey continues with efforts to enhance energy security. However, it is questionable that energy sector reforms, which have been formalized in 2001 with two laws restructuring electricity and natural gas markets, have contributed much to enhancing energy security yet; nor is it clear that restructuring alone would be sufficient to enhance energy security—additional policy instruments, such as supporting energy efficiency, renewables, and nuclear, are probably necessary. The objective of the restructuring process is primarily introduction of competition in order to reap the benefits of increased productivity over time. In the Turkish case, one could also add the objective of transferring the financial burden of investments from the public budget to the private sector. However, the Turkish case vividly demonstrates that these objectives alone do not constitute a comprehensive energy policy. Electricity restructuring was based on privatization, which was itself based on raising revenues rather than ensuring a competitive market.

I. Atiyas et al., *Reforming Turkish Energy Markets*,
DOI: 10.1007/978-1-4614-0290-9_5,

After 10 years of reform, only less than a quarter of the market is competitive with no efficiency gains; a state utility continues to control close to half of generation capacity in the country. Privatization of 21 distribution regions have been delayed until 2008 (except for three regions that were privatized in 2006) and the results in terms of reduced system losses and improved reliability are not readily visible yet. The lack of timely and publicly available data on these critical metrics makes it harder to assess the effectiveness of the reforms independently.

A state entity, BOTAŞ, continues to dominate the gas supply market as the holder of most legacy long-term contracts, which are the most significant stranded costs in the system. The efforts to transfer some of its contracts to private entities failed and hence, there is not much competition in the wholesale gas market, without which retail competition envisioned in the 2001 restructuring law is not possible. Although BOTAŞ may have been resisting to release some of its market power, it was also unrealistic to expect suppliers to switch to private counterparties forgoing the Treasury guarantees on take-or-pay clauses of their agreements with BOTAŞ. This constraint on BOTAŞ' ability to transfer some volumes to private importers might explain why EPDK never fined BOTAŞ for failing to reduce its market share to mandated 20%. It would have been difficult to hold BOTAŞ responsible for unwillingness of counterparties such as Gazprom to renegotiate with new partners.

However, private enterprises could have been allowed to import to create competition. For example, a private company built an LNG import terminal with a capacity of six billion cubic meters per year on the Aegean coast near an industrial complex and was ready to import in 2002 but the terminal was not given an import license until late 2008 and only for spot cargoes although it was provided with a storage license in 2003. The deliberate delay in the licensing of the terminal is often associated with a political desire to protect BOTAŞ and may have been necessary given the take-or-pay contracts of the company with often state-owned suppliers from Russia, Algeria, Nigeria, Iran, and Azerbaijan; the volumes of these contracts were sufficient to meet demand for at least the 2000s. Perhaps more damaging to introducing competition was the 2008 agreement with Egypt to import gas; ETKB signed it but transferred the responsibility of the contract to BOTAŞ. According to the 2001 NGML, BOTAŞ could not sign a new import contract until its share fell below 20%; the law was amended in 2008 to allow the Egypt deal. Although no gas import from Egypt has started and no import licenses have been awarded yet, giving the import responsibility of this contract to BOTAŞ is inconsistent with the spirit of NGML and the goal of introducing competition to the gas market.

As some of the earliest contracts started to expire and the country's gas consumption continue to increase, private entities are slowly starting to negotiate or sign their own import contracts either as spot LNG cargoes or as long-term pipeline contracts.

The addition of renewables to the extent it can be done at reasonable cost and without undermining the reliability of grid operations will help to diversify the country's generation portfolio and may in turn help reduce gas imports. However, as discussed in Chap. 4 , there are multiple challenges faced even by hydro and wind, most cost competitive and technologically proven options. Still, the Renewables

Law of 2005 and implementing regulations and amendments since then have been laying the foundation for development of renewable generation capacity in Turkey as demonstrated by more than 1,600 MW of new wind capacity and close to 3,000 MW of new hydro capacity built since 2005. With the current level of feed-in-tariffs, not much solar capacity can be expected in the near future; there are no licensed solar facilities. There is a 600 MW cap on solar construction until the end of 2013. There is more interest in geothermal with an installed capacity of 114 MW and 11 facilities with an installed capacity of 315 MW under construction but geothermal potential is much more limited than solar, wind, or hydro.

Although Turkey's energy intensity is not as high as other rapidly growing economies, the country still has opportunities to adopt energy-efficient technologies and programs, which would help to reduce energy imports. The Energy Efficiency Law of 2007 and many amendments and regulations call for involvement of many governmental entities in implementation of energy efficiency programs and raising awareness among the public as the change of consumer behavior is often central to success of these programs. Large industrial users are already responding to high energy prices of the 2000s by adopting technologies and practices that use less energy but economy-wide impact can be harnessed only when the public at large embrace energy efficient behavior and restrain the urge of owning a car, moving to a bigger house, and spending more for the sake of consumerism as more and more people join the ranks of middle classes. Public outreach is critical. It is also essential to monitor the building industry to ensure that they are following the highest possible energy efficiency standards that have been developed.

Finally, Turkey is closer to its first nuclear power plant than it has ever been since the Akkuyu site was first licensed in the 1970s. The addition of nuclear plants, with a goal of 5% nuclear by 2020, would help to diversify the country's generation portfolio. However, as discussed in Chap. 4, many question, especially in the wake of the Fukushima accident in Japan, the country's institutional readiness for a nuclear facility, let alone at a site near an active earthquake zone.

1 The Need for a Cohesive Long-Term Energy Policy

Taken together, Turkey seems to be following a strategy of diversification of energy types and import sources to enhance energy security but a cohesive long-term energy policy seems to be lacking. It is desirable for ETKB, together with stakeholders (universities, consumer groups, environmental groups, professional associations, EPDK, private companies) to develop such a long-term energy policy. Various organizations such as DPT, ETKB, EİE, and EPDK have strategy documents but these technocratic analyses, albeit useful, are not based on a stakeholder process where pros and cons of various options and system impacts are evaluated. Any energy security-focused approach should evaluate multiple criteria. For example, APERC (2007) focuses on availability, accessibility, affordability, and acceptability. In Table 5.1, we provide a summary evaluation of the options currently available to Turkey across these four dimensions based on the analysis presented in the previous chapters of this book. These evaluations form the basis of the policy recommendations discussed in the rest of this chapter. Grading (+/−) is subjective but reflects our understanding of the current energy security situation in Turkey; and it is meant to provide an easy way to compare different fuels across the four dimensions.[1]

2 Improving Competition and Efficiency in Energy Markets

Looking ahead, there is a number of measures that can be adopted in order to facilitate and increase the quality of the restructuring process in the electricity industry.

2.1 Institutional Measures

The management of the restructuring process can be improved and made more transparent and accountable. To its credit, the EPDK often does undertake public consultations before finalizing regulations. This process can be made more formal, and comments and views provided by different stakeholders may be made public. More importantly, one of the key measures in this regard is to require the EPDK to provide detailed justifications for its decisions. Finally, appointments to the Board of EPDK can be made more accountable. One way to do this would be to hold parliamentary hearings for the candidates.

2.2 Competition

Prospects for competition in electricity generation may be greatly improved by corporatizing the portfolio companies, appointing skilled managers, and requiring that they behave in an independent and competitive manner in the market. It is not necessary to wait for their privatization for competition to develop. At the same time, full transparency of the financial accounts of the corporatized entities would help in establishing a level playing field.

[1] This approach is based on USAID (2008), authored by Dr. Gülen and his colleagues at the Center for Energy Economics.

Table 5.1 Key dimensions of energy security for Turkey

	Availability	Accessibility	Acceptability	Affordability
Natural gas	++ No significant domestic resources; upstream frameworks outdated and unattractive; almost complete import dependence; but globally both conventional and unconventional resources are large and widely available; significant exploration potential remains; LNG is becoming more global	+ Need for new infrastructure both upstream, pipelines and downstream (e.g., storage); investment barriers though less than oil; Turkey has access to pipeline gas and LNG from multiple sources	++/– Cleaner burning and more efficient than oil and coal; power plants cheap and quick to build/import dependency	– ➔ + Rising costs due to oil-indexed pricing but can be moderated with LNG availability from low cost sources and moving away from oil-indexed pricing in future contracts
Hydro	++ Large resources available/risks due to climate change and sharing water with riparian countries	++/– Some capital and infrastructure constraints	+/– Resistance from local communities (ecological, social and archaeological impact); conflicts with downstream countries	++ Higher capital but lower operation cost than most fossil fuel options
Wind	++ Resources available across Turkey but best in certain locations	– ➔ + Legal and regulatory frameworks emerging; FITs and local content bonus help	++ Mostly no direct emissions; direct ecological impact considered low except the risk to migrating birds	– ➔ + Higher economic costs than fossil fuels but declining; oil-indexed pricing of gas is high helping competitiveness of wind
Solar	++ Resources available across Turkey but best in certain locations	– Legal and regulatory frameworks emerging; but FITs and local content bonus too low	++ Mostly no direct emissions; direct ecological impact considered low except for solar thermal that requires large amounts of water	– Costs are still high but declining especially for PV modules

(continued)

Table 5.1 (continued)

	Availability	Accessibility	Acceptability	Affordability
Nuclear	+++	−−	−−	+
	Global uranium resources available, though uranium processing is constrained	Institutional capacity lacking; non-competitive selection prevented comparison of alternatives	Strong local opposition to Akkuyu site near an active fault line; raised concerns due to the Fukushima accident and non-transparent selection process	Highest capital but lower operation cost compared to most fossil fuel options; but the price offered by the developer of the Akkuyu site is quite competitive
Coal	++	++/−	−−−	++/−
	Domestic resources are mostly lignite; resources available worldwide; Turkey started imports	Some capital and infrastructure constraints (ports, ships, trains)	Emissions (SO_2, mercury, GHG); pending IGCC and CCS	Cheap but environmental regulations and CCS can add to the cost
Biofuels	+/−	+/−−	+/−	−/+
	Limited supply capacity	Natural conditions (land, soil quality, water resource, plant type); distribution infrastructure constraints	Depends on feedstock and market; competition with food; water depletion; deforestation; fertilizer use	Cannot compete without subsidies but high fuel prices and taxes in Turkey may help if biofuels are exempted
Oil	−−	−/+	+/−	−−
	No significant domestic resources; upstream frameworks outdated and unattractive; almost complete import dependence; globally both conventional and unconventional resources are available but concentrated in geopolitically challenging regions	Rising geopolitical risk and investment barriers/Turkey's location allows for imports from multiple sources via pipelines or tankers	Most convenient transportation fuel/rising concerns about dependence on OPEC and GHG emissions	Oil price seems to have been stabilized at a higher plateau; highest taxes on fuels are in Turkey

Source Authors

It has been argued above that prospects for the development of retail competition are weak unless some degree of real-time pricing becomes possible at the retail level. It would be worthwhile for EPDK to undertake a study on whether providing subsidies for the installation of smart meters is economically and socially warranted. Similarly, a study on the pros and cons of full ownership unbundling between distribution and retail supply companies would be very useful.

So far unilateral market power has not been a major concern in the electricity industry. However, that does not preclude the possibility that this may become an issue once generation assets are privatized. Moreover, transmission constraints are more likely to become binding as siting of new plants is increasingly guided by proximity to energy sources, especially renewable sources. It would be useful for TEİAŞ or EPDK to monitor the state of transmission constraints, and make this information available to the public. In addition, it is necessary for the authorities to consider whether formal mechanisms of market monitoring and market power mitigation are necessary.

In the natural gas industry, increases in gas storage capacity, especially large-scale underground facilities, in multiple locations would greatly facilitate the transition to a more competitive market structure. In addition, it would help manage seasonal fluctuations and hedge against the risk of supply cuts.

2.3 Resource Adequacy

Currently the responsibility for resource adequacy in electricity ultimately rests on EÜAŞ. This has been more of a default option rather than a well-thought and justified strategy. Concerns for resource adequacy have declined as a result of the slowdown in demand that came about in 2008 and 2009. Many countries have instituted various forms of capacity mechanisms to address the resource adequacy issue. The ETKB or EPDK or both should examine the pros and cons of instituting such a mechanism in Turkey.

2.4 Tariffs and Distributional Concerns

Cross subsidies across consumer groups have no good economic or social justification and they should be ended. Given the high level of income inequality in Turkey, affordability of energy for poor households will remain an issue. Manipulating electricity prices is not an efficient way to deal with energy poverty. These are also households that are likely to be affected by any upward adjustment in prices that may occur as tariffs become more cost-reflective. A well-thought mechanism needs to be devised to protect the poor from price increases and to ensure that energy becomes or remains affordable.

3 Diversification Strategies

Diversifying types of energy fuels and technologies as well as import sources (if imports are large) is a standard strategy for improving energy security. It can be difficult to assess how much diversification is sufficient. In IAEA (2005), a joint report by the International Atomic Energy Agency, United Nations Department of Economic and Social Affairs, International Energy Agency, Eurostat and European Environment Agency, four social, 16 economic, and 10 environmental indicators are identified. Among the economic indicators are energy use per capita, energy intensity, reserves-to-production ratio, share of renewable energy, and net import dependency that are central for the energy security debate. These criteria are collected to evaluate sustainability, a much larger topic than energy security. A set of more concentrated energy security indicators can be developed based on the Shannon-Wiener Index, a measure of biodiversity.[2] Indicators can be structured somewhat differently to reflect policymakers' preferences regarding factors of interest (e.g., political stability of import sources) as well as technical considerations such as statistical normalization. For our discussion on Turkey, the following statistics can be of value:

1. Diversification of energy supply sources:

$$-\frac{\sum_{i=1}^{6} a_i \ln(a_i)}{\ln(6)}$$

where a_i is the share of each of our six primary energy sources (oil, natural gas, coal, nuclear, hydro and renewables) in total energy consumption.

2. Net import dependency:

$$1 - \frac{\sum_{i=1}^{6} (1 - m_i) a_i \ln(a_i)}{\ln(6)} \Big/ \text{Div}$$

where m_i is the share of import for energy source i.

3. Net oil import dependency: net oil imports/total energy demand.
4. Net gas import dependency: net gas imports/total energy demand.

---

[2] For example, J.C. Jansen et al. (2004), von Hirschhausen (2005), and APERC (2007).

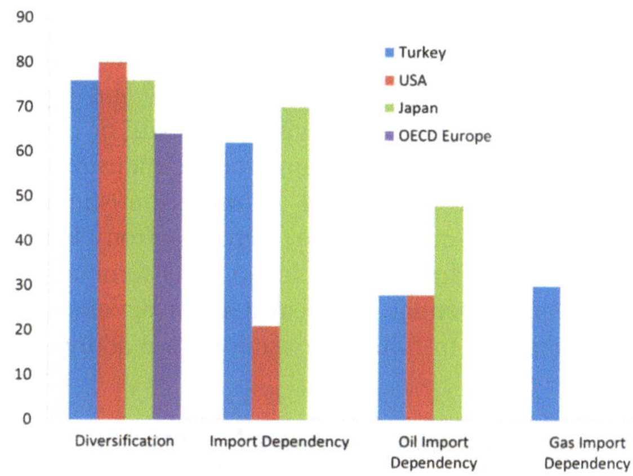

Fig. 5.1 Energy security indicators. *Source* Authors' calculations for Turkey based on IEA (2010); Jansen et al. (2004) for OECD Europe; APERC (2007) for Japan and USA

Turkey scores fairly high in terms of these criteria (Fig. 5.1). Overall diversification index value is 76, which is the same as Japan's, a little lower than that of the US and significantly higher than that of OECD Europe. Japan, as an industrialized country with even less domestic energy resources than Turkey, is often seen as a success story in terms of energy security. Scoring as high as Japan is an indication of Turkey's success as well. Japan achieves that high score with nuclear while Turkey achieves it via domestic coal and hydro.

Turkey's import dependency is high because, like Japan, both oil and gas are almost fully imported. Individually, net import dependency for oil and gas is 28 and 30%, respectively. Since oil consumption is a smaller share of the energy portfolio in Turkey than it is in Japan, Turkey scores much better than Japan but this can change as Turks continue to increase car ownership and miles traveled. In any event, the net oil import dependency index can be a bit misleading because oil products do not have ready substitutes at the necessary scale as transportation fuels. As such, Turkey is vulnerable to oil price shocks as any other importer. But, Turkey does not subsidize petroleum products; in fact, the country imposes some of the highest taxes on gasoline in the world. Smuggling of petroleum products along the Iraqi and Syrian borders is a problem but probably declining in significance as the market continues to grow. In short, the demand is not artificially inflated. Building strategic petroleum reserves, improving availability and convenience of public transportation, requiring improvements in fuel efficiency, and pursuing alternative transportation fuels such as natural gas (CNG or LNG) and biofuels as well as electrification of transportation can help reduce oil import vulnerability. None of these strategies is sufficient by itself but as a portfolio, they can be more effective. Although the role of public agencies is clear in terms of creating the frameworks to facilitate investment in these alternatives, the private sector has to raise most of the capital necessary for these investments in a competitive environment to ensure that energy security is achieved at least cost.

Gas import dependency is slightly higher than oil import dependency but at 30% should be manageable. Although Turkey imports almost all of its gas, the share of gas in total energy picture is relatively small. Unlike oil, with no large-scale substitutes as transportation fuel, gas has alternatives for power generation in coal and hydro. Still, existing gas-fired capacity and their contracts create a stranded cost that cannot be easily or quickly substituted.

Clearly, there are other important dimensions to evaluating Turkey's energy options than those captured in these statistics. Environmental impacts (from greenhouse gas emissions to mercury, from land use to water use), safety of operations (e.g., for nuclear plants), long-term cost of energy, reliability of import sources, and potential for local content development among others are all valid considerations.[3] In following sections, we address some of these dimensions.

3.1 Natural Gas: A Central Fuel

In its efforts to diversify types of energy fuels and technologies, natural gas, though almost fully imported, should remain as an important piece of the puzzle. Turkey is located at the crossroads of existing or potential energy supply routes and is surrounded by sea; as such the country has relatively easy access to both pipeline and LNG imports. The availability of natural gas has been improving as reserves and supplies are increasing globally with the increased production of unconventional fields (shale, tight sands, coalbed methane) as well as new conventional fields. Increased production is impacting LNG trade: traditional oil-indexed pricing of LNG contracts is being replaced by gas-on-gas competition at least in Western Europe; in all likelihood, this shift will moderate the cost of natural gas.

Natural gas is the lowest emission fossil fuel, making it more acceptable to public especially if it is replacing coal facilities without state-of-the-art emission control equipment. Gas-fired power plants are most efficient and cheapest and quickest to build, making them ideal for maintaining resource adequacy. To the extent the fuel can be procured competitively, low capital cost of gas-fired plants will also help keep electricity prices low.

However, to take advantage of these benefits of natural gas, Turkey has to focus on two major areas. First, the country should continue to diversify sources of imports via private importers by completing the implementation of the NGML. Russia still dominates with 46% of the imports. Currently, there are multiple pipelines and two LNG import terminals, one of which is not being fully utilized. The large number of private entities with spot LNG import licenses is promising as these volumes can help break the dominance of oil-indexed pricing of BOTAŞ' contracts. But, more LNG terminals and long-term import licenses are needed. There are also many transit pipeline projects, which would allow Turkey to access gas from additional sources but the pricing of these contracts should move away from oil indexing. Such diversification of sources and importers will help increase liquidity in the Turkish natural gas market and move to gas-on-gas competition

[3] For example, see Foss (2011).

and to lower prices than those in oil-indexed contracts. Diversification would also reduce the risk of supply cuts as experienced in 2006 and 2007 when Russia stopped gas flow to Ukraine and Iran could not send agreed volumes to Turkey. Since gas-fired power generation is large and supplies the peak load, gas availability is critical for power sector reliability as well. In addition to diversifying import options, the transportation and, especially, storage infrastructure should be expanded to add flexibility to the market. Additional LNG import terminals would also help by providing storage services.

Second, Turkey remains underexplored for fossil fuel resources, especially offshore and unconventional resources such as shale gas. Reforming the upstream frameworks to attract more experienced investors to explore oil and gas in both onshore and offshore, and both conventional and unconventional could lead to significant discoveries of valuable hydrocarbon resources. However, the upstream reforms should be accompanied with development of world class environmental regulations related to oil and gas exploration and production. More importantly, the legal and regulatory framework should reflect global best practices that capture the adjustments made due to the Macondo accident in the Gulf of Mexico; and there should be no question about the independence and authority of environmental regulators. Turkey's natural, ecologic, and historical sites and coastlines that are an increasingly important source of tourism revenue (about $20 billion) should not be risked in a haphazard way. Privatizing or corporatizing TPAO, the national oil company, seems necessary. At the least, Turkey might want to create a commercially oriented arm of TPAO that can be at least partially listed in the stock market to explore both domestically and internationally (perhaps, a re-organized Turkish Petroleum International Company, an affiliate of TPAO). Examples of successful, partially privatized national oil companies include Petrobras, Statoil, and increasingly Chinese companies CNOOC and CNPC; their models can be pursued for TPAO.

3.2 *Hydro: Potential and Risks*

Turkey already has almost 16 GW of installed hydro capacity, most of which are based on large dams. The remaining potential is also large; the projects in the licensing process or under construction can double the installed capacity. However, some caution is warranted with hydro expansion. Perhaps partially driven by climate change, but certainly impacted by inefficient irrigation practices, water scarcity is a growing problem in Turkey as it is globally. Syria and Iraq depend almost fully on Euphrates and Tigris rivers for their freshwater needs and had conflicts with Turkey in the past, often blaming Turkey for deliberately cutting water flows. Turkey has many dams on both rivers and more are under construction or planned as part of the Southeast Anatolia Project. International standards and laws are emerging regarding the use of the water of rivers that cross multiple countries. Although their impact on Turkey's hydroelectric facilities is yet uncertain, Turkey should follow closely and participate in these processes to protect its rights.

Increasingly, small-scale hydro facilities are being built. There are concerns that companies building these facilities do not follow best environmental practices. Although an environmental impact assessment is necessary, policing is reportedly weak. The standards for small-scale hydro facilities are not up to international standards. Most visibly, local communities in many locations strongly oppose these facilities, including several bloody altercations with security forces. If local communities cannot be convinced of the benefits of these projects and companies' commitment to protection of their environment via public hearings and civil negotiations, these projects should not be forced upon them. These small facilities cannot be expected to add much to country's energy security.

3.3 Wind and Solar: Expansion Aware of Their Shortcomings

Other than hydro, Turkey has large potential wind and solar resources. Since the 2005 Renewables Law, about 1,600 MW of wind capacity has been developed but no significant solar capacity is built yet. As the capacity of wind and solar facilities increase, the Turkish electricity grid and market will start facing certain challenges. The expansion of these renewables should be pursued considering these challenges fully.

Wind and solar are intermittent, have low capacity factors, and cannot provide base load service reliably. In many locations around the world, wind does not follow load throughout the day; hence it has low load factor but conditions in Turkey are not publicly available yet. If wind blows during peak hours more regularly, wind can be more valuable for the Turkish system but it will remain variable. Solar is typically available during peak hours.

Most renewables are difficult and costly to scale up; the largest wind turbine design is now five MW but turbines of 1.5 to 2.5 MW are more commonly used. For example, given a capacity factor of 35%, one needs to build more than 200 windmills to generate the same amount of electricity as a 500-MW gas-fired plant with a 75% capacity factor. With low load factors and scalability limitations, generation from intermittent resources cannot increase their share in generation in any significant way, especially during peak hours, in a time-frame consistent with Turkey's economic growth. Without significant share of generation, these technologies can only yield limited benefits in terms of lower emissions.

Intermittent resources require back-up generation, which is typically supplied by gas-fired plants, either open or combined cycle. Such cycling impact the economics of these plants negatively, some of which may choose to retire. But in Turkey, hydro can provide a cleaner and cheaper back-up option.

Integration of variable generation from renewables cause challenges to system operators. Among the problems reported by system operators in different locations are: voltage regulation as wind ramps up or down almost instantaneously and somewhat unpredictably; and forecast inaccuracy requiring expensive ancillary services. These problems can and are being solved by system operators but seem to impose a natural upper limit to how much intermittent capacity can be reliably added to an electricity system—a range of 20–30% is often given for wind.[4]

Wind but especially solar remain more expensive than conventional technologies; wherever they have relatively high penetration (Germany, Denmark, Spain, Texas) subsidies ranging from $20 per MWh to several hundred dollars per MWh have been necessary. A certain level of subsidy can be considered by the Turkish government to support most promising technologies but the support should be transparent and consistent to create a predictable investment environment. The ending of such subsidies in many European countries after the financial crises of 2008 is exemplary of how unrealistic support programs can fail. The total burden of these subsidies to the Turkish government should be weighed against other public services expected from the government such as education, health services, and roads. From the perspective of energy policy, a particularly relevant comparison could be the ranking of returns on investment by the government on such subsidies versus investment on public transportation and/or energy efficiency.

3.4 Nuclear: Only when Institutionally Ready

Nuclear can be pursued but, in the absence of a national energy policy document as discussed above, it is not proven that Turkey needs nuclear energy from an economic, energy security, or environmental perspective. In any case, the country's first nuclear facility should not be built until safety concerns of the public are addressed satisfactorily. It does not appear that Turkey has the required human resources and institutional capacity in place; the legal framework is based on a five-page law with no details on prevention of accidents and radiation leaks, waste management, and decommissioning at the end of the plant's life. For example, an independent regulatory agency to oversee safety is necessary. This agency should be staffed with experienced professionals who are trained in most current nuclear technologies and safety procedures. A "safety culture" needs to be established across all public entities responsible for the safe operation of nuclear facilities and waste management—best practices can be obtained from IAEA and similar agencies in other countries.

The Akkuyu project seems to be moving forward despite the opposition of the local populace. This approach is misguided; public engagement is necessary, especially in plant sites. The Fukushima accident changed the rules of public engagement even in Japan, where traditionally utilities were able to coordinate their actions with government with minimal communication with the public. Governments and companies can ignore such public opposition at their own peril.

The selection of the technology of the first nuclear plant is crucial. A standard technology that can be duplicated in the future and that will be familiar to

---

[4] For example, see Chap. 4 and references cited there in USDOE (2008).

regulatory and utility professionals would facilitate further expansion in the future. A proven technology with multiple operating sites around the world is preferable; Turkey should not be a testing ground for a new technology or first of its kind plant. These requirements necessitate transparency in tender and licensing processes as well as during construction and operation of the plant. The selection of the Russian state company to build one of the firsts of its kind facility without a competitive bidding process does not meet these criteria.[5]

3.5 Coal: Constrained and Lower Emission Use

Coal is quickly becoming the fuel of the last century in most OECD countries. Climate change concerns are clearly a driver since coal-fired power plants emit large amounts of greenhouse gases. But perhaps a more imminent driver is impact on local populations due to emissions of sulfur dioxide, particulate matter, and mercury, which cause acid rain, pulmonary diseases, and developmental handicaps, if plants do not have emission control equipment. Turkey's own coal production is mostly lignite, which typically has much lower heat content than other coal types. Lignite plants are less efficient and their emissions per unit of electricity generated are higher as compared to other coal plants. With the most advanced control equipment, some of these emissions can be lowered but expenses may not be justified given their heat content and efficiency limitations. Turkish coal fleet is relatively young; some of the oldest plants have been retired and most others have flue-gas desulfurization scrubbers but not all have equipment to capture mercury, cadmium, and particulate emissions. It is also reported that operators do not always run emission control equipment to manage costs. Turkey might want to consider gradual retirement of lignite plants starting with the oldest, without negatively impacting system reliability. At the least, the installation of state-of-the-art emission control equipment should be mandated and strongly enforced on all plants and new builds. Only the lowest sulfur coal should be used. As EÜAŞ starts transferring some of its coal plants to the private sector, these environmental improvements should be presented as a condition of the privatization scheme.

3.6 Transportation: Biofuels, Electricity, and Natural Gas as Alternatives to Oil

Although we did not discuss the transportation sector and oil much in this book as we focused on electricity and natural gas markets and reforms in these sectors, there are close linkages in terms of emerging technologies and substitutability of

[5] See EDAM (2011) for a detailed discussion of the selected technology and other considerations.

various energy options. Also, the holistic long-term energy policy we asked for earlier in this chapter cannot ignore the transportation sector; Turkey's dependence on oil imports remains a macroeconomic and energy security challenge. As such, diversification of transportation options is also necessary. Oil market is more uncertain than the emerging global market for natural gas; although resources (including unconventional) are available, geopolitical risks are much higher primarily due to concentration of major oil suppliers in the Middle East and especially around the Hurmuz Strait. Although alternatives to oil products used in transportation (gasoline, diesel, and jet fuel) are many, they all face significant technical and economic challenges but as a portfolio they can offer some relief.

For example, Turkey can continue to pursue biofuels (biodiesel or ethanol) but in addition to domestic production, imports can be considered if they are cheaper. Given some of the environmental challenges faced by Turkey (e.g., locational water scarcity, top-soil erosion), it may not be feasible or even desirable for Turkish farmers to switch to fuel crops from food crops. It is also not advisable to produce fuel crops that are water intensive or use a lot of fertilizers as the environmental damage from these practices could be significant. Turkey may consider crops such as jatropha, switchgrass, or others that can grow in lands that are not suitable for food crops and that do not require too much water or fertilizers. Biodiesel from waste oil and industrial algae production are other alternatives. Many of these options remain expensive and some are still in experimental scale but high oil prices and high fuel taxes in Turkey can encourage these fuels.

Natural gas can be an alternative transportation fuel in the form of compressed natural gas (CNG), LNG or diesel from the gas-to-liquids (GTL) process. But these alternatives will not be competitive with oil products as long as Turkey imports its gas via oil-indexed pricing for natural gas. In any case, the market for natural gas vehicles will, for the foreseeable future, be limited to fleet vehicles that can refuel at their central location as it will be expensive to develop a distribution network similar to gasoline stations.

Electric vehicles and plug-in hybrids are also increasing in popularity. Although they remain expensive and there are concerns related to batteries such as recycling of used batteries, access to resources of lithium and other materials used in battery manufacturing, small EVs are attractive solutions for congested city traffic both in terms of relieving congestion and reducing emissions. Again, fleet applications can be the first step. Another issue is the impact of increased use of EVs and their charging on the electricity system. Although not an issue for a long time to come, eventually, large amount of charging during system peak hours can hurt reliability.

4 Energy Efficiency

Energy efficiency is often seen as the low-hanging fruit in terms of reducing energy consumption and emissions. Although the accounting of these benefits often turn out to be more complicated than first imagined, energy efficiency can yield high benefits at low cost if well-thought-out programs are cleverly and rigorously implemented. Turkey initiated this momentum with the passage of the Energy Efficiency Law in 2007 and following implementation efforts seem to be serious. There is a visible public education and outreach effort, which is absolutely necessary for energy efficiency programs to be adopted by larger segments of the population and yield desired benefits.

There are efficiency standards for buildings; implementing agencies must ensure that these standards are highest possible from a technological perspective and that builders and property owners comply with these standards with strict monitoring and high penalties. Building starts should be combined with smart architectural and urban designs with planned developments and mass transit availability and convenience.

Given that Turkey depends on oil imports and most of the imported oil is used in the transportation sector, it is important to develop fuel efficiency standards for vehicles that increase over time. A challenge is the tax revenues the government collects from the sale of gasoline, the price of which has been highest in Turkey among the OECD countries. Hopefully, these tax revenues do not create an obstacle to implementing fuel efficiency, alternative fuel, and public transportation policies. There is now a "cash for clunkers" program, which should help remove inefficient, old vehicles from traffic, which would also help with reduction of emissions. The new emission labeling may also convince some environmentally conscious customers preferring more efficient vehicles; but direct emission limits could be more productive.

Overall, Turkey has opportunities to follow a much more efficient energy consumption path as the country is building new infrastructure or replacing old ones and as emerging middle classes chose their cars, appliances, and lifestyles.

5 Conclusion

Although not endowed with rich hydrocarbon resources, Turkey has been taking advantage of its hydro and lignite resources for decades. As the country continues on its path of rapid development, however, its energy needs have been increasing commensurately. The diversification of its energy options with natural gas imports since the 1980s have yielded energy security and environmental benefits; but import dependency on non-competitive suppliers and cost of imports, which are high due to indexing gas price to that of oil, remain as concerns. The geographical location of Turkey allows the country to source gas from multiple producing regions, both as LNG and pipeline gas. Also as a transit country for gas pipelines, Turkey stands to gain from deals initiated by consumers in Europe. The sector reform seems to be finally allowing competitive importers to emerge, which should help wean the country of oil-indexed pricing of gas imports. Reforming the upstream investment frameworks could lead to increased production of oil and gas in Turkey as long as necessary measures to protect significant environmental damage are taken.

With recent laws, there is increased interest in new hydro facilities, especially small ones, as well as renewables such as wind, solar, and geothermal. Except for hydro and wind, the contribution of these renewables will be relatively small in the near future; even wind facilities have to prove themselves in terms of supplied electricity rather than installed capacity. Turkey is also close to its first nuclear facility. Renewables and nuclear will arithmetically help country's energy diversification but institutionally there are challenges, especially for nuclear.

The legal framework consists of a five-page law, which does not cover critical safety and waste management standards. There is no provision for a new independent regulator to oversee nuclear operations' compliance with such standards. The investor company and technology was selected via an intergovernmental agreement between Russia and Turkey rather than a competitive process during which the technology, safety, and economic criteria could have been transparently evaluated and the public could have been engaged. The opposition of the local population, which only intensified after Fukushima, is being ignored by the officials.

This unwillingness to engage the public is unfortunately a long practiced tradition of officials; it is also being witnessed during opposition to many small hydro facilities. There is a "culture of secrecy" in state institutions, which remain heavily involved across the energy value chains as operators, importers, and investors. The Council of Ministers is directly responsible for some key decisions on the energy sector. In the past, the government interfered with the independence of EPDK as the regulator; especially in setting electricity and gas prices for end-users, although this practice seems to become less routine. Most recently, a decision by the Council of Ministers subjected all independent regulators, including EPDK, subject to audit by relevant ministries. Under such an environment, pursuing energy projects via intergovernmental deals or despite public opposition creates a non-transparent rent-seeking environment, where companies affiliated with media companies or otherwise affiliated with the political system may end up with projects. This opaque, non-market transaction space is the most troublesome aspect of the Turkish energy scene. A national long-term energy policy developed via a transparent and large stakeholder process could help address some of these concerns. The analysis provided in this book suggests that such a policy will necessarily be multidimensional, both focusing on the development of competition and addressing additional concerns that competition alone may not be able to solve. Clearly, the state (mostly via ETKB and DPT) has an important role in development of this policy and, perhaps, in international negotiations for imports, and support for renewables; but the market and private investors under the supervision of EPDK, which might need to be further empowered with clarity on its independence should be able to meet Turkey's energy needs. The reform process that started in 2001 with EML and NGML needs to be completed to ensure competitive supply of electricity and natural gas. In addition, the competitive process needs to be supplemented with measures to deal with problems such as market power, resource adequacy, diversification of energy types and sources, energy security, and distributional problems.

References

APERC (2007). *A Quest for Energy Security in the 21st Century: Resources and Constraints.*

EDAM (2011). *The Turkish Model for Transition to Nuclear Power.* Edited by Sinan Ülgen, Ekonomi ve Dış Politika Araştırmalar Merkezi.

Foss, Michelle Michot (2011). *The [Energy] Webs We Weave*, Center for Energy Economics, The University of Texas at Austin. http://www.beg.utexas.edu/energyecon/thinkcorner/Think%20 Corner%20-%20Energy%20Webs.pdf (last accessed on January 4, 2012).

IAEA (2005). *Energy Indicators for Sustainable Development: Guidelines and Methodologies.*

IEA (2010). *Energy Policies of IEA Countries: Turkey 2009 Review.*

Jansen, J.C., W.G. van Arkel and M.G. Boots (2004). *Designing Indicators of Long-Term Energy Supply Security* for the Netherlands Environmental Assessment Agency.

von Hirschhausen, Christian (2005). *Strategies for Energy Security – A Transatlantic Comparison*, German Institute for Economic Research.

USAID (2008). *Energy Security Quarterly*, prepared by the Center for Energy Economics (The University of Texas at Austin) with input from PA Government Services Inc. http:// www.sari-energy.org/Energy_Security_Quarterlies/ESQ1_January_08.pdf (last accessed January 4, 2012).

USDOE (2008). *20% Wind Energy by 2030.* http://www.20percentwind.org/20p.aspx?page=Report

Glossary

APERC Asia Pacific Energy Research Center

bcm Billion cubic meters

BO Build Operate

BOT Build Operate Transfer

BOTAŞ Boru Hatları ile Petrol Taşıma Anonim Şirketi (Petroleum Pipeline Corporation)

Btu British thermal unit

DPT Devlet Planlama Teşkilâtı (State Planning Organization)

DSİ Devlet Su İşleri (State Hydraulic Works)

EIA Energy Information Administration

EİE Elektrik İşleri Etüt İdaresi Genel Müdürlüğü (Electrical Power Resources Survey and Development Administration)

EML Electricity Market Law

EPDK Enerji Piyasası Düzenleme Kurumu (Energy Market Regulatory Authority)

ETKB Enerji ve Tabii Kaynaklar Bakanlığı (Ministry of Energy and Natural Resources)

EU European Union

EÜAŞ Elektrik Üretim Anonim Şirketi (Electricity Generation Corporation)

GDP Gross domestic product

GW Gigawatt

GWh Gigawatthour

I. Atiyas et al., *Reforming Turkish Energy Markets*,
DOI: 10.1007/978-1-4614-0290-9,

IAEA International Atomic Energy Agency

IEA International Energy Agency

İGDAŞ İstanbul Gaz Dağıtım Anonim Şirketi (İstanbul Gas Distribution Company)

IMF International Monetary Fund

IPP Independent power producer

kr Turkish Kuruş, one hundredth of a Turkish Lira

kWh Kilowatthour

LNG Liquefied natural gas

mcm Million cubic meters

MTA Maden Tetkik ve Arama (Mineral Research and Exploration)

mtoe Million tons of oil equivalent

MW Megawatt

MWh Megawatthour

NGML Natural Gas Market Law

MYTM Milli Yük Tevzi Merkezi (National Load Dispatch Center)

OECD Organization for Economic Cooperation and Development

PMUM Piyasa Mali Uzlaştırma Merkezi (Market Financial Reconciliation Centre)

TAEK Türk Atom Enerjisi Kurumu (Turkish Atomic Energy Authority)

TEDAŞ Türkiye Elektrik Dağıtım Anonim Şirketi (Turkish Distribution Corporation)

TEİAŞ Türkiye Elektrik İletim Anonim Şirketi (Turkish Transmission Corporation)

TETAŞ Türkiye Elektrik Ticaret ve Taahhüt Anonim Şirketi (Turkish Electricity Trading and Contracting Corporation)

TL Turkish Lira

TOR Transfer of Operating Rights

TPAO Türk Petrolleri Anonim Ortaklığı (Turkish Petroleum Corporation)

TWh Terawatthour

USDC Unit service and depreciation charge

Index

I. Atiyas et al., *Reforming Turkish Energy Markets*,
DOI: 10.1007/978-1-4614-0290-9,

MIX
Papier aus verantwortungsvollen Quellen
Paper from responsible sources
FSC® C105338

If you have any concerns about our products,
you can contact us on
ProductSafety@springernature.com

In case Publisher is established outside the EU,
the EU authorized representative is:
Springer Nature Customer Service Center GmbH
Europaplatz 3, 69115 Heidelberg, Germany

Printed by Libri Plureos GmbH
in Hamburg, Germany